THE SURVIVAL OF THE SELF

The Survival of the Self

ROBIN HARWOOD
Georgia State University

Routledge
Taylor & Francis Group
LONDON AND NEW YORK

First published 1998 by Ashgate Publishing

Reissued 2018 by Routledge
2 Park Square, Milton Park, Abingdon, Oxon, OX14 4RN
52 Vanderbilt Avenue, New York, NY 10017

Routledge is an imprint of the Taylor & Francis Group, an informa business

A Library of Congress record exists under LC control number: 98072855

ISBN 13: 978-1-138-36511-7 (hbk)
ISBN 13: 978-1-138-36514-8 (pbk)
ISBN 13: 978-0-429-43091-6 (ebk)

Contents

Permissions

Permission to quote from the following sources is gratefully acknowledged.
Cherry: "Can My Survival be Subrogated?" 1984 *Philosophy* © Royal Institute of Philosophy, reproduced by permission of Cambridge University Press; *Journal of Indian Philosophy* Vol. 18 1990, pp 1-18, "The Self in Deep Sleep According to Advaita and Visistadvaita" by Michael Comans, with kind permission of Kluwer Academic Publishers; *Some Must Watch While Some Must Sleep* by Dement, ©1974 by W.H. Freeman and Company. Used with permission; Ehman, "Temporal Self-Identity" by permission of *Southern Journal of Philosophy*, *Philosophical Studies* Vol. 52 1987, pp 427-433, "Personal Identity and Time Travel" by Douglas Ehring, with kind permission of Kluwer Academic Publishers; Filice, Carlo,"Sustained Causation and the Substantial Theory of the Self." Reprinted by permission of the *International Philosophical Quarterly*, Vol. 26, No. 2, 1986, p.101; Flew: "James Giles on Personal Identity" 1992 *Philosophy* © Royal Institute of Philosophy, reproduced by permission of Cambridge University Press; Flew: *The Logic of Mortality* by permission of Basil Blackwell; Forman: "Pure Consciousness Events and Mysticism" by permission of *Sophia*; Giles:"Bodily Theory and Theory of the Body" 1991 *Philosophy* © Royal Institute of Philosophy, reproduced by permission of Cambridge University Press; Korsgaard, Christine M. "Personal Identity and the Unity of Agency" *Philosophy and Public Affairs* Copyright © 1989 by Princeton University Press. Reprinted by permission of Princeton University Press; McKay and McKay: "Explicit dialogue between left and right half-systems of split brains" Reprinted by permission of Dr. V. MaKay and Macmillan Magazines from *Nature*, Vol. 295 Copyright 1982 Macmillan Magazines Limited; Madell: "Derek Parfit and Greta Garbo" *Analysis* by kind permission of Geoffrey Madell; *Philosophical Studies* Vol. 70 1993, pp 305-321, "Having the Experience: the Next Best Thing to Being There" by Raymond Martin, with kind permission of Kluwer Academic Publishers; Moody: "William of Ockham" in *The Encyclopaedia of Philosophy* Copyright © 1967 Macmillan, Inc. by permission of Macmillan Library Reference USA, a Simon and Schuster Macmillan Company; Parfit: "Personal Identity" by permission of *Philosophical Review*, Parfit: *Reasons And Persons* by permission of Oxford University Press; Perry: "The Problem of Personal Identity" in *Personal Identity* (Ed. Perry, J.) Copyright © 1975 The Regents of the University of California, by permission of University of California Press: Robinson: "Personal Identity and Survival" by permission of *Journal of Philosophy*, Shear: "The Experience of Pure Consciousness" *Metaphilosophy*, by permission of Blackwell Publishers; Stone: "Parfit and the Buddha: Why There Are No. People" 1988 by permission of *Philosophy and Phenomenological Research*; Taber: "The Mimamsa theory of self-recognition" by permission of *Philosophy East and West*.

Acknowledgments

I want to express my gratitude to Mr. Michael Proudfoot, who guided the research through all its stages. He read and discussed with me the whole manuscript, and offered useful suggestions to improve it. Thanks are also due to Dr. David Oderberg, for his helpful comments and criticism, and to Mr. John F. Parise, who converted my sketches into respectable diagrams.

Special thanks should go to Mrs. E. L. Harwood for her support, and to Ms. Miho Matsumoto, without whom I would not have been able to complete the work.

1 Introduction

In this book I shall give an account of personal identity derived from the Butler-Reid position. Most accounts of personal identity attempt to find the necessary and sufficient conditions for a person at one time to be identical with a person at another time. I shall argue that from the first person point of view one necessary condition of personal identity is the survival of the Self.

My claim is that a normal human person is a combination of a Self, a mind, and a body. The Self is the centre of consciousness and agency. It is the subject of experience and the agent of deliberate action. The mind includes both the present mental events and the structure of memories, beliefs, desires, etc., that underlie the events. Bodies and minds are compound entities that change over time, but the Self is a simple, continuant entity that does not change. For a person P1 at time t1 to be identical with a person P2 at time t2, the Self of P1 must have survived from t1 to t2 and be the Self of P2. Although this is a necessary condition, I do not regard it as a sufficient condition.

The problem of personal identity stems at least in part from the fact that persons are in fact compound entities. When we think about ourselves or about other people, we usually regard a person as being the Self-mind-body combination, or (if we do not have the concept of the Self, or do not regard it as distinct from the mind) at least as the mind-body combination. Thus, if any great or sudden changes are made in any one of the three we are inclined to regard the original person as not being identical with the resulting person. If, for example, a person's mind is totally destroyed, and replaced by another mind, and then this mind plus the Self is transferred to another body, we are inclined to judge that the original person no longer exists, even though the new person has the same Self as the original. When the judgment is made from the third person point of view the judgment that the original person no longer exists is even more likely, since even if we believe in Selves there is no way of knowing that the same Self has survived and is associated with the new mind and body. In order for survival of the Self to be a sufficient condition for personal identity, it would be necessary to show that being a Self was sufficient to be a person. But this seems to run counter to our usual way of thinking of persons.

Nor will I attempt to find a set of sufficient conditions for personal identity. Minds and bodies are mereologically variable entities. Their identity is only identity in Butler's "imperfect" sense. A set of sufficient conditions would consist, at best, of the necessary condition of survival of the Self, plus a long and complex disjunction of conditions for psychological and physical continuity. Borowski (1987) argues that such a set would be unbounded. If he is right, the attempt to produce one is misguided, but even if he is wrong, and a set of sufficient conditions for personal identity could be produced, it would be a task beyond the scope of this book.

Is there such a thing as the Self? The best argument against the existence of the Self is the fission argument. The second best is the argument from its intermittent existence. There are also Unger's deconstruction arguments (in Unger 1990) to show it cannot be a simple entity. I shall deal with these arguments in the course of presenting my argument..

In this chapter I shall discuss the nature of the Self, its unity, and its identity. In the next, I shall give some arguments for existence of the Self, and its distinction from the mind. I shall show that we can have direct experience of the Self as conscious subject and a conscious agent. (In fact, the whole of this book acts as an argument for the Self by showing that the idea of the Self leads to an account of our survival and identity that is more satisfactory than those accounts which exclude the Self.)

In the third chapter I shall discuss some accounts of unity of consciousness, and suggest that the idea that the Self is the unifier of conscious experience provides a better account of unity of consciousness than the alternatives. In the fourth I shall argue that the Self is continuous entity. It is continuously conscious throughout its existence. It is continuously attached to the same mind. I shall suggest that we are aware of existing, and of our own continuity, even while asleep. This awareness of being oneself is constant, and therefore usually unnoticed, throughout life. Nonetheless our tacit knowledge includes the knowledge of our own continuity.

The fifth chapter will show that our concerns for survival are that this continuity of the Self shall not cease. We know our life is a continuous stream of experience. When we want to survive, we want the future experiences to be part of the same stream, in the way that our present experiences are part of the stream. The stream is sustained and unified by the persisting Self. I shall also discuss the distinction between replicas and survivors, and show that neither Parfit's (1991) Relation R, nor Brennan's

(1988) S - relation, give an adequate version of survival. Finally, I shall show that my account can deal with some of the famous puzzle cases.

Fission and fusion will be discussed in the sixth chapter. The fission argument is that the logical possibility of fission shows that survival without identity is possible, and that therefore the Self is not simple. I shall show that this is putting the cart before the horse. Only by assuming that there is no simple Self can we begin to make a case for the logical possibility of fission, and even than there are good reasons for believing that fission is not possible. I shall argue similarly against fusion, to conclude that fission and fusion of persons are impossible. In case my arguments for this are not accepted, I also offer alternative argument to the effect that the fission products can be identical with each other, so that we still need not accept the possibility of survival without identity.

Arguments against the neo-Lockean views of personal identity are distributed throughout the book. In the seventh chapter I concentrate on showing that personal identity is not accountable in terms of bodily identity or continuity, and that bodily identity is not logically necessary for the continuity of the Self.

The final chapter will not only show that memory provides evidence that there is a permanent Self, but also show that we gain knowledge of our own personal identity from memory because we have knowledge of our Self continuity. A person's memory comes to him as being part of the stream of experience had by his own Self.

Throughout this book I shall give priority to the first person point of view. I am concerned with persons, and as Madell (1981) and Matthews (1990) pointed out, persons have a first person point of view. They have views on what they are and what they want to continue. Self concern is a primitive concern, not derived from any other concerns. This shows that there is something special about personal identity. The identity and survival of persons is not the same as the identity of a ship or a piece of clay, so arguments that apply to ships may not be appropriate for persons.

(Here I should, perhaps, insert a disclaimer. Although from time to time I make reference to various ideas and arguments from Indian philosophy which I have found useful, I have no expertise in Indian philosophy, and rely uncritically on secondary sources. I do not intend that my versions of the ideas and arguments should be taken as authoritative accounts of the Indian sources.)

The Mind Body Problem

I have tried to make this argument conformable to all ideas about the relationship of mind and body. My own beliefs are rather mystical, and so I am inclined to believe that the Self is something non-physical, but my argument does not require this. If the physicalists are correct, the Self might be a specific part of the brain, or a specific brain process, or an organization of brain activity. Then, if that part of the brain is destroyed, or the process ceases, or the organization is disrupted, the Self will then cease to exist. Consciousness will be snuffed out. However, this seems to be a contingent truth (if truth it be) and not a necessary one. From the first person point of view it is not obvious that the Self has any connection with the brain at all. It is this logical distinction that I try to bring out in the seventh chapter. Some of my arguments depend on the logical possibility of dualism, but not on the claim that dualism is true. Books and articles are still being produced in support of dualist positions, so it seems that, in spite of many attempts over many years, the incoherence of dualism has not been definitively shown. I think that the logical possibility of dualism can be accepted.

The Nature of the Self

I shall use and argue for a minimal view of the Self as a subject/agent. My general principle is that the Self is the way it seems to be and that we need strong reasons for considering it to be otherwise. When we examine ourselves, and thus examine what the Self seems to be, we find it is a unified entity that is the subject of awareness of the phenomenological states and experiences that arise in normal waking consciousness, mystical states, dreaming, sleep, and perhaps various other states. The Self is not the same as its thoughts, actions, or feelings. It remains the same when all its thoughts and operations change. The Self is also the agent of deliberate actions. In these two roles it directs and is aware of thoughts, and other mental processes. It is a continuant, with an unbroken existence.

McGinn (1982) points out that theories of personal identity that exclude the Self fail, and from this concludes that the Self is not to be explained in terms of any materials these theories invoke. Thus, the Self is not the body, not the brain, not a construction from psychological relations.

The Self is (to quote Kupperman, 1984) "not constructed to unify elements of empirical consciousness" but something "having a primitive matter-of-fact unity." Although I will from time to time use the language of substances, and refer to the Self as substantial, this is just a manner of speech. "Substance" gives the impression of something passive, solid, and opaque. The Self seems active and transparent. It seems better described as a point of view than as a substance.

Self and Mind

Bradley (1928) gave an excellent analogy that can be used for the relation of the Self to the mind. He asks us to imagine ourselves suspended over a river at night, looking down at an illuminated area of the river, and observing the flow of the water and the objects floating in the water. The illuminated area consists of a brightly lit area that can change in size and position, and an area of dimmer light reflected from and surrounding the main light. This analogy fits our experience extremely well. The river is the mind, with all its contents, and the combination of the light and the observer is the Self. The illumination and the observation are, of course, consciousness. The analogy misleads slightly in making the observer and the light into different things, while consciousness is one thing only.

Being aware of the contents of the mind is to illuminate them. The bright patch of light is attention, which can be focussed or diffuse. The dimmer light is what Evans (1970) referred to as unprojected consciousness, the awareness of mental items that are not being attended to. Bradley pointed out that the dimmer light gives a little illumination upstream and down stream, analogous to the way our awareness is spread over time, giving us direct awareness of what is happening "just now", but also an awareness of "just past" and "just future".

The stream of consciousness is the stream of mental events that are illuminated by the Self. They are unified in to a single awareness by there being one Self which is aware of them. Consciousness is a unity, so its contents are unified.

The Self also is the source of agency. An important point that Bradley does not include in his analogy is that the attention is under the control of the will. By exercising agency, attention can be focussed tightly, or diffusely. It can be focused on varying contents of the mind, and held on one item, moved deliberately from one item to another, or allowed to flit more or less randomly from item to item. The Self controls at least some aspects of mind and body. Deliberate action, directed thought, are both under the control of the will.

The Self is a Simple Entity

McGinn (1982) suggests that the difficulty of producing adequate criteria for personal identity is evidence for the concept of the Self being primitive and irreducible. I will go a step further, and claim that it is not only evidence for the simplicity of the concept, but also for the simplicity of the thing conceived, the Self.

In order to show that the Self is a simple entity I adapt an argument from Lowe (1991). The argument consists in showing that the Self has no parts, which involves trying to prove a negative. Proving a negative is a notoriously difficult project, so Lowe argues that the various possible candidates that seem as if they could be parts cannot in fact be parts. Following this pattern, I shall show that the Self as I conceive it does not have parts.

First, I have suggested that the Self can be regarded more as a point of view than a substance. Now a point of view is not the sort of thing that can have parts.

Second, I regard the Self as being a subject/agent. As a subject, the Self is conscious, and as an agent it can exercise agency. Consciousness has no parts, and neither has agency, so the only possibility is to attempt to separate agency from consciousness. Such a separation runs directly counter to our experience of ourselves. The unity of consciousness and agency is as primitive as the unity of consciousness.

I shall discuss agency and the Self in more detail the next chapter. Here I shall simply point out that in normal waking consciousness and mystical states, attention has to be controlled, directed, relaxed or withheld. These are all deliberate acts, so agency is involved in these forms of consciousness. Consciousness is, of course, involved in agency. When we perform a deliberate acts, we are aware not only of being the source of the power, but also of consciously performing the act. The faculties of consciousness and agency have no possibility of existing independently. They are in fact abstractions from the lives of persons, and so do not qualify as parts of the Self. The idea of consciousness and agency existing independently of each other is implausible, and so we need arguments to show that they can be separated before we accept the claim that they can be regarded as parts of the Self.

To quote Moody's encyclopaedia entry on the philosophy of William of Ockham:

> We are aware of the soul only as that which thinks and wills; and since the person who thinks is not other than the person who wills, the terms "intellect" and "will" refer to precisely the same subject, and not to distinct faculties within that subject.
>
> … If it is only by intuitive cognition of our own acts that we are aware of ourselves as intelligent beings, it is only in this way we are aware of ourselves as voluntary agents free to choose between opposite actions. (Moody 1967, p. 315)

Third, psychological states or processes cannot be parts of the Self. The psychological states and processes are part of the mind, and I shall argue below that the Self and the mind are logically distinct entities.

Fourth, from the first person point of view, parts of the body cannot be parts of the Self. It may in fact be the case that there is a section of the brain that is the physical base of consciousness and agency, and that the section of the brain involved is a compound entity, but that parts of that section are not parts of the Self. The Self is an entity known only from the first person point of view, and so its parts can only be known from the first person point of view.

I cannot think of any other feasible candidates for the position of parts of the Self, and so it seems that the Self has no parts. Lowe suggests that the burden of proof that the Self has parts lies on the opponents of the idea that the Self is simple. It is up to them to offer more convincing candidates for the parts.

The simplicity of the Self implies it is indivisible. I shall take up the issue of indivisibility in the chapter on Fission.

Also, the simplicity of the Self corresponds to the unity of the Self.

Neither its Presence nor its Survival is a Matter of Degree

The unity of the Self implies that its presence is an all or nothing matter. It cannot be partly present, since it has no parts. By being a unity, it can not include anything which is not itself, and so the Self is set apart from all other things. This makes it an individual.

Since the Self is either present or not, its survival cannot be a matter of degree. Unger (1990) has attempted to show that the subject can be partly present, that it can fade away, and so that its survival can be a matter of degree. He argues against the absoluteness of experience and the absoluteness of the subject from a physicalist stance, but his arguments do not succeed.

In order to show that consciousness can fade away slowly, rather than being either present or absent, he argues from the basis of a brain being dismantled while still functioning.

Unger makes much use of the idea of "zippering" "Zippering" is an imaginary procedure in which radio transceivers are attached to neurons in such a way that, when the neurons are separated from each other, the transceivers continue to transmit the impulses between the neurons in such a way that each neuron receives exactly the same impulses from the other neurons that it would have received were it not separated from them. If the separation is done slowly, a living, functioning, brain can be divide into two halves without the function ceasing or being impaired during the process.

Unger asks us to consider a functioning brain, with conscious experience, being divided into halves by the zippering process. It is then divided into smaller and smaller parts, until it is a scattered collection of neurons, each connected by the appropriate radio transceivers. Eventually, Unger claims, there will be no conscious experience. He offers two reasons for this. First, there will no longer be a subject to have the experience. Second, the connecting devices become more and more complex, in order to make sure that the right signal arrive at the right part of the neuron at the right time and in the right order. As a result of this complexity, the nature of the causal process changes. The cells contribute less and less to the process, the communicators contribute more and more.

Unger's first reason is obscure. He claims that a brain that has been divided into halves but is still connected by radio can be a subject, and uses this claim in his other thought experiments. Now if a brain with separated halves can be a subject, this implies the principle that there is nothing about separation of parts that prevents the parts from being a subject when they are linked in the appropriate way. By this principle it seems that a quartered brain, or a brain divided into eighths, could still be a subject. Why does this principle not apply when the parts are exceedingly small?

The second reason is stronger. However, as the connecting devices become more complex, they will, almost certainly, eventually form a machine as complex as that of the initial brain. Now physicalists suggest that the brain is a biological machine whose operations generate consciousness. It seems feasible to suggest that if a non-biological machine performs the same operations, they would also generate consciousness. Alternatively, if consciousness is a feature of a non-physical Self, whether Cartesian, Plotinian, or Samkya, there seems no *a-priori* reason why such a Self should not be associated with a complex machine. Thus, it seems possible that the conscious experience of the initial brain will have been passed across the machine. The net effect is that of adding a prosthesis to the brain, so that the whole machine becomes a conscious subject, or has the conscious subject associated with it. The case does not compel us to suppose that the conscious experience would fade.

Unger has two arguments against the absoluteness of the subject. The point of these arguments is to show that the subject comes into being gradually, and can gradually cease to exist.

The first argument is that there is no subject before conception, but, after the slow process of development from zygote to full human being, there is a subject associated with the body. At what stage does the subject come into being? Since all the processes are gradual (even conception is a gradual process) it seems reasonable to presume that the subject come into being gradually.

I find this a strong argument, but answerable. If consciousness is an emergent property, why must it emerge gradually just because the physical structure it supervenes upon comes into existence gradually? Why can it not be the case that the subject (whether immaterial or a physical process) comes into being instantly when the zygote has reached a certain stage of development.

The second argument is a spectrum of decomposition. If we take away a single cell of a person, the person will still remain, and be a subject. But if this procedure is followed, eventually there will be just one cell, and finally no cells. If the Cartesians are right, the subject will still exist, but if the physicalists are right, there will be no subject. At which stage in the procedure will the conscious subject cease to exist? We predict that it will cease at some stage in the decomposition of the brain. If there is one particular cell whose activity is essential for the brain to be conscious, and whose removal would lead to unconsciousness, we can add artificial stimulators to the brain so that they would provide the right sort of stimulation to the rest of the brain to keep it conscious when that cell is removed. At what stage would there first be no conscious being?

But it seems perfectly possible that, for consciousness to exist, a minimum number of cells arranged in a particular way and operating in a particular way is required. When the correct arrangement is set up, there will be consciousness. As soon as the arrangement ceases, consciousness ceases. It goes out instantly. If artificial stimulators can provide the appropriate stimulation to keep consciousness going this, again, is shifting consciousness, from a brain to a brain prosthesis. While the prosthesis continues to function, the subject continues to exist.

Unger claims that continuous capacity for consciousness is necessary for his existence, but not sufficient. What is sufficient is the continuity of his core psychology, including the capacity for reason. When the decomposing brain can no longer reason, it is no longer him. It is only a subject, not him. Therefore he fades into a another, subpersonal subject. But in fact it is not another subject. It is the same subject, with diminished capacities. He becomes an irrational being, but he remains the same subject.

Unger's arguments are not strong enough to make me give up the intuition that the Self is simple entity, with a basic unity. We seem entitled to the conclusion that the Self should be conceived as the subject/agent described above.

The Identity of the Self

I have hinted that the identity of the Self is "perfect philosophical" identity, because the Self is a simple continuant entity. Here I shall adapt arguments from MacKenzie (1983) and Lowe (1991) in support of the claim that the fact that the Self is simple makes it impossible for there to be criteria for its persistence through time.

Imagine an Epicurean atom, immutable and eternal, which is large enough to be seen. It was on the table yesterday, and is on the table today. If I am asked "Is this the same atom that was on the table yesterday?" I can answer "The atom that was here yesterday has not been removed and replaced by a cardboard copy." I can add "I spent a sleepless night watching it." This is answering the epistemological question about the evidence I have for the identity of the atom.

However, if I am asked the ontological question "What makes this atom the same atom as was here yesterday?" I have no answer.

I have an answer to the question "What makes this table the same table as was here yesterday?" For a complex object made up of particles, such as the table, the answer is that all the particles that made up the table yesterday are still present, in the same arrangement, and none have been added. But of course this answer will not apply to the atom. It *is* a particle.

An answer of the sort "there is a continuous spatio-temporal path on which the present atom and yesterday's atom both lie" is simply a way of translating "same atom" into the terminology of four-dimensional ontology.

The answer "being itself, being the same atom" seems obvious and vacuous, but there is no other answer. The fact is that there are no *constitutive* criteria (as distinct from evidential criteria) for the identity of simple objects. Constitutive criteria apply only to complex objects. Since the Self is a simple entity, without constituents, the same considerations apply.

The Self is the only simple entity directly known to us, and it is the persistence of the Self that forms the ground for our notions of time and identity. The concept of identity comes from our experience of our own identity. I know it is the same atom because I have been watching it. If I do not believe that I retain my identity, that the person who started watching it is the same as the person who is watching it now, I would not form the concept of identity.

The question of the relationship between survival and identity has been raised by Brennan (1988) and Parfit (1991). Both of them claim that survival is a more basic relation than diachronic identity. Identity can, they allege, be defined in terms of survival. However, when a simple continuant entity is involved, there is no difference between survival and identity. Only when there is discontinuity, replacement of parts, fission, or fusion, can a logical wedge be inserted between survival and identity. Since I claim that a Self is a simple entity, for the Self survival and identity amount to the same thing. I shall not, therefore, give any detailed discussion of whether survival really is more basic than identity.

One Self

Zuboff (1990), Clark (1991), and Vendler (1984) have all suggested that there is only one Self, or at least, in Vendler's view, that it is not the case that there is a distinct, independent Self for each person. I will call this the One Self theory. It haunts this book, although I shall give no detailed discussion of the idea. Vendler has argued that since the Self is neutral, so that there is no distinguishing characteristic to make one Self different from another, and there is no spatial separation of Selves, there is no sense in saying there is more than one Self. However, as McGinn (1993) has pointed out, spatial separation is a basic difference. There is nothing to distinguish between one part of space and another except for the fact that they are spatially distinct. It is perfectly possible that other distinctions are also basic. The distinction between one Self and another may be also basic. I will proceed on the assumption that there is a distinct Self for each person.

I have sketched a view of the Self as a unified subject/agent which is an essential part of a person, the other parts being mind and body. (I do not deny that there may be more to the Self than consciousness and agency, but I will not argue that question.) I have argued that the Self is a simple entity, and so the identity through time of this Self is the same as its survival. The survival of the Self cannot be a matter of degree, because the Self is either present or absent. This is the concept of the Self I shall develop and argue for throughout this book.

2 The Self from the First Person Point of View

In this chapter I will show that there is a logical distinction between the Self and mind, and then show that we can have direct experience of the Self as the centre of agency and consciousness, and give an account of the subject of experience. After that I will deal with some of Unger's arguments against the idea of a Self. The Humean idea of the bundle Self and the Kantian idea that we could have no acquaintance with the Self were both arrived by examining ordinary waking consciousness. The argument for the direct experience of the Self is based on the experience of pure consciousness, which is usually obtained through meditative practice. This is a contentious issue, so I shall append a brief defence of pure consciousness.

The Distinction Between Self and Mind

The first part of my task is to show that the Self exists separately from the mind. I will do this by using arguments from Knox (1969, 1970) and Woodhouse (1970). The arguments are not strict proof, but the collective force is considerable.

Argument 1

I can imagine the world seeming to be very similar to the way it is now, but populated entirely by robots, which act similarly to the way we do. This is a world without consciousness and subjectivity. (From reading *Consciousness Explained* (Dennett, 1992) I suspect that Dennett would say that if they act exactly the way we do then there would be as much subjectivity as there is now, or at least that the claim that there was no subjectivity is incoherent.) This is a world which could be completely described from the third person point of view, and in which the third person point of view is the only one that needs to be considered. But it is not the real world.

The real world includes conscious mental states, attached to various bodies. If we give a complete third person description of the real world we have to list all the conscious states and say which bodies they are associated with. But this complete description still lacks an essential feature. It does not say which collection of conscious states is *me*. Nor can a third person description include that feature. No matter how detailed the descriptions of the collections of conscious states are, there is no way that I can deduce which one is mine without introducing the first person point of view into the description.

If a description of X does not include the information that I am X, there is no way of deducing "I am X" from the description. For example, I cannot deduce from the *description* "a befogged student of philosophy looking at a computer screen" the *fact* that "I am that student" without already knowing "I am befogged and looking at a computer screen"

Suppose all the states of a mind (that is, the ordered totality of experiences and dispositions possessed by a person) are determined and could be predicted. It would then be possible to predict that there would be a mind with exactly the contents my mind has now. It would be possible to predict that there is someone exactly like me. However, this does not make it possible to predict that this person *is* me, that the states of mind are mine, that the experiences are mine.

In the case of physical objects to say that one particular *f* could not have been predicted as against some other *f* is empty, since there is no intelligible difference between one *f* and another *f* exactly like it. However, this does not extend to persons. If I were replaced by a person exactly like me in every physical and mental characteristic, to the extent of having exactly the same mental states, this would be undetectable to another person, but not to me. From the first person point of view I am not replaceable. The implication of this is that I am not a collection or instantiation of a set of characteristics; I am whatever it is that has the characteristics.

Argument 2

Suppose exactly similar twins with exactly similar mental states faced each other against exactly similar backgrounds. The contents of their visual fields would be exactly similar. The total contents of their conscious minds would be similar. From the third person point of view the locations of their bodies would be sufficient condition for the awareness of the difference between them. An outside observer (looking down on them, perhaps) could distinguish between the two persons present, by seeing that there was one to the North, and one to the South. Of course, if they were switched round when the observer was not watching, he would not know the difference.

However, from the first person point of view, nothing in the description of the bodies would determine in whose visual field the other's body is an object. No characteristic about the body of the twin to the North would determine that the body represented in his visual field was that of the twin to the South. The conscious state of each twin would be the same. Simply analyzing the content of the conscious states would not be sufficient to determine "this state is the state of the twin to the North, and this state is the state of the twin to the South." Not even the twins could determine which visual field was his from the content alone. Thus, each twin's awareness of his own numerical distinctness could not be fully analyzed in terms of spatial distinctness. If the criterion for deciding in whose visual field the other's body is an object were spatial distinctness there would be no distinction between the two points of view, and this would destroy the concept of a subject of experience. In order to distinguish spatially between oneself and another, the distinction between "my point of view" and "another's point of view" is a necessary prerequisite. (Woodhouse, 1970) Thus, the "mineness" of experience cannot be deduced from the characteristics of the experience. The full description of the contents of experiences does not imply that they are mine. (Unless we claim that "mineness" is part of the content. But that is to concede the point that the third person description of the content is incomplete.)

Argument 3

I may begin my life with very little in the way of mental content. I would have very little "individuality", in the sense of having very ill-defined personality or character. If it were the case that my distinctness from other persons depended on mental content, I would not be clearly distinct from other people beginning their lives. Now it may well be the case that from the third person point of view one baby is very much like another (though it is not wise to suggest this to the parents of the babies) but it seems improbable that each baby is not, or does not have, a subject of experience distinct from that of the other babies.

The contents of my mind can resemble those of another mind to a greater or lesser degree. My present mental state may more resemble that of the Prime Minister than the mental state I had last week. Thus, if my distinctiveness depends on my mental content, my distinctiveness from the PM is a matter of degree. Sometimes I am less distinct from him than other times. (A gruesome thought!) When there is complete similarity (as in the case of the twins, above) then there is nothing (from the first person point of view) which makes me individual. Yet I am at all times a distinct person from John Major. I seem to be completely distinct from any other person. I am myself simply by being myself, not by having certain ideas, memories or beliefs.

Argument 4

Suppose I know that every one of my ideas, memories, beliefs, etc., will change radically, and then I will be tortured. I would still feel fear of the torture before the changes take place. This shows that my concern for the future is not that the future experiences will be accompanied by a particular set of experiences, but that the future experiences will happen to me. Even if all the characteristics change I am still worried about the experiences, so I am worried about the experiences happening to something other than the set of characteristics. (I will give an expanded version of this argument in the chapter on survival.)

The conclusion I draw from the arguments above is that what makes a certain person me is not discovered through examination of experiences and dispositions. That aspect or element that most decisively distinguishes one self-conscious individual - me - from another does not depend on the characteristics of my mind, nor on any particular instances of these characteristics. I am not just this collection of characteristics and memories, but something, an «I», that has the collection. What makes me the particular individual I am is being the Self I am, being the something that has the collection, the something that experiences the collection from the first person point of view.

This shows that the Self is distinct from the mind, and not just a combination of any of the various contents of the mind. The source of individual uniqueness is not in traits.

Vendler's Argument

Vendler (1984) uses the same insight to argue for a Transcendental Self. The Transcendental Self is the subject of experience that cannot be an object of experience. Thus, it cannot be named or described. Vendler further argues that the Transcendental Self is an agent, in that it determines causal chains, but is not itself a cause. It exists, but is not an item in the world. It is not the case that each person has their own individual Transcendental Self. It is the same Transcendental Self that provides the centre of consciousness and agency in each person. He claims that our natural concepts are not strong enough to take the burden of understanding it.

As I said in the introduction, I do not intend to pursue the question of whether the Self is transcendental, or whether there is an individual Transcendental Self for each person. Nor will I give or defend Vendler's account of agency. I am interested in establishing that there is a distinction between Self and mind, and that the Self is the centre of consciousness and agency.

We can start Vendler's argument from the question of how I locate myself in the world. The full third person point of view description of the world is complete and yet leaves out which bit, which body with an associated set of conscious experiences, etc., is me. Of course, in fact I have no doubt about which bit of the world is me, but I want to provide a justification for my belief. To find out which is me requires me to match the experiences I have with those of a body. Experience comes unbidden, popping up into consciousness. This experience is first integrated, and then recognized as being appropriate for this body. Experience and agency combine. I turn my head, and feel the appropriate kinaesthetic sensations, as well as seeing the change in the visual field. I see an item, stretch out a hand to touch it, and see and feel a hand that is part of this body reaching out. As I feel the object, I see the hand touching the object. This body is the one I have direct control over. The experiences I have match those I imagine to be appropriate for this body, but are in fact richer than those I imagine, so this is my body.

By treating Self-location in this way, I find I can imagine being in someone else's position, and having their thoughts, feelings, etc. Of course, I might be inaccurate in the details of the imagined version, but that does not affect the principle. Indeed, in order to represent another person's mind, I cannot imagine that mind without imagining that it is in some specific ways like my own. I have to represent it as having consciousness and agency. This means I have to represent it from the first person point of view. If I cannot so represent it, I cannot represent the consciousness and agency of another mind at all, and I am then pushed into solipsism.

Let us suppose, purely for the sake of argument, that the PM is not a computer graphic, or a rather unconvincingly constructed robot, but a real person. What is involved in entertaining this fantasy? I imagine that he has a conscious mind. And that requires me to attribute to the PM a first person point of view, like my own. If I succeed at imagining what it is like to be John Major, I will be imagining that I am John Major. To do this I reverse the procedure for locating myself in the world. In imagining being John Major, I first imagine the objective details of his body, then fill in the details of what it would be like to be in that position. I similarly imagine that I have his ideas, his emotions, etc. Of course, I also imagine that I have the same direct control over his body and thoughts that I have over my own.

This is imagining being John Major, not imagining Robin Harwood's mind has migrated into John Major's body. I do not imagine that John Major has my thoughts, ideals, intellect, etc. (improving though this would be for him) and I do not imagine that Robin Harwood is Prime Minister (improving though that would be for the world in general). I imagine, depressingly, that I have the ideas thoughts, feeling, memories, or perceptions that John Major has. I imagine that my subjectivity and agency is attached to John Major's body. I imagine that I am "hooked" to John Major's life. I imagine seeing the world from John Major's physical and mental point of view.

If I imagine a world without cats, I am imagining a different world, but in imagining the world in which I am John Major I am not imagining a different world. If I were John Major, to a third party observer, everything would seem to be as it is now. There is nothing in the objective features of the world that would show the difference. Only from my point of view would there be a difference. My point of view would be that of John Major. It would be John Major's experience that came unbidden, and it would be John Major's body over which I would have direct control.

What I imagine is not a possible stage of Robin Harwood's life. The conscious life of a person is a single phenomenon spread out in time. Robin Harwood's consciousness is conscious of a connected sequence of experiences, actions, etc., matching the history of Robin Harwood's body. Similarly, the consciousness of John Major is conscious of a connected sequence of experiences, actions, etc., matching the history of his body. What I imagine is being conscious of a state in the series determined by the history of John Major's body.

Even though Robin Harwood imagines this, I am imagining that I am not Robin Harwood, and although it is not the case that I am John Major, I can imagine that I am John Major. This shows that the «I» that I can imagine being John Major instead of Robin Harwood is logically free of its association with the body and mind of Robin Harwood.

But the logical dissociation of the «I» from the body and mind of Robin Harwood implies that the «I» is not the same as Robin Harwood. If they are not the same, what is the relation between the «I» and Robin Harwood? Being Robin Harwood is one possible state for «I», being John Major is another. Robin Harwood is a state that «I» can be in. The statement "I am Robin Harwood" means that Robin Harwood is the bit of the universe the «I» is anchored to. Being so anchored is to be in the state of being Robin Harwood.

What is this «I» that I can imagine being John Major instead of Robin Harwood? When I imagine that I am anchored to John Major nothing specific is left of being Robin Harwood. Only the general framework of human consciousness and agency is left. This framework, the «I», is the (Transcendental) Self. It is a subject/agent without content. Vendler uses the analogy of a TV screen. Whatever image is shown on the screen is constrained by the shape of the screen, and the number of lines used to form the image. In the same way, conscious experience is constrained to be experienced from the a point of view of a subject. Of course, the TV screen is a thing in experience, and there the analogy breaks down. The «I» is a format or schema for experience.

The analogy gives rise to an objection. I view the TV screen, but when I imagine being John Major, the imagining is a set of images, etc., in Robin Harwood's mind. It is part of Robin Harwood's mind. Analogously, Robin Harwood's mind is a *picture* on the screen. Therefore one or part of one picture contemplates another picture.

Now it is certainly true that the Robin Harwood mind contains the act of imagining John Major. However, it is also true that it is the contentless «I» which performs the act of imagining. I can represent my mind, or another mind, or another's mind in my mind. Just as the eye cannot see the eye, I cannot represent the «I» that views the show and creates the representation.

Vendler's view may be a minority view among modern Western philosophers, but I suspect that the majority of the world's philosophers hold or have held such a view. Regarded as conscious subject at least, Vendler's version of the Transcendental Self is very similar to the view of the Self in Neoplatonism, and in the Islamic and mediaeval philosophies that descended from Neoplatonism, and similar to the view of the Self in many Eastern traditions.

However, it does not have to be regarded as dualist. For the purpose of this book, which is to examine the problem of survival and personal identity, we need only consider that a Self exists, and is the basis of our conceptions of ourselves. We do not need to presume that it is in fact separable from the body or realized in some other way than the patterns of brain activity, so long as we recognize that it is not logically necessary that it be so realized.

Hannay (1987) offers some criticisms of Vendler's argument, some of which are criticisms of the account of agency. The main criticism of the basic argument is that it presupposes that solipsism is not true. This seems a reasonable presupposition to me. Neither solipsism nor its negative can be proved, because they are not the sort of claim that can be proved. However, solipsism is not a position I can seriously believe, and, like all skeptical positions, it is ultimately a barren position. I am, therefore, prepared to disregard it, and accept the presupposition.

These arguments for the logical distinction between Self and mind have given a picture of a Self that is a contentless centre of consciousness and agency. Examination of the phenomenology of consciousness and agency supports this picture.

Phenomenology of Experience

As Madell(1991) points out, this idea of the Self does not come from reifying grammatical features, but from experience. The concept does not arise because there is a pronoun "I" in English. We have a dummy pronoun "it" in expressions such as "it is raining" or "leg it", but we are not inclined to posit the existence of an «it», whereas we are strongly convinced that there is an «I» that the pronoun refers to.

The belief comes from the fact that we experience ourselves as a unified centre of action and experience. Experience does not come as a scatter of «I» thoughts, but as a coherent whole. I drive, watch the traffic, hear noises and feel cold all at the same time. I cannot genuinely doubt that the same «I» performs the actions and has the experiences. The «I» that watches the traffic is the «I» that drives. The same «I» has each of the experiences of feeling cold and hearing noises. I also cannot genuinely doubt that I am not any one of the actions or experiences. I am not the watching, or the driving, or the feeling cold. Nor do I believe, pretheoretically, that I am the total of these. My experience includes awareness of myself as the subject acting and having the experiences. I cannot doubt that I, the subject, exist, as an entity distinct from the experiences.

To doubt that I am the subject that I take myself to be requires me to accept a philosophical theory that tells me that my experience is misleading. I cannot doubt that the experiences are experienced together. I have to accept the possibility that this impression of being a subject distinct from the experiences might be an illusion resulting from the fact that the experiences come and go. I have to accept that I do not exist as a subject distinct from the bundle or stream of experiences.

(However. if I am under the illusion that I am aware of myself as a subject then I exist to have the illusion. There is at least the entity that has the illusion, even if the entity is a compound of experiences which includes the illusion. Now this illusion is persistent. Such a persisting mental state could in fact do a lot of the work that a persisting Self does in establishing Self identity. Nonetheless, it seems doubtful that a mental state could be a subject.)

The Self is always an agent, even when the agency is not being applied. Agency does not seem compatible with the idea of there just being a conscious mind made up out of bits and pieces. It is partly because the Self is so active that I am loath to refer to it as a substance.

Examination of the phenomenology in detail supports this impression of the Self. We can have direct experience of the Self, not as an object of consciousness, in the way that a pain is an object, but the experience of being an agent and a subject

The Self as the Centre of Agency

This lengthy treatment of Filice's (1986) argument is little more than a paraphrase. It shows that we are in fact aware of the causal and controlling aspect of the Self. I deal with it at length because I consider the agency of the Self to be very important, and I use it as part of some of my other arguments.

Action is so intimate a part of Self that Filice offers as an incomplete definition of the Self "the occurrent source of physical/psychic conscious-intentional actions". A familiar argument here is the sense of the Self as decider when an action is decided on. (Campbell, 1951) However, the aspect considered here is not the decision to perform an action, but the doing of a continuous action. Examination of continuous bodily and mental action reveals that there is a sense of active, continuous causation.

First, I will consider two types of bodily activity, and show how they differ. The first bodily activity (Case 1) is activity that is not consciously controlled, and the second (Case 2) is activity under continuous control.

Case 1: I take a gasp which triggers a coughing fit. I deliberately gasped, and knew the coughing would follow. The initiation of the event was a conscious and deliberate choice, and the event engages my concern as it occurs. Nonetheless, it is something I suffer. It proceeds on its own. I am not controlling it.

Case 2: I am deliberately juggling a ball. This is not just a state triggering another state, or a chain of events. I sustain and experience a causal contribution during the whole event. I can control the length of the event, as well as some variations within the (very limited!) range of my juggling skill.

The gasp in Case 1 is an action, but the coughing is the result of the action. I do not act when I cough (in this case). It just happens to me. It would be difficult for me to stop coughing. Case 2 is an action in the primitive sense. Case 2 is not just a case of standing causal conditions (e.g. the electricity passing through the filament causes the glow) but is dynamic. I have no difficulty in stopping juggling. Thus, in case 2, I am aware of myself as a continuous cause.

This experienced causation cannot be just a set of event-like states (beliefs, desires, intentions, tryings, etc.) with me being either a passive bearer of these states or a totality of these states. In case 1 only one psychological event (event like state) is necessary, and I would only experience one state. However, in case 2 a series of short events is necessary. I experience the series, and the experience of the series of states creates the feeling of continuous causation.

Now if one state is not experienced as a feeling of causation for the subsequent coughing, we need an explanation of why a series of states is experienced as causation for the juggling. Alternatively, if one state is needed to experience causation for the gasp (but not the coughing) but a series are needed to make up the feeling of continuous experience of causation for the juggling, the question arises of *how many* states are needed to make up the series. Furthermore, the feeling is not experienced as a series, but as continuous.

Nor can it be a long-lasting desire or intention which gives the experience of continuous cause. I need not experience desire or intention while juggling. They may be subconsciously present, but we need a reason to posit this.

The position becomes even clearer when we consider mental activity, such as thinking, deliberate imagining or visualizing, or attending. When these are continued for some time, I am aware of myself as cause, as the source of control, and after a little while I feel I have to exert more and more mental effort to sustain the activity. The very term "mental effort" shows how natural it is for us to regard ourselves in this way.

When I concentrate my attention on understanding a knotty argument or on following my breath, I am directly aware of being the active cause. (Following the breath is a meditation technique. It involves focusing the attention on the sensation of breathing, and not attending to any other sensations, perceptions, or ideas.)

A Humean attempt to analyze the directing of attention into a series of states seems unfaithful to experience, and inadequate to explain the experience. The experience is not simply one of a succession of states, but of effort and control.

> Being aware of effort and control is in fact very different from being aware of a throbbing toothache, or of a recurrent image. (Filice 1986, p. 101)

Toothache and recurrent images are experiences which one cannot help feeling. Effort and control are different from these in the following ways.

(a) They contain the awareness of a power being exerted
(b) One experiences oneself as being immersed in the exertion, not as neutral or detached
(c) One feels oneself as the source, not as the receiver; neither oppressed nor overwhelmed by the power.

The relevant features of sustained willed attention are continuity, sustainment, and will-like personal causation. They point to the Self as being something continuous and causal, not a sum of beliefs, desires, etc.

Desires, impulses and obsessive thoughts can be felt as foreign, oppressive, or imposed. Sustained causation cannot be felt as something imposed. It is very different from desires and impulses. I can, in fact, reject or try to prevent actions or ideas that I desire. I can try to overcome my impulses.

While I am sitting in the library concentrating on a philosophical argument, a beautiful young woman in exiguous garb drifts past and at once my concentration evaporates and my attention shifts away from the argument. Then I have to struggle to control my attention and bring it back to philosophy. This is not simply a matter of conflicting desires. There are two stages. In stage one I have the desire to read philosophy, and the conflicting desire to hang up philosophy (unless philosophy can make a Juliet) and look at the young woman. My attention shifts to the young woman on impulse. In stage two I reassert control over my attention, reconstruct my concentration, and return to the philosophical argument. At this stage I am aware of exerting effort to overcome the unphilosophical desire. I have the same two desires, they still conflict, and I also have the feeling of exertion. Perhaps the relative strengths of the two desires has changed, but this provides no explanation for the feeling of exertion.

There are three good reasons for believing that sustained willed attention is indeed like this account of it.

(1) It is a common experience. If it is deceptive, the deception is very deeply hidden.
(2) We also know the opposite phenomena. We know discontinuous attention, non-focussed attention, and, of course, uncontrolled attention, as in the library example above.
(3) It is not possible to imagine cases where we think attention is focussed, continuous, and sustained, when it is not. Nor can we imagine cases where we think we are directing the flow of attention when we are not.

Filice points out that while the phenomenology does not directly exhibit a Self, it does provide evidence of a Self which is causal, continuous, and unified.

Nonetheless, we do have direct experience of being an agent, which is one sort of direct experience of the Self.

Direct Experience of the Self as Consciousness

Shear (1983) presents an argument to show that it is in fact possible to have direct experience of the Self as consciousness. Shear's argument is that the experience of pure consciousness is the experience of the Self. Normal waking consciousness is condition of

I am conscious of an object.

In pure consciousness the state has become

I am conscious.

Normal subject - object experience, which is dual experience, ceases, and only non - dual experience remains. This state can be remembered afterwards.

> One remembers simply that one was, *without being aware of anything*, without even noticing *that* one was awake. Yet one was awake, aware, not unconscious – this one remembers. In memory it is clearly distinguished from unconsciousness, as for example, from the 'blackout' of deep sleep; it is clearly distinguished from unconsciousness because one remembers being awake, just simply consciously being. (Shear 1983, p. 59)

Forman (1986, p. 49) described the state thus:

> the subject is awake and conscious, but without an object or content for consciousness - no thoughts, emotions, sensations, or awareness of any external phenomena.

This description stems from his own experience. I have experienced the state several times, although not recently, and my experiences, so far as I can recall it, fits this description. In Nagelian terms, it is "what it is like to be an experiencer".

Pure consciousness is identifiable by the total absence of any empirical content. In this state one is aware of existing, but not of anything else. There is no thinking, no perceiving, no mental activity of any kind. Although sustained mental effort is usually needed to attain the state, there is no sense of agency while in the state. There is no thought "I have achieved pure consciousness." Nonetheless, one is awake, and will report afterwards that one was not asleep.

This shows that consciousness is not reducible to a series of conscious experiences. If it is possible to be conscious without being conscious *of* anything then consciousness is not just a collection of experiences, but something of which experiences are a state.

Shear argues as follows that pure consciousness is direct experience of the Self.

(1) It is a well accepted assumption (*a*) that the experience of the Self is necessarily present in every experience. Only an experience without determinate qualities can accompany all other experiences. There can only be one such experience for if there were two, what would make the difference between them? Pure consciousness is the only possible experience that can satisfy this requirement. Therefore the experience of pure consciousness is uniquely able to fulfil the condition of assumption *a*, and therefore pure consciousness is the experience of the Self.

(2) By *a* the experience of the Self must be in pure consciousness. But pure consciousness is experienced alone, contentless, and without parts. Therefore the experience of the Self must be the whole of the pure consciousness experience. There is no part of the experience which is not experience of the Self.

I would point out that this does not imply that the pure consciousness experience is experience of every aspect of the Self. There may well be aspects of the Self (e.g. agency) which are not comprehended in the experience. Even if one can see nothing but the iceberg, it may still be only the top of the iceberg that one sees. Pure consciousness is the experience of the Self as consciousness.

The weakest part of his argument is the assumption *a*. Shear claims that *a* is intuitively plausible, so I will attempt to justify his claim.

If there is an experience of the Self, it cannot be a dual subject - object experience, but rather the experience of the subject being an experiencer. The Self is the subject, not the object, and cannot be an object of experience. The subject is present as an experiencer in every experience, so it seems likely that the experience of the Self will be present in every experience. To deny *a* requires that an explanation be given for why the experience of the Self is absent from some experience.

The process of reaching the pure consciousness state is one of withdrawing attention from the contents of consciousness, until the stage is reached in which no contents are attended to. Thus, there are no objects of consciousness. The attention is focussed down to a point. (Traditionally referred to as achieving "one-pointedness of mind".) This means that pure consciousness is not a dual experience. This fact gives added strength to the claim that pure consciousness is the experience of the Self. It is exactly the sort of experience one would expect the experience of the Self to be.

Pure consciousness is unchanging, so although it is present in all experience it is not noticed because attention is given to the changes. Nonetheless, Shear suggest that we gain our common sense idea of the Self at least in part from the presence of pure consciousness.

> We are suggesting, in short that our intuitive notion of the Self as constant and unchanging and present somehow in all of our experiences reflect a vague, subliminal awareness of pure consciousness as the constant all-pervading 'background' of all our experience. (Shear 1983, p. 61)

The background is only noticed when all the other contents of consciousness have been eliminated.

The experience of pure consciousness at once provides observable support for the idea of the Self as a unified entity and reveals it as being the sort of thing that we intuitively believe.

The Subject of Consciousness

In the state of pure consciousness there is no sense of subject, and no feeling of agency. Agency is required to attain the state (by controlling the attention) but it is latent when pure consciousness is achieved. In normal waking consciousness we have a lively sense of the subject of consciousness. To explain this I will adapt Evans' (1970) account of the subject of consciousness.

Evans uses a very traditional first person view of consciousness. Normal waking consciousness is commonly described in analogous terms to vision or spotlight. As we saw from Bradley's version, this is an appropriate analogy. The structure of normal waking consciousness is that of attention focussed on one of the contents, with the rest of the contents present but unattended to. This is like a spotlight with the centre of the beam clearly illuminating the item in the centre of the being, but also casting some light on the items around the centre. The focus of the beam is variable. It can be tightly focused on a single item, or spread more diffusely over several items. The analogy with vision is similar. The centre of the field of vision can be moved to illuminate various items. The item in the centre of the field is clear and in focus. The items around it are less distinct, and the items at the periphery of vision are noticed only if they move, and then only as an awareness that something is moving. In order them to be clearly distinguished they have to be brought into the centre of vision to be examined.

However, these analogies each only give one side of the picture. The spotlight illuminates, but does not perceive. Sight perceives, but does not illuminate. Consciousness does both. When an item becomes part of the content of consciousness it is at once illuminated by consciousness and known to the subject.

These analogies led Evans to describe normal waking consciousness as polarized into projected and unprojected consciousness. Attention picks out one section of the contents for detailed examination, while the rest is merely present. The content picked out for attention is projected consciousness, and the remainder is unprojected consciousness. Thus, while I am concentrating my attention on this paragraph, I am only vaguely aware of the feel of the chair under my bottom. I am only vaguely aware of the slight ache in my knee. Even though I have been concentrating my attention on writing, when I broaden the focus of my attention, I am not surprised to find that my knee aches. I have not been attending to it, but nonetheless it was part of the contents of my consciousness, and so I had some awareness of it. If a burst of toothache were to hit me now, I would surprised, because there is no awareness of toothache in my conscious at the moment. If I shift my attention to the ache in my knee, I know that it is not too bad, and will shortly stop with just a little rest. I can shift my attention to the feel of the chair. There is no sense of surprise about the feel of the chair, even though I can now analyze it in more detail. When a particular item is attended to, it is much more detailed than when it is not attended to. A pain when attended to can be known to vary rhythmically in intensity, to be spread over a certain area, to have a variety of other qualities. An orange blob can, when attended to, be seen to have a certain shape, texture, size, and variation in shade. The more the item is inspected, the more detail is revealed. This phenomenology of the attended contents and the unattended contents is well known.

Evans claims that the subject - .object feel of normal waking consciousness comes from the awareness that there is the distinction between the attended object and the undifferentiated mass of unattended contents. By being picked out by attention, the item attended to is separated from the rest of the contents and so set in opposition to them. The rest of the contents, which Evans classes as the unprojected consciousness, are the subject, while the attended item is the object. This gives the subject-object polarity of normal waking consciousness.

Evans' conclusion is that the mass of unprojected consciousness is the Self. Unprojected consciousness cannot be the object of attention, just as the Self cannot. It lies behind every normal waking consciousness experience, as the Self seems to. We have a lively sense of the presence of the Self. We also have a constant awareness of the contents of unprojected consciousness.

Now Evans regards consciousness as the aggregation of the total contents. An unattended item is part of consciousness, and an attended item is also part of consciousness. This means that the contents of the mass of unprojected consciousness changes with every shift of attention, and one part of the subject becomes object, and then reverts to being part of the subject when attention shift to another part of the contents. Yet at all times the object is part of the total field of consciousness.

This does not square with the intuition of the Self as something constant and unchanging. Nor does it make it possible for us to recognize the Self in memory.

Nonetheless, I think Evans is right to the extent that the sense of being a subject arises from the division of the content of consciousness into the attended and the unattended. Since the experience of pure consciousness shows that consciousness is logically distinct from its contents, I think that the subject is not the aggregate of contents but is consciousness itself. The polarity comes from the feel of agency associated with directing the attention. In normal waking consciousness agency directs attention at particular content, and thus makes this content the object. The remainder of the contents cannot be subject, since they are just contents of consciousness. Nonetheless, the awareness of their presence shows that consciousness extends beyond the object. It is the sensation of agency using the attention to separate out the object that creates the contrast between the subject/agent and the object of attention. Thus, consciousness (distinct from its contents) is the subject.

This conclusion seems to be supported both by the phenomenology of pure consciousness and by the phenomenology of letting our minds go blank in the usual sense. In the state of pure consciousness there are no contents to be picked out, and so no contrast between the attended and the unattended. Nor is there any activity. There is, therefore, no sense of being a subject/agent. It seems, also, that the sense of being a subject/agent is strongest when we are concentrating attention on an activity or idea. When we allow attention to lose its focus and drift then we are less aware of being a subject/agent.

Thus, we can have direct experience of the Self, an experience which can lie behind and within our normal experience to give us the Self - knowledge that we seem to have. The Self is the source of consciousness and agency. We note that agency is not an attribute of the Self, but is the Self acting. Consciousness is not an attribute of the Self, but is the Self being aware. Normal waking consciousness is sufficient to be a subject, and attention shows that agency is intrinsic to consciousness. Therefore we can regard the Self as the subject/agent. Now it may be that there is something which is conscious and an agent, or it may be that consciousness is the agent. If the former, then there is something which is undetectable lying behind consciousness and agency. However, it is sufficient for us to proceed with the Self as consciousness and agency.

A Defence of Pure Consciousness

It is very difficult for me to accept arguments against the possibility of pure consciousness. Since I have had the experience of pure consciousness, I am inclined to take the experience as evidence that such an experience is possible, and disregard arguments against the possibility. Nonetheless, I will try to meet the main objections to the possibility of pure consciousness, and to show that the burden of proof rests on those who deny the possibility of pure consciousness.

The Claims as Evidence

There is evidence for the possibility of pure consciousness in the experience which seems to be that of pure consciousness. For those who have had the experience, the experience is the best evidence, but for those who have not had the experience the claims of others can count as evidence.

Forman uses the following argument to defend the claims against the suggestion that those who report it are mistaken or misdescribe their experience. If a sane, honest, intelligent person claims to have experienced it, that is evidence for it. The claim can always be contested, but what else could count as evidence for pure consciousness? If this sort of claim is not permitted to be evidence, then nothing else will or can be permitted as evidence, and so the assertion that there is no pure consciousness becomes an empty claim. Those who doubt the possibility of pure consciousness have perhaps not attempted or succeeded in the mental discipline needed, but pure consciousness is very widely reported by people from many different backgrounds and cultures who have practiced the discipline a little. (Forman 1986)

Pendleton (1988) suggested that the reports were of experience that had been reflected on, in being remembered and described. By the principles of the phenomenologists (Pendleton quotes Husserl) the reflection modifies the experience, and so the reports would be of the modified experience. Forman (1991) pointed out that this argument could be used against all first person reports of pure consciousness experiences, and therefore cast doubt on any claim. Then the assertion that there is no such thing as pure consciousness would become an unfalsifiable assertion. Also, Husserl's argument is that reflection alters the experience. For Pendleton's argument to work the alteration would have to be complete reversal. If, before alteration, it was an experience *with* content, and yet after alteration pure consciousness is reported as being an experience *without* content, this is an 100% change in the nature of the experience. If such a change can occur between having an experience and reflecting on it, then doubt is cast on all other reports of any sort of experience. (Forman 1991)

Meeting the Main Objections

The main objections are as follows:

(1) All experience is mediated.
(2) All consciousness is intentional.
(3) All consciousness must have empirical content.
(4) Consciousness is identical with its contents.
(5) There is no difference between an experience without empirical content and no experience at all.

If these objections are based on generalization from ordinary experience, then they fail immediately, because there is an experience which is an exception to all of them. To have any force, they must be established by other means.

(1) All Experience is Mediated.

The argument from mediation of experience is that all experience is inextricably bound up with its cultural and conceptual context, and thus varies according to that context. Thus, the nature of the experience which I interpret as pure consciousness is, in fact, determined by the context, and is shaped and coloured by the context. It is not, therefore, a experience of *pure* consciousness.

The argument is dealt with in detail by many of the contributors in Forman 1990, but I will make a few points about it here. The idea that cultural context can and often does influence our experience seems to me to be a truth verging on the Self-evident, but the claim that it must always influence all experience seems something which needs to be proved.

(When this cultural relativism is taken to the extent of claiming that cultural context determines or even constitutes experience it then seems to me to be Self-evident nonsense. "Stat rosa pristina nomine, nomena nuda tenemus" may be a fine ending to a novel (Eco, 1984), but it is dubious epistemology. I am not a modern man, let alone "post-modern".)

The experience of pure consciousness counts against the thesis of mediation. Although ordinary experience may be mediated by concepts, etc., the experience of pure consciousness is one in which no concepts are consciously used, and is arrived by expressly removing and disregarding concepts. The onus of proof lies on those who claim that pure consciousness is a mediated experience.

(2) All Consciousness is Intentional

Proponents of the thesis of intentionality have always had difficulty with such things as emotions and pains, but even if we accept that normal consciousness is always intentional, this does not exclude the possibility of a state of consciousness which is not intentional.

To guarantee the impossibility of objectless consciousness, we have to make consciousness identical with its objects, but then we could not formulate the thesis of intentionality.

The thesis of intentionality is claimed to be a phenomenological description of the fundamental nature of experience, not as a logical truth. This being the case, it denial is not illogical, and consciousness without an object is a logical possibility.

Even if the thesis of intentionality is regarded as a logical truth, we can still say that it is only a logical truth about normal waking consciousness. Perhaps it is true, and even necessarily true, that all people who are awake and in normal waking consciousness are conscious of something, but that does not imply that normal waking consciousness is the only form of consciousness, or that any form of consciousness must be consciousness of something. If it is not a logical truth about other forms of consciousness, then it is logically possible that it is not true about those other forms of consciousness. (Woodhouse, 1990)

(3) All Consciousness must Have Content

The basic notion of consciousness seems to be "not in one of the modes of unconsciousness." These modes include dreamless sleep, under anaesthesia, coma, death, and inanition. Consciousness seems to be the basic condition for experience, but the notion does not entail that there be any experience or other content. To claim that all consciousness must have content requires claiming that, in spite of appearance, there is content in the experience of pure consciousness, or that the experience of pure consciousness does not exist. Neither of these seems acceptable, since both involve denying that the experience of pure consciousness is what it seems to be. If this denial is made without evidence or reason it is merely begging the question. (Prigge and Kessler 1990. A similar notion of consciousness is found in O'Shaughnessy 1986. I will later to claim that consciousness continues during sleep, anaesthesia, and coma, but that will not affect the argument here. The distinction between me, now conscious, and my chair, now, presumably, unconscious, remains.)

(4) Consciousness is Identical with its Contents

The phenomenology of consciousness is that of constant consciousness with changing contents, of consciousness as a canvas on which the various experiences and ideas are painted (O'Shaughnessy 1986).

The core of Mark Woodhouse's argument against the identity of consciousness and its contents is as follows:

First, consciousness is not logically identical with its contents. If consciousness were logically identical with its contents then we would not distinguish between a person being aware of a succession of phenomena and a person having a succession of awarenesses over the same period. Since we do distinguish the two ideas, there must be a logical distinction between consciousness and its contents.

We make a distinction between consciousness and the objects of consciousness. This distinction is used in the thesis of intentionality - that all consciousness is consciousness of something, that is, that it has an object. The object may be an idea , a perception, an emotion, etc. Now if consciousness is identical with its contents, it must be identical with its objects. All contents are actual or potential objects. But in such a case there would be no point in saying that consciousness must be consciousness of an object. The thesis of intentionality collapses. We would not be able to conceive of an intentional content. Clearly we can, so consciousness and content must be logically distinct.

(Also, it seems to me that if consciousness is identical with its contents, but it is not identical with its objects, the object would no longer be part of the contents of consciousness, and so we could not be conscious of the object.)

If we attempt to claim that consciousness is identical with all its content except the current object, the result is that an item becomes part of consciousness when attention is shifted away from it, and then ceases to be part of consciousness when it is attended to, while persisting throughout these changes.

Second, consciousness is not contingently identical with its contents. Hume, James, and Bergson developed theories which claimed that consciousness was identical with its contents. But if a Humean account of consciousness were true, we would surely feel consciousness as coming in short pulses. On a Jamesian view, we would be aware of it being passed on from one set of mental contents to the next. Neither of these are the case. (I discuss this more fully in the chapter on continuity of consciousness.) Bergson cannot account for the unity of the awareness of the changing states of the mind. It is the fact that there is an enduring consciousness distinct from its contents which enables us to experience change, to recognize that one experience came after another, or that two experiences are simultaneous.

(5) *There is No Difference Between an Experience Without Empirical Content and No Experience at All*

When we wake from dreamless sleep, we are inclined to consider that we remember no experience at all. However, on emerging from pure consciousness, we can clearly remember the experience. We are constrained to describe it in negative terms because our language is based on describing experience with content. Nonetheless, we can state that we were conscious during the period of pure consciousness. Thus, we can make a distinction between what we remember as no experience, and experience that is difficult to describe.

These arguments show that pure consciousness is a genuine possibility. Even without personal experience of pure consciousness, the reports provide suitable evidence for the reality of the phenomenon. Those who would deny it must provide reasons strong enough to convince not only those who accept pure consciousness on the evidence, but also to convince those of us who have experienced it.

3 Unity of Consciousness

The unity of consciousness question is usually understood to be about the fact that I see the road ahead and the surrounding fields, hear my wife say "Waaa! Pooo! Agriculture!", and smell the cause of this exclamation at the same time. All three items are perceived by the same me as a single complex sensory experience. But I am also driving the car. I am also feeling rather cheerful because the traffic to Edinburgh is lighter than I expected. I am also calculating the likely time of arrival in Edinburgh. If asked what bit of action I performed in controlling the car just at the time of the exclamation, I would probably not remember (indeed, I do not – this example is taken from Real Life) and if I did I would have had to search my memory for it diligently. The driving was not conscious in the same way that the calculating was. It had been, in a sense, handed over to a subordinate system. I can recall feeling cheerful, but had I been asked about my mood at the time, I would have had to pause and examine the memory just as diligently as I do now. I was not immediately conscious of being cheerful, rare though the condition is. Clearly, there are bits of my mental activity that do not form part of my unity of consciousness, and yet can be regarded as belonging to me at the time. Some of these are accessible to my consciousness, others (the alleged murky motives of the subconscious, for example) are not.

In this chapter I will give an account of unity of consciousness in terms of the Self as I have described it, and then discuss some attempts to explain unity of consciousness without invoking the idea of a Self. These will be

(a) the Humean view,
(b) the "just so" account,
(c) an account basing unity of consciousness on unity of agency, and
(d) unification by the brain.

I will then discuss the alleged division of consciousness in "split brains" and explain why such cases fail to show that there is no Self. Finally, I will argue that we are justified in accepting the account of unity of consciousness in terms of a unifying Self.

Unity of Consciousness and the Self

The unity of consciousness and the phenomenology of consciousness gives rise to the idea that there is a centre to the mind, a Self. However, a account is needed of how the Self unifies the mind.

The view of the Self as consciousness/agency, given in the preceding chapter, can provide such an account. Once we have recognized that there is a distinction between consciousness and its contents, and that the experience of pure consciousness shows that consciousness is undivided, consciousness can be regarded as a field or a ground on which the various contents appear. It then becomes clear that the contents of consciousness are unified by being contents in a single field. Using the spotlight analogy again, the light illuminates a set of items which are unified by being illuminated in a single patch of light.

The concept of the unified Self provides the simplest explanation for the unity of consciousness and the unity of agency.

Humean Connections

Hume"s account has been criticized so much that I will only give a brief criticism here. Hume claimed that there were three relationships between "perceptions" that united them into a single consciousness, viz., resemblance, causation, and contiguity.

Resemblance of your perception and mine of the film we are watching together does not make them belong to one mind. Resemblance should unify your perception of Mickey Mouse with my perceptions of Minnie, even though we are watching different cartoons in different cinemas, without unifying my perceptions of Minnie with the rustle of the crisp packet coming from the seat behind mine.

Even if we consider my perceptions alone, it is not clear how the perceptions resemble each other. What characteristics do they have in common? The sight of my computer, the taste of chocolate, the sound of a jet plane, and feeling cold are very different perceptions. They do not seem to resemble each other and yet they are all unified in my consciousness now.

Causation can provide vertical, but not horizontal linking. It does not explain why my philosophical musings are unified with the taste of chocolate.

Each of these could probably be fitted into a causal chain with a preceding state either of the mind or of sense organs, but they have no apparent causal connection with each other. The taste does not cause the musings, nor the musing the taste. Since they are contemporaneous, it is difficult to see how there could be any causal connection between them.

Further, as Stroud (1977) pointed out, there can be chains of causation in which A's perception of the enemy causes A to signal B, who signals the order to attack to C. C's perception of the order was caused by A's perception of the enemy, but the perceptions are not in the same mind.

(Stroud also claims that the careful Humean analysis of causation breaks down here. Hume only gives rather vague remarks about it. Stroud considers that if the Humean analysis of causation is applied it does not work. Perception G is not always followed by perception H, and without this uniformity or regularity we cannot see them as causally connected.)

Contiguity, in the sense that sound and vision come together, is the very fact to be explained.

It seems possible that Hume meant that there is only one event at a time, but they follow so quickly, and there is such rapid alternation between them that they appear to be simultaneous, and hence unified Since there is only one at a time, there is no problem about how they can actually be simultaneous. However, the simple succession of ideas is not enough to make them ideas in the same consciousness. Furthermore, surely the *appearance* of simultaneity is itself a mental event that encapsulates several different events. This would be a higher order thought.

The suggestion that perceptions that reflect the world from a common perspective are thereby linked together will not do either. We can have several perspectives and still bring the perceptions together. I can quite easily imagine sitting in a hot bath, wearing virtual reality goggles which show me scenes of the snow falling in the mighty forests of British Columbia, and being restrained from singing the Lumberjack song by the fact that my Walkman is playing the sounds of a railway station, without losing unity of consciousness. Nor, as Brooks (1985) points out, do moods and feelings have a perspective. Indeed, it is difficult to see how they could be said to reflect the world, so the "common perspective" explanation will not work for them.

The contents of consciousness are so varied and so disparate that it seems unlikely that any set of relationships could exist between them that would suffice to unify them. It is much more likely that they are unified by being related to the Self.

Thoughts of a Higher Order

Proponents of the higher order state theory of unity of consciousness claim that the various contents of consciousness are united by being the objects of higher order states. Thus, when I am listening to music and thinking about philosophy at the same time, there is a "sound of music" state, a "philosophy thoughts" state, and a higher order state of "I am thinking and listening" Carruthers (1986) claims that not all the states of consciousness belonging to the same mind are joined by a higher order state of consciousness. I am aware of the music and aware of what I am thinking without being aware of what I am *simultaneously* hearing and thinking. I hear a crescendo, and the music reaches fortissimo at the same time as I have an idea, without my being aware that the idea and the fortissimo are simultaneous. I later may be able to recall the sequence of the music, and the sequence of the thoughts, without being able to correlate them with each other. There is no higher state of consciousness, or collection of higher states, that contains both.

Nor can the higher order state theorist fall back on saying that unity of consciousness consists in the capacity to have such a higher order thought. It is quite conceivable (indeed, almost certain) that if I tried to keep track of the music and my thinking at the same time I would find myself incapable of thinking about philosophy.

"Just So" Stories

Dainton (1989) and Parfit (1991) seem to claim that unity of consciousness is an ultimate fact. It just is the case that some mental events are united in consciousness. Now there do seem to be ultimate facts, but appeal to ultimate facts is an appeal of last resort. Unity of consciousness does not seem to be sufficiently ultimate to justify the appeal. Consider the variety of items which are somehow unified.

> I have a visual experience of seeing a slimy frog in my hand.
> (Sense experience)
>
> I have a tactile experience of feeling a slimy frog in my hand.
> (Sense experience)

I sense the weight of the frog.
(Sense experience)

I have an aural experience of hearing the frog's croak from where my hand is.
(Sense experience)

I have an emotional experience of disgust at the thought of following tradition and kissing the frog.
(Emotional experience)

I am trying to decide how big a kiss will suffice for the transformation.
(Mental act)

There is no evident reason why these items should combine to form a single complex experience/act. The four sense experiences come through different modalities. The emotion emerges unbidden from the depths, whereas the mental act is my own performance, under my control. Also, there is the fact that on the one hand, some items can change, while the others remain the same, but on the other hand there are items which, if they change, lead to changes in other items. The frog can stop croaking, without affecting the colour, sliminess, or the disgust I feel. I can give up the idea of kissing it, which might make the disgust fade, but will not change the feeling of the weight of the frog.

The disparate nature of the items and their relationships seems to demand a fuller account than the appeal to ultimate facts.

Dainton says the unity of consciousness is a fact to be recognized. He also claims that consciousness has a continuous passive awareness of its own unity, and justifies this claim by the experience of unfocussed attention. In this state the unity of the disparate items in the field of consciousness becomes obvious, since the distinction between foreground and background items (or, in Evans' terms, between projected and unprojected consciousness) is less marked. All this is acceptable as far as it goes, but it is not sufficient to be an act of the unity of consciousness. Consciousness can only be passively aware of its own unity if it is a unity to begin with.

Parfit does not clearly explain what unifies simultaneous experiences into one and the same stream of consciousness. He says that several experiences just can be the objects of a single state of awareness (Parfit 1991 p. 250). If the basic mental events are experiences, thoughts, ideas, etc., then it seems the acts of awareness are constructions of the basic mental events. This leaves no explanation for how the mental events are brought together to form these states of awareness.

(If the states of awareness are the basic mental events, then during waking time there is a single continuous state of awareness which has extended overlapping experiences as its objects. But such a state of awareness seems to be an ephemeral subject of experience, and so the experiences are unified by being had by the same subject.)

Oaklander (1987) interprets Parfit as offering a higher order state theory, and brings the objection that the acts of awareness are among the things to be unified. The state of awareness A1 of experiences Λ and Ξ is itself an experience. I need a higher order experience A2 to unite A1 with its objects (experiences Λ and Ξ), and then A3 to unite A2 with A1 and so on.

Matheson (1990) thinks this is a misinterpretation. He offers two reformulations of Parfit's position.

(1) If two experiences are such that one is an awareness of the other, then those two experiences belong to the same person.

(2) If two experiences bear the co-conscious relation then these two experiences belong to the same person.

However, Matheson's (1) seems to have two possible meanings. The first meaning is that Experience Λ is an experience of the taste of lemon, and Experience Ξ is an awareness of Λ. This makes Ξ a higher order thought. What is the difference between an experience of the taste of lemon (Λ) and an awareness of an experience of the taste of lemon (Ξ)? If "awareness of an experience of the taste of lemon" means that the experience Λ is the object of attention, it does nothing to unify the contents of consciousness which are not attended to. Also, how does having Ξ help us to unite Λ with the visual experience of lemon meringue pie (Π) even when Π is also being attended to?

The second meaning is that experience Π is the visual experience of lemon meringue pie plus an awareness of Λ; that is, the awareness of Λ is part of and included in Π. But this raises the question of how an awareness of Λ came to be part of and included in Π in the first place.

Matheson's (2) is a return to the "just so" position. "Bear the co-conscious relation" is simply another way of saying that they are unified.

Parfit's view seems to be unsatisfactory regardless of whether it is interpreted as a "just so" view or a higher order state view.

A Special Case of Unity of Agency?

In a recent paper, Korsgaard (1989) says that unity of consciousness is a special case of unity of agency, and unity of agency is forced on us by our being embodied. There is, she says, no need to postulate a unifying Self or subject.

I find it difficult to understand her account of unity of agency, and so my presentation of it may be flawed, and the criticism I make may be invalid. However, even if I have misinterpreted Korsgaard's account of unity of agency, and my criticisms fail, her account of unity of consciousness is independently vulnerable to other criticisms.

Unity of Agency

Although we consist of (among other things) a group of psychological functions, we regard ourselves as unified agents because the group needs to become unified in order to act. There are two factors imposing this unity.

(1) We have one body, so we need to eliminate conflict between desires, otherwise action would be impossible. Only one project, one set of desires, can be carried out at a time to avoid the left hand working at cross purposes to the right. If the body does not act in a unified and coordinated way no project will be possible. Thus, unity is necessary for action.

(2) To eliminate conflict between desires we need to deliberate between the desires. One set of desires has to be chosen as that which is to be carried out first. To deliberate, we take the deliberative standpoint, and unity is inherent in the deliberative standpoint. When we deliberate between choices, it is *as if* there is a "me" who chooses for *reasons based on a self concept, a principle expressive of the Self.*

Korsgaard stresses that this "me" is not a metaphysical entity, and seems to imply that this idea of there being a "me" is derived from the deliberative stance. The necessity of making choices imposes the need for identification with a "unifying principle", and to identify with a principle in this way is to be unified.

The deliberative stance leads to the idea of a continuous Self. A merely present Self cannot be an agent. It must identify with something from which its reasons are derived, and this is most likely to be something that leads into the future: i.e. the idea of a continuous Self. We need to identify with a *continuous* Self in order to take the deliberative stance. To make a choice, one must identify with the *unifying principle,* and choices always lead to the future. The things a person chooses to do take up time, therefore they need a continuous person. Therefore the present Self's reasons are not independent of the future Self.

E.g.: My present study of philosophy is not independent of the idea of "my" future self being a lecturer in philosophy at the Elmer Gantry Baptist University and Live Bait Store.

Thus the person must regard himself as being a continuous person, and indeed must regard himself as being a deciding Self.

Unity of Consciousness

Unity of Consciousness is a special case of unity of agency. Consciousness is a *feature* of certain actions: perceiving, looking, attending, thinking, moving voluntarily, etc. It is not a state which makes them possible nor a feature of a subject. If you can perform the activities, you are conscious. Voluntary movement is moving consciously. You do not need to be conscious that you are moving. Being "engaged in a conscious activity" is not the same as "being conscious of an activity." (Korsgaard 1989, p.118)

Practical necessity requires the various activities to function together. Unity of consciousness is the ability to coordinate and integrate the activities, and the lack of perceived difficulty in this cooperation. It does not require a common subject of conscious experience, but it does require unity of agency.

Criticisms of the Account of Unity of Agency

The first difficulty is the relationship between the deliberative stance and the idea of there being a "me" who deliberates. Here the argument seems a bit confused. At one stage Korsgaard seems to be referring to an over-arching desire or moral or prudential principle as the unifying principle, but then she says we identify with it.

Now I interpret "identify with X" as meaning that I say "X is me" or "that which is good for X is good for me". The latter means "that which gives feelings of satisfaction, happiness, etc., to X gives similar feelings to me." But I cannot identify with a moral principle in this way. I cannot think "I am the principle 'follow the Shari'ah'". I cannot say "that which gives feelings of satisfaction, happiness, etc., to Free Trade gives similar feelings to me." Free Trade is an abstract concept. Abstract concepts do not have feelings.

Moral or prudential principles are not persons, and the differences between them are such that only the most confused thinker would think of himself as being such a principle. Identification can go no further than thinking "I am a person who follows and applies a principle completely and to the exclusion of all other ideas". The same considerations apply to desires.

The "arbiter among conflicting desires" (Korsgaard 1989, p. 119) cannot be a desire or a principle. When deciding, the arbiter *applies* a principle or tests desires against the main desire to see if they will help to satisfy it. The desire or principle cannot be the arbiter.

Further, if the unifying principle is not just the strongest desire it is difficult to understand how it would become the unifying principle in the first place. It seems to me that it would need to be chosen on the basis of some other principle or desire. But then we must ask how that other principle or desire becomes the basis of the choice. It seems to lead to a regress.

This leaves Korsgaard without an account of how the unifying principle unifies the bundle of psychological factors, and how the idea of there being a "me who decides" arises. Some other concept of "unifying principle" is needed.

The unifying principle has to be the idea of a continuous Self, of being a continuously existing unified entity. But this leads Korsgaard to the position that the sense of being "me deciding" is derived from identifying with the idea of the continuous Self. So the idea of the continuous Self must be logically prior to that of the deliberative Self, not derived from it or the result of it.

Criticism of the Account of Unity of Consciousness

My first criticism turns on the claim that consciousness is a feature of certain actions such as perceiving, thinking etc. Korsgaard here is arguing against the conception of consciousness as "something like a room, a place, a lit up area, within which we do our thinking, imagining, remembering, and planning..." (p. 116) Instead of considering experiences and asking what unifies them, Korsgaard wishes to characterize consciousness in terms of activities and dispositions.

One difficulty here is the question of why conscious activities differ from activities which seem similar in every respect save that they are not conscious. If I give up trying to solve a problem, and set it aside, later the solution pops up. Now this is clearly the result of unconscious thinking. What is it that differentiates unconscious thinking from conscious thinking, and conscious acting from unconscious acting? The feature of being conscious is the self-evident and unenlightening answer.

Consciousness does not seem to be an intrinsic feature of thinking, but if it is an extrinsic feature then there is a question of how conscious thinking acquires the feature of consciousness.

If consciousness is an intrinsic feature of conscious activities then some account should be given of activities which can be made conscious, and conscious activities which can become automated and carried out unconsciously. Normally breathing is carried out unconsciously, but attention can be directed to it, and then the sensations and actions become conscious. Many skills are practiced as conscious activities at first, but later become automatic and are carried out while the attention is directed elsewhere.

Korsgaard's account of consciousness as a feature of conscious activities does not seem appropriate for these well known phenomena, whereas the traditional view of consciousness as a sort of light, which illuminates some mental activities and experiences and which can be directed to include or exclude various items, is intuitively more satisfactory.

My second criticism is that, while thinking is clearly an activity, perception and emotion do not seem to be activities. Certainly, there is no strong sense of agency about emotions. They appear to rise unbidden and impose themselves upon us. Agency is involved in directing attention to various perceptions, but the perceptions themselves are just there. I open my eyes, and there is a visual field full of images. While I direct my attention on the images, I still perceive the pangs of hunger from my stomach, the itch in my ear, the sound of the wind. Agency is not obviously involved in perception or emotion.

My third criticism is that even if we do regard perceptions, etc., as actions, unity of consciousness still cannot be reduced to a special case of unity of agency. The argument Korsgaard uses only shows that there does not need to be a single subject/agent, a Self, for coordinated action.

"The unity of consciousness consists in one's ability to coordinate and integrate conscious activities." (Korsgaard p. 118) This seems to imply that a common psychological subject/agent is necessary to co-ordinate and direct the activities, but Korsgaard denies this. She bases her claim that a subject/agent is unnecessary for the integration of psychic functions on the example of "split-brain" patients, pointing out that it is possible for the hemispheres to communicate with each other by means other than the corpus callosum, and compares this with two people integrating their functions by communicating to become effectively a single agent. This may show that two or more subject/agents can integrate their functions and unite their agency by communication, but it does not show that there can be integration of functions in the absence of any subject/agents at all. The split-brain example gets its force through tacitly regarding the hemispheres as subject/agents. Korsgaard's argument does not show that there can be agency without subject/agents to communicate.

If there is no subject/agent, how do the various psychic functions become integrated? Certainly not through communicating with each other. Subject/agents may communicate, but functions do not seem the sort of things that communicate. What information would a psychic function communicate? How would it understand the communication from another function? How would it act on the information received? Psychic functions are, rather that which is communicated when subject/agents communicate with each other. The functions, the desires and the intentions, are the content of the communication.

Korsgaard claims that the integration of the functions requires unity of agency. Again, the fact of having a single body means that the "various psychic functions must work together. The 'phenomenon' of the unity of consciousness is nothing more than the lack of perceived difficulty in the coordination of psychic functions." (Korsgaard 1989, p. 119)

However, accepting that embodiment means that the functions must work together goes no way toward explaining how they do work together. Lack of difficulty in co-ordinating the functions does not clarify how the various conscious functions and activities come together as a single complex state of consciousness. A group of people can coordinate their activities and functions without thereby creating a state of consciousness that unifies their various mental states.

Korsgaard further claims that the sense of being the subject of unified consciousness is just the "unity inherent in the deliberative standpoint. I regard myself as the employer of my psychic capacities in much the same way that I regard myself as the arbiter among my conflicting desires." (p. 119)

Of course, this claim is vulnerable the difficulties that arose in consideration of the unity in the deliberative standpoint. The fact that there is such a sense of being a subject is *prima facie* evidence for being a subject. Korsgaard has not given an alternative explanation for that sense, and her account of consciousness and its unity fails.

Unification by the Brain

Brooks (1994) argues that the various mental states are unified by the brain. Each state is an activity in the brain, and these activities are organized into a unified field of consciousness by the brain, perhaps by them all being referred to a particular region or activity which constitutes the Self. Now this may be what happens in the brain, but from the first person point of view it is certainly not obviously a necessary condition. I will argue later that we can imagine unity of consciousness in disembodied persons and in persons with two unconnected brains.

"Split Brains" and the Unity of Consciousness

Experiments with commissurotomy patients show that under the experimental conditions contradictory responses can be obtained from the patient in a way that suggests that information presented to one hemisphere is not available to the other hemisphere.

The results of the experiments led philosophers to speculate that these cases are cases of actual division of persons, or divisions of minds. Brian Garrett (1990, p. 180) says "the impossibility of hemisphere bisection and transplantation appears to be merely technical". Parfit goes even further and claims

> it is a fact that people with disconnected hemispheres have two separate streams of consciousness – two series of thoughts and experiences, in having which they are unaware of having the other. (Parfit 1991, p. 247)

Parfit argues that the division of consciousness which results from commissurotomy shows that unity of consciousness is not explained by ownership of a subject, and regards this as evidence for his reductionist view of the mind. He claims that people with disconnected hemispheres of the brain have two streams of consciousness, each of which stream has its own unity of consciousness, and that this means that unity of consciousness is not explained by a single subject being conscious.

Parfit bases his argument on a "simplified imaginary version of the evidence." But this version is fiction. The real evidence is more amenable to interpretations that do *not* imply separate streams of consciousness.

Neither the facts nor the informed opinion of neurophysiologists support Parfit's wide ranging claims. Parfit quotes Sperry's early statements as justification for his belief, but Sperry later changed his mind, and now does not believe that commissurotomy creates dual streams of consciousness. (Sperry 1985) Both Gillet (1986) and McCloskey (1986) point out that even when Parfit is referring to the empirical evidence he uses his imagination on Sperry's reports, giving an example of an experiment that did not actually happen. McCloskey also points out that the best that can be drawn from the evidence is that there are two streams of experience, but that this is not the same as having two unities of consciousness, and that Parfit assumes the unity of each stream is such that it is incompatible with being the relatively independent stream of one dissociated subject.

(In criticizing the philosophical theories based on commissurotomy cases, D. Robinson (1982) pointed out that epistemic contradictions can be induced in normal subjects, and gives a brief historical survey of theories of multiplicities of Selves based on cases of epistemic contradictions and multiple personality. He claims the epistemic contradictions can be explained in terms of information processing, and that multiple personality does not imply multiple Selves.)

Furthermore, there is plenty of evidence to count *against* the idea that commissurotomy creates two distinct streams of consciousness or two minds. First, it is important to note that the effect of there being two distinct streams of consciousness is noticed mainly in the special experiments. Outside the experimental situation there is little sign of disunity, and that as time goes by there is less sign of disunity even in the experiment. The split brain re-integrates its experience. The integration is so complete that it was at first thought that the operation had no effect other than to prevent epileptic fits passing from one side of the brain to the other. In daily life the patients seem to be fully integrated people, to such an extent that it was, for a long time, thought mysterious that such a major operation could be performed on the brain without markedly affecting behaviour.

Second, the patient acts in a very integrated way *during* the experiment, only showing disunity in respect of a very few ways carefully selected by the experimenter. Also, the patients themselves are, as Gillet points out, often aware of internal conflict. The patients think of themselves as one person who makes strange mistakes. They try to reintegrate the information they receive and use a wide variety of tactics to overcome the errors they make. There is a constant attempt to re-integrate experience and information, and to struggle with the confusions they find they have. The actual results of the experiments can be just as well, and I claim better interpreted, as that of a single person trying to overcome confusions.

The patients do not regard themselves as two mutually independent streams of consciousness which happen to be in the same body. The hemispheres do not seem to recognize the existence of each other as separate minds. Rather, they seem to try to support each other, and show a resistance to disunity.

In one experiment, MacKay and MacKay (1982) attempted, without success, to set up explicit dialogue between the hemispheres. They noted that the patient addressed the experimenter rather than the other hemisphere, and that there was no conflict between the hemispheres.

MacKay and MacKay point out that to say that there were two persons or minds present after the operation implies each hemisphere has, not just a stream of experience, but a "terminal of dialogue", a centre (or at least a stream) of conscious awareness who can be argued with, met, interrogated, informed, etc. Each "terminal of dialogue" must be not only a receiver of sensory information and generator of bodily movement, but also an evaluator. If there are two persons or minds present after the commissurotomy operation, dialogue between the two minds should be possible.

Neither in the experiment conducted by the MacKays, nor in the other experiments was there recognition by one hemisphere of the other hemisphere as a separate person. There was no sign of independence at the level of will, where priorities are evaluated.

> Our evidence is consistent with the null hypothesis that at the higher levels of supervisory evaluation J. W. has not two half-systems but one undivided system, presumably associated with deep neural structures not surgically separated. (MacKay and MacKay 1982, p. 691)

They report that the patient asked several times "Are you trying to make two people out of me?"

Third, J. Robinson (1988) cites experimental work by Trevarthen that indicates that commissurotomy patients can in fact make judgments that require integration of information delivered separately to the visual half-fields, indicating that there is a common awareness of both hemispheres.

> Trevarthen claims that the two hemispheres cannot be regarded as two separate and independent spheres of consciousness, because the brain stem plays an essential role in the production of consciousness and its unification, even in commissurotomy patients. (Robinson 1988, p. 327)

The evidence seems to *undermine* the claim that commissurotomy divides one mind, or even one stream of consciousness, into two. An alternative explanation for the experimental results is needed.

J. Robinson (1988) suggests that the apparent split of consciousness can be explained by attention switching and automatism. Each hemisphere can make some responses automatically without conscious attention, and conscious attention can be directed to either hemisphere, but not always to both at once.

Kinsbourne (1980) gives a similar explanation, and expresses the idea as one consciousness utilizing a variable data base. He also uses the idea of a single centre of attention switching back and forth between hemispheres.

D. MacKay (1987) has a theory similar to those of Robinson and Kinsbourne, but one directed more at accounting for the contradictory actions of the commissurotomy patient in trying to perform the experimental tasks. He points out that the brain seems to operate on at least two levels, which he calls the executive level and the supervisory level. On the executive level, the brain organizes activities and evaluates them in terms of current criteria. The supervisory level deals with (among other things) adjustment of priorities and criteria of evaluation.

It seems that the operations of the executive level can perform complex actions without being conscious. When a person is riding a bike while looking for a particular house, the riding is done unconsciously, at the executive level. The supervisory level is involved with the conscious search for the house.

Similarly, I am consciously thinking of how to express my ideas in clear words. I am not consciously directing my finger movements to hit the keys, nor am I concentrating on spelling. All that direction is done at the executive level.

The two hemispheres of a commissurotomy patient's brain can each think on the executive level independently of the executive level thinking of the other hemisphere. The supervisory level is not divided. Thus, the supervisory level decides "perform the experimental task" and leaves the details to the executive level. Each hemisphere then performs the task according to its capacities and information. Since each hemisphere has different information and capacities, they sometimes perform contradictory actions.

Thus, using the idea of conscious attention only being able to attend to one hemisphere at a time, and the idea of conscious supervisory thinking leaving the detailed execution of action to the unconscious executive thinking, we can explain the odd behaviour of the commissurotomy patient without denying a single centre of consciousness and agency, and account for the high level of integration that the patients show. A person with a "split brain" is better described as oddly absent-minded than as being two persons.

There seems to be one Self which tries to integrate the experience and actions of the two hemispheres. The integration is in fact evidence for the fact that the system has a strong desire to reintegrate itself and has very flexible powers to do exactly that This combination of desire and power is more consonant with the idea of there being a controlling Self than with Reductionism.

Unity of Person

The unity of consciousness question can be related to the larger questions of the unity of the mind and unity of the person. I have separated the mind from the Self, and claimed that the person is made up of the Self, mind and body. It is not vital to my theory that a person have a unified mind or that he have a unified empirical Self. Thus a person with multiple personality syndrome may not have a completely unified mind, but he can still have a single Self which makes various aspects of the mind conscious at any given time.

An Adaptation of Broad's Argument

Examination of the phenomenology of experience and of action has established that there appears to be a Self, an actor/subject which is not a collection of mental states, but is a distinct entity. Postulating this entity gives an explanation for unity of consciousness that fits the phenomenology of unity of consciousness. I have shown that there are serious problems with some of the theories that attempt to explain unity of consciousness without invoking a Self. The Self appears to be a unified source of agency and of consciousness which is the centre of the mind, and which unifies the mind by being the centre. The question I will consider now is whether we are justified in accepting the impression given by the phenomenology.

Broad (1925, p. 585) offered the following argument for the mind having a centre. I will interpret it as referring to consciousness and unity of consciousness, rather than the whole conscious and unconscious mind.

(1) The contents of the mind are either related by being a unity of system or by being a unity of centre.
(2) There appears to be a centre.
(3) There is no reason why a set of items which are related to each other by being members of a set unified by a unity of system should appear to be unified by a unity of centre. (If the centre were hard to identify, it would not be surprising for the set to appear to be unified by a unity of system.)

Therefore:

(4) The contents of the mind are unified by there being a centre.

Premise (2) seems to be true in regard to consciousness, at least. The phenomenology of consciousness is such that there does seem to be a centre. Premise (3) is questionable. Anderson (1978) offers a situation which appears to be one of unity of centre but is in fact unity of system. The situation is that of a blind choir standing in a circle. They cue each other by tapping with their feet. One member has his back to the audience, and is waving his arm. He appears to be the director, but he is not. To avoid seeing the score as being the centre, Anderson suggests that they are making up the piece as they go along. She points out that this is not a very good analogy for the bundle theory of the mind. The director who appears to be the centre is in fact not part of the system. The idea of there being a mental state which is not part of the system and yet appears to be the centre of the system would be difficult for the bundle theorist to accept. However, we can include the director in the system by having his arm movements cued by foot taps from the rest of the chorus. He than becomes an epihenomenon. By analogy, this mean that the bundle of the mind includes a mental state which is produced by the others and appears to be the centre, but which actually has no effect on the other mental states. This gives us a system which appears to have a centre but in fact has not. I would need a good reason for believing that the mind is like this, and that the apparent centre is in fact causally impotent.

Anderson changes (2) to say "there appears to be a *substantive centre to the mind*". (3) can then be replaced by (3') below.

(3') There is no reason why a unity of system composed only of mental experiences should appear to be a unity of centre where the centre appears to be a mental substance.

To claim that (4) follows from this seems to derive too much from appearances. The fact that there appears to be a centre is a good reason for believing that there is a centre, but it does not prove that there is a centre. The argument does not include any proof that the unity of consciousness is not a unity of system, only the fact that it does not appear so. Appearances can be deceptive. There could be a good reason for a unity of system appearing to be unity of centre even if no-one has yet discovered that reason. (Of course, the onus of proof is on the objector to supply such a reason.)
I will replace (4) by (4') below.

> (4') There is no reason to believe the unity of conciousness is a unity of system, and there is reason to believe it is a unity of centre.

When this argument is combined with the strength of the impression of the Self in phenomenology, it gives good reason for believing that the phenomenology is not deceptive, and that unity of consciousness is the result of the various items being unified by a Self.

4 The Continuity of the Self

> ...for the interruptions of this sense of continued identity by sleep, inattention or otherwise seems from its being afterwards renewed to prove the point more clearly, as it seems to shew that there is some deep inward principle which remains the same in spite of all particular accidental changes. (Hazlitt, 1969, p. 83)

For the Self to be the constitutive criterion of identity and survival it has to have unbroken existence during the lifetime of a person. It must not be possible for the stream of experience to move from one subject to another, or for one Self to be replaced by a subsequent Self with or without an intervening period in which no Self exists.

There are two problems to deal with here, the first (raised by Kant) being that it is possible for the stream of consciousness to move from one subject to another, and the second, a criticism against Descartes, that since there is no consciousness during sleep, the Self ceases to exist.

Kant (1929, p. 342, A 364) suggests, in his famous footnote , that the whole state of a subject can be transmitted to another subject, along with its consciousness. Thus, "we can conceive a whole series of substances" each transmitting its states to the next until the "last substance would then be conscious of all the states of the previously changed substances, as being its own states" without the final substance being identical with the first of the series.

I am not convinced that this suggestion is coherent. Certainly, it is easier to write the words than to conceive of what is actually supposed to happen. First, each substance must persist for a definite time, for if they each existed for an instant, without duration, they would not exist at all. However, this immediately concedes the principle of a continuous Self. Second, the time gap between the end of one substance and the beginning of the next must also have duration. If there is no duration there is no time gap at all between one substance and the next, and if there is no time gap, what is it that distinguishes one from another? A series of qualitatively similar entities that come into and go out of existence with no time gap between the members of the series seems not to be a series at all but a continuously existing entity. If there is no time gap between the substances, or if they overlap with each other, some other principle than time must ensure that their existence is separate. It cannot be space. Consciousness and agency are not spatial, so from the first person point of view the Self is not a spatial item. The only principle that I can think of is the connection between them that transfers the states of on to the next. I will discuss this in some detail below.

During normal waking consciousness and pure consciousness there is no sensation of consciousness or agency being handed over from one subject to the next. Nor is there any sense of consciousness being anything other than continuous. When I am acting in a sustained way (as in holding my attention on a topic) there is no sense of agency being intermittent. The sense of continuity of experience and agency during normal waking consciousness seems so strong that even the bare logical possibility of the continuity being illusory is difficult to accept, and there is no reason to believe that there is any discontinuity.

The message of experience is not that the Self is a series of entities extended through time, but rather that time sweeps past the Self. My experience is not one of being at a point in time, but of the present at once becoming past and the future becoming a new present. To recognize that time is flowing, I need to be directly aware, not of a point or instant without duration, but of an extent of time. To use a visual analogy, if I were watching a train go past, my field of vision would have to have a finite width in order to recognize that there was anything moving at all. If my vision were narrowed to a line, perhaps by watching the train through an exceedingly thin slot, I would not be able to tell that the there was any movement. For colour, and therefore change in colour, to be perceived requires extension in two dimensions. I would therefore need a two dimensional field of vision. With the imperfections of human vision, the slot would have to have a certain minimum width for me to detect change. In the same way, the extent of time of which I am directly aware, the specious present, has to extend over a finite duration.

My experience of the present includes the period of time from the just fading awareness of the past to the just coming future. In Ehman's words:

> ..let us...with James and Husserl distinguish between explicit memory and our immediate awareness of what has "just past". The present is always in a process of turning into a just now present, and that into a more distant present until it fades out of our actual consciousness. There is an analogous distinction between explicit anticipation and our immediate awareness of

> what is just about to occur. The present is always open to an immediate future that is in the process of becoming present. (Ehman 1974, p. 334)

The Self that is having the experience is always at the at the peak of the now. It is, to adapt James' words, perched on "a saddleback, with a certain breadth of its own ..., and from which we look in two directions into time." (James, 1891, p. 609) This experience always includes the immediate awareness of what has "just past" and the immediate awareness of what is just about to occur. But what has just past was, just previously, the peak of the saddle back. The Self that was aware of the fading past when the past was present must be the same as the Self that now is aware of it as the just past. If it were not the same Self, the span of time the Self is aware of would have a beginning or an end. At the moment a new Self came into being, it would not have experience that extended into the past. There would be an experience of beginning. An old Self would not have experience that extended beyond its existence. It could not be aware of the future becoming present. However, experience is continuous. There are no beginnings and no ends to time.

The final experience of a Self just before extinction would be that of the "just now" and the "just past", but the "just future" would be that of the end of experience, and so there would very quickly be no "just future" in the span of experience. The Self would be aware of a contracting span of time, of diminishing specious present.

The first experience of a new Self as it came into existence would be one of "just now" and "just future", but no "just past". As the "just now" became "just past" the span of time the Self was aware of would expand. Now if this Self received the final state of the previous Self at the same time as it came into existence, it would at once be aware of a span of time expanding, and one contracting, of a present with past and no future, and a present with future but no past. Perhaps these conflicting experiences would combine harmoniously to create the illusion of continuous existence, but it seems much more likely that the Self persists. The hypothesis of a persisting Self provides a theoretically simpler explanation of the experience of continuity. To be aware of the continuous passage of time the Self must persist, and in being aware of the passage of time it is aware of its own continuity. (I shall return to this topic later.)

For consciousness and agency to persist unbroken either the consciousness and agency are distinct from the substance, and so it is the numerically identical consciousness and agency that is passed from one substance to another, or each substance takes over the contents of the consciousness and continues to exercise the agency in the same way.

If the same consciousness and agency are passed from one substance to another, then the bearer of identity is the consciousness and agency. Consciousness remains the same throughout the changes in content, and so consciousness is as much persisting substance as the Self is, insofar as the substantiality of the Self consists in it remaining the same throughout change. Consciousness and agency are inseparable from the Self. While consciousness and agency persist, the Self persists. The Self is being passed from one substance to another, but the Self persists. Thus, the series of substances is not a series of Selves.

Let us consider, for one dizzy moment, that consciousness is nothing more than the totality of the current conscious experiences. Each substance must be capable of consciousness and agency. The various states and events of consciousness and the activities of agency are propagated from the beginning to the end of its period of existence by some means. I will call this standard propagation. Each substance must pass the total state of consciousness and the activity of agency to the next substance. The important question is what happens at the junction between the substances.

If the total state of consciousness and the activity of agency is passed across by standard propagation, then in what way is the first substance distinct from the second? If it were possible to join together two copper wires in a such a way that the joint presented no greater impedance to the signal than any other part of the wires, and that the joint was undetectable by any other means, what sense would it make to say that there were still two wires rather than a single long wire? By analogy, then, if there is no detectable difference between propagation of the total state of consciousness and the activity of agency during the period of existence of one substance and the propagation between substances, the distinction between the two substances must lie in some other distinction. The substances we are considering are Selves, regarded as subjects of experience and agents. If they have any other characteristics, they are extraordinarily difficult to detect. To sustain the claim that there are two distinct substances would require a God's eye view that can detect those other characteristics.

Of course, the total state is a state of the substance, and so the second substance actually gains a qualitatively similar state, rather than the numerically identical state. Similarly, when the activity of agency is passed over, the second substance starts to perform qualitatively similar activity to that of the previous substance.

Suppose that the substances do not pass over the total state of consciousness and the activity of agency by standard propagation. If there is a time gap separating the substances, it seems that at the junction between the substances, which are the subjects of experience, there would be neither subject of experience nor agent, and hence neither experience nor action.

If one substance begins its existence before the other has ceased, it seems there would be two subjects of experience and two agents, with uncertain results both for experience and action. If the propagation requires the total state of consciousness and the activity of agency to be passed over in some other form than standard propagation, it ceases to be in the form that it is in when it is experienced. In order to maintain experience one substance has to continue to maintain that total state in standard form, while the next one takes it up. Perhaps by exquisite timing the first substance ceases to maintain the total state at exactly the moment that the second substance begins to experience it, so continuity is maintained.

Foster's Argument that Co-personality Entails Consubjectivity

John Foster, in *The Immaterial Self*, (1991) argues against the possibility of someone's mental states being transferred from one subject to another. That is, that stages of the one person's mind cannot belong to different thinking substances, and stages of the one thinking substance cannot belong to different persons. Co-personality entails consubjectivity.

For the sake of clarity, I will first give an informal version of Foster's argument, and then a formal version.

Informal Version

An experience has to be had by a subject. At least some experiences have to be extended through time to be experienced at all, and so the subject has to last as long as the experience. (Indeed, the idea of an experience that lasts only an instant, and is experienced by a subject that lasts only an instant seems to be incoherent. For an experience or a subject to exist at all seems to me to require that it exist for a certain duration.) At any one time a subject can have several experiences together. The sound of the radio, the smell of coffee, and the sight of the coffee filter all are had by the same subject at the same time. One experience will cease (the sight of the filter) and another start (the taste of the coffee) but the experience of the sound of the radio and the experience of the smell of coffee continue, and are experienced by the same subject as the taste of the coffee.

Sound has to be experienced by the same subject in order to be experienced at all, so the subject T (in the diagram below) that experiences the taste has to be the same subject as the subject F which experiences the sight of the filter since they are both the same subject as that which experiences the sound and smell.

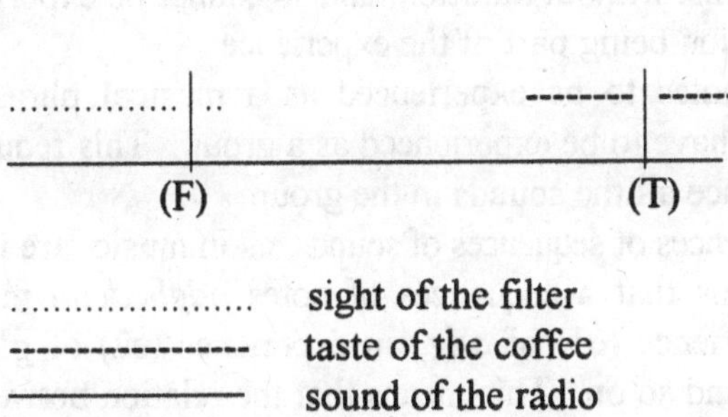

Since the whole stream of experience is made up of overlapping experiences, the subject must always be the same subject.

Formal Version: Principles and Definitions

Foster starts from the principle (P1) that whatever relation makes simultaneous mental items co-personal (that is, part of a synchronically unified consciousness of a single person) should have a natural affinity with or should be of the same type as whatever relation makes serial items co-personal (that is, part of a diachronically unified consciousness of a single person). It should be possible to develop the one relation into the other. The relation he takes for simultaneous co-personality is strict co-consciousness.

Definition 1. Experiences are strictly co-conscious iff they are part of a single complex experience.

This means experiences are elements of a single episode of consciousness and are accessible to the same introspective awareness. Thus, in the version above, the sound of the radio, the smell of coffee, and the sight of the coffee filter are all part of my experience at a given time, and are accessible to my introspection. This makes them part of a single complex experience, and so they are co-conscious.

Foster then argues that at least some experiences have to be temporally extended to be experienced. Examples of these are motion and sound. Motion is not experienced as an object in a series of positions in space, but as a change in position. Now change takes time, and to be experienced as change, the experience has to be extended in time. For a note to be experienced as a note, it has to be experienced as having duration as well as pitch volume, and timbre. A sound cannot exist without duration, and so cannot be experienced as a sound without duration being part of the experience.

For a group of notes to be experienced as a musical phrase the experiences of each note have to be experienced as a group. This requires a single subject to experience all the sounds in the group.

Further, the experiences of sequences of sounds, as in music, are in fact overlapping. This means that a sequences of notes *adgbcdcaa* may be experienced as an experience (e1) of *adg*, an experience (e2) of *gbc*, an experience (e3) of *bcd*, and so on. This means that the relation between e1 and e2 is that of strict co-consciousness, since they both contain *g* as a component. Similarly for e2 and e3, which both contain *b*. If e1 and e2 and e3 are not parts of a larger total auditory experiences in the way that the experience of *d* is part of e1, then e1 and e3 are connected by an experience with which they are both co-conscious. Similarly, a chain of connected experiences would connect *adg* with *caa*.

In the case of more complex music, there is counterpoint and harmony with other chains of notes, which form even more complicated overlapping structures. In a performance of opera splendid music overlaps and coincides with the hideous honking and screaming of the singers, the visual imagery of the movement on the stage, the discomfort caused by the hard seat, the longing for a stiff drink, and the wondering how much longer it will last. The relation between all these is that of being serially co-conscious.

Definition 2. Experiences are serially co-conscious iff they are strictly co-conscious or connected by links of experiences which are strictly co-conscious.

Serial co-consciousness provides a relation of the right kind for co-personality of experiences in an unbroken stream of consciousness.

A *stream of experience* is a sequence of overlapping experiences. A *total stream of experience* is a stream of experience which is not part of a larger stream.

The relations defined above are all C-relations.

Definition 3. Experiences are C-related iff they are either strictly or serially co-conscious.

The relation of co-personality can thus be defined in terms of C-relations. Experiences are co-personal iff they are C-related. Streams of experience belong to the same person iff they are co-personal.

Formal Version: the Argument

There are two cases to consider.

Case i: Strict co-consciousness.

Since any experience belongs to a subject, if two experiences are strictly co-conscious, then they are parts of a single complex experience of a single subject.

Case ii: Serial co-consciousness.

In the description of experience of sound given above, e1 and e2 are strictly co-conscious and therefore, from case i, consubjective. Similarly e2 and e3 are consubjective. An experience is just an experiential state of a particular subject, and so consubjectivity is transitive. Therefore e1 and e3 are consubjective. Serially co-conscious experiences are consubjective.

Streams of experience which are C-related are therefore consubjective, and so co-personality is simply consubjectivity. The stages of a person cannot move from one mental substance to another. While there is an unbroken stream of consciousness, there is a single abiding subject.

This argument depends on the idea that it is not possible for two subjects to share the same experience. Certainly, if experience is seen as being in an "adjectival" relationship to the subject, so being a state of the subject, it seems that two subjects can no more have the same experience than two cars can have the same dent in their mudguards. If experience is seen as being an event or action of the subject, two subjects can carry out two token performances of an action, but not the same performance.

Unger's Argument for Shared Experience

The idea that it is not possible for two subjects to share the same experience is a widely held belief about experiences. However, Unger (1990, Ch. 6, p. 170ff.) has put forward two cases to try to demonstrate, first, that it is possible for two persons to have numerically the same experience, and second, that it is possible for one continuous experience to be first had by one person, and then passed over to be had by another person.

The first case starts with two exactly similar persons (total twins) having two exactly similar experiences. They are each sitting in a silent room, looking at a blue wall. The upper and lower halves of their brains are slowly separated and transceivers are fitted to the nerve endings so that the direct nerve connections are relayed by radio connections. This is done slowly, and in a piecemeal fashion, so that only a few connections are broken at any one time. (This is the process Unger calls "zippering") The twins do not have any change in their experience during this process, so that their experience at the end of the separation is the same as it was at the beginning. The situation can be diagrammatically represented as follows:

U = upper brain L = lower brain ↑ = radio communication from lower to upper brain ↓ = radio communication from upper to lower brain

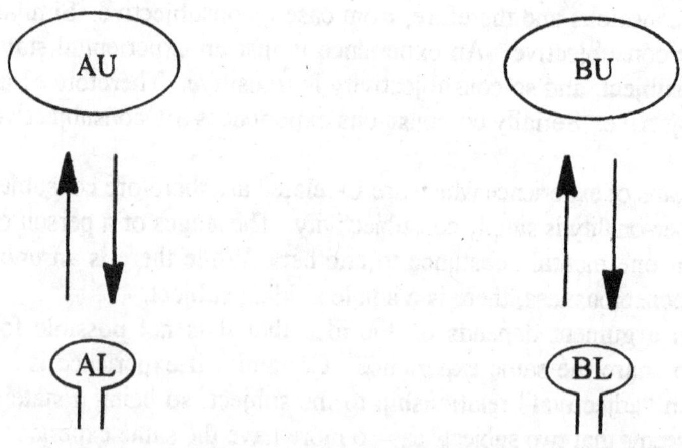

At the flick of a switch, the radio communications are adjusted so that for five minutes AL receives combined input from AU and BU. There is no difference in information content between the input from AU and BU, and the

intensity is (presumably - Unger does not state this) adjusted to make the final input to AL indistinguishable from the input it previously received. Similarly, BL receives combined input from AU and BU. AU and BU also receive combined input from AL and BL. This can be diagrammatically represented thus:

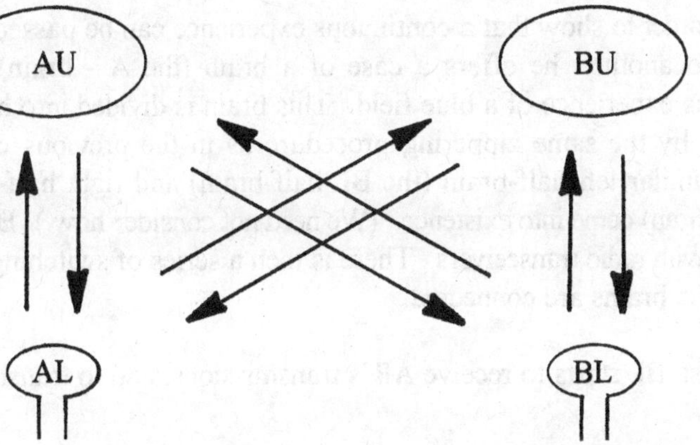

This situation lasts for five minutes, and then the combined input is stopped. During this time, Unger claims, A and B have numerically the same experience.

This claim founders upon the fact that we have no satisfactory account of the relation between consciousness, conscious experience, brain activity, and information flow.

If, for example, there is a "seat of consciousness" in the brain stem, so that only information that passes through that part of the brain gives rise to conscious experience, then there will be two seats of conscious each with information giving rises to two numerically different experiences. If one brain stem suddenly died, the other would continue to have the experience and not notice any change.

If consciousness is a result of the activity of a whole brain working as a unit, no prediction can be made about the effect of having a brain and a half or two brains working together. If conscious experience is a result of there being a certain pattern of information flow between upper and lower brain, it seems at least as likely that there will be *four* conscious experiences associated with the combined brains as that there will be one. In that case, one conscious experience will be associated with the combination AU — AL, another associated with AU — BL, another associated with BU — AL, and yet another associated with BU — BL. Each of these experiences will be in a stream of consciousness as distinct from the others as Unger's stream of consciousness is from mine.

Unger's case fails to show that one experience can be shared by several subjects.

In order to show that a continuous experience can be passed from one subject to another, he offers a case of a brain (the A - brain) having a continuous experience of a blue field. This brain is divided into halves (AL and AR) by the same zippering procedure as in the previous cases. An exactly similar left half-brain (the BL-half-brain) and right half-brain (the BR-half-brain) come into existence. (We need not consider how.) BL and BR are fitted with radio transceivers. There is then a series of switchings altering the way the brains are connected.

First, BL starts to receive AR's transmissions, and to transmit to AR.

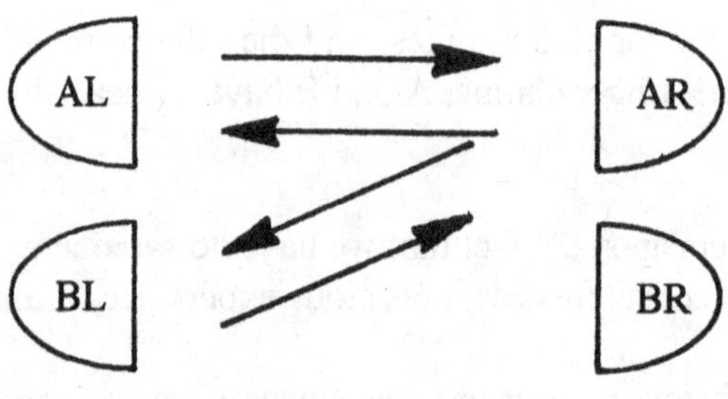

AL then ceases to send and receive transmissions.

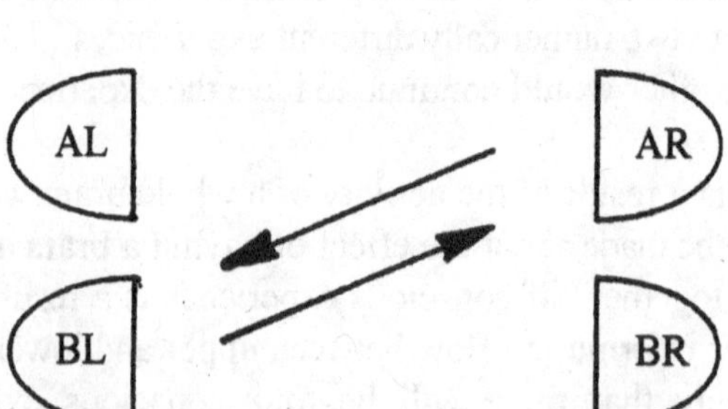

BR starts to receive BL's transmissions, and to transmit to BL.

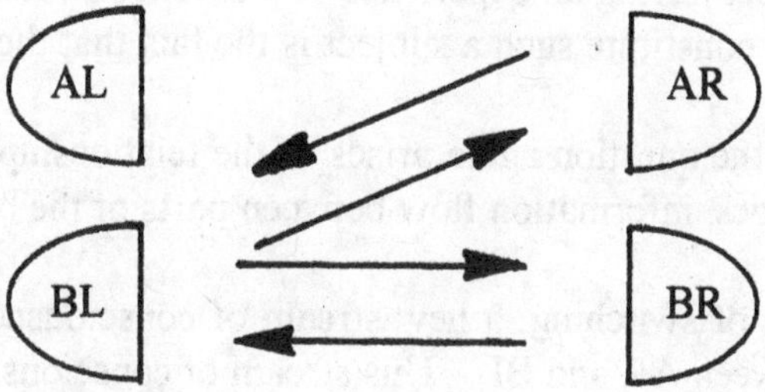

Finally, AR ceases to send and receive transmissions.

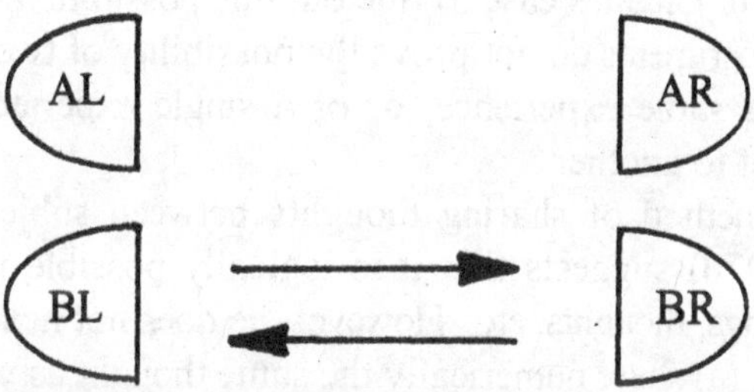

AL and AR are put together again. BL and BR are also put together.

Unger claims that in this case the experience of blue was first an experience of the A-brain but then became that of the B-brain.

This case founders for similar reasons to the previous case. The A brain is experiencing a blue field. If the halves of the B-brain are exactly similar to the halves of the A brain, then they are in the state of a brain having an experience of a blue field. The question arises of how the experience is induced and maintained in the A-brain in the first place. If the experience results from the eyes attached to the A brain looking at a blue wall, then when there is no contact with the eyes (by the third stage), surely there would be no experience of a blue field. The B-halves would each need an eye attached, looking at the same field. Corresponding arrangements would have to be made if the experience is artificially induced. This means that the cause of the experience being that of a blue field would not be the connection between AR and BL. This connection can only be the cause of the state of BL becoming part of a *conscious* experience. If the B-half brains were joined together they would constitute a subject having an experience of a blue field. It seems the only reason they do not constitute such a subject is the fact that they are not connected.

But in this case the question again arises of the relationship between brain states, brain activities, information flow between parts of the brain, and conscious experience.

In the first stage of switching, a new stream of consciousness could come into existence between AR and BL. This stream of consciousness may include an experience of a blue field, but it is a numerically different experience from the experience in the stream of consciousness between AL and AR. Of course, the stream of consciousness between BL and BR would constitute a third stream of consciousness.

There is nothing in Unger's case to rule out this possibility.

These thought experiments do not prove the possibility of two subjects having numerically the same experience, or of a single experience being passed from one subject to another.

An alternative method of sharing thoughts between subjects is by telepathy. Morick (1970) suggests that it is logically possible for me to directly know your feelings, thoughts, etc. However, he does not make it clear what this involves. Do I (a) share numerically the same thought as you, or do I (b) have a thought which is qualitatively similar to yours. If (b), I have knowledge of your thoughts by some means other than deducing them from your words or actions. Perhaps your thoughts exert a casual influence on my mind to bring it into the qualitatively similar state to your mind. This seems to be a fairly direct way of knowing your thoughts. If Morick means (a), this is simply to claim that it is logically possible for two subjects to be in the numerically same state. The conceivability (and possible reality) of telepathy does not support the claim.

One subject can no more have another subject's thoughts. feelings, or experiences, than (as Morick puts it) one stick of dynamite can have anther stick's explosion.

Foster's argument, then, shows that the Self can be regarded as continuing at least as long as conscious experience lasts.

Strawson (1966) claims that the hypothesis of a series of conscious subjects is as likely to be true as the hypothesis of a single persisting subject, and that the one is as good an explanation for the nature of experience as the other. Even if the above arguments do not show that the hypothesis of a series of conscious subjects is incoherent, they do show that it is no more than a bare logical possibility. It is so unlikely to be true that we need not consider it further.

Our Knowledge of Our Own Continuity

Not only are we continuous beings, we have knowledge of the fact. To show this I adapt an argument from Bolton (1992), which he attributes to Butler.

I am aware of my own existence now, in the "just now" of the specious present. I also know that I persisted from the "just past". But when that "just past" was the "just now", I knew I persisted from the time that was the "just past". That time is now the time I remember in short term memory. Thus we have successive temporal states A (the time I remember in short term memory), B ("just past") and C ("just now"). I arrived at B accompanied by the knowledge that I had persisted from A to B(based on the experience of my own continuity from A to B) and I arrived at B accompanied by the knowledge that I had persisted from B to C (again, by the experience of my own continuity) as well as the knowledge that I persisted from A to B. Thus I have knowledge that I persisted from A to C. This knowledge accumulates as I continue from C to D, D to E, and so forth. Knowing my own existence at any time leads me to know my own continuity. This knowledge is extended in time automatically. It is usually tacit knowledge, and it is knowledge without phenomenal content, just as the knowledge of body position is knowledge without phenomenal content.

The Self in Sleep

The problem now is to show that the Self continues to exist throughout periods of dreamless sleep and unconsciousness. To do this I will argue that there is a certain basic level of consciousness which does not cease during sleep. Of course, it is not the same as normal waking consciousness, but it is not a total absence of consciousness either.

There is a tendency to conceive consciousness and unconsciousness as being states analogous to off and on in a computer. Actually people can be in a variety of different states. The following list is not intended to be exhaustive

1: Coma or deep unconsciousness, as induced by powerful anaesthetics or trauma.
2: Dreamless sleep.
3: Dreaming.
4: Hypnotic trance.
5: Normal waking consciousness.
6: Pure consciousness.
7: Cosmic consciousness. (As described by the mystics)

I have not experienced 4, or 7, and have only had limited experience of 1 and 6. Nonetheless, the existence of the other states is sufficient to make it clear that there are a variety of different conditions. The states themselves seem to be fairly stable, with unstable borderline conditions between them. One can be asleep or awake, but it seems that one cannot remain too long in the transition state, pleasant though it is. Five of them are states that include conscious experience, in the sense that there is a "something it is like" to be in them. There are subjectively experienced mental states in them. It seems unlikely that the remaining two are totally lacking in any subjectively experienced mental states whatsoever.

Normal waking consciousness itself can be divided into at least three varieties.

(i) Waking unfocussed consciousness. (The condition of going about one's normal business without thinking about it or anything else.)
(ii) Waking absorption in a task.
(iii) Waking Self consciousness.

However, these distinctions are not relevant here. There may well be distinctions between coma and the state caused by anaesthetic, but they also are not relevant.

In discussing the Self during sleep there is a conceptual issue and a procedural issue to deal with. The procedural issue is that of the onus of proof. It is usual to claim that it is harder to prove the negative than the positive. If the positive cannot be proved, the assumption is that the negative is true. However, if the normal belief is the positive, then the onus of proof is more heavily on the negative. In the case of sleep we assume the positive in our daily lives, that is, that the Self awake today is a continuation of the Self who was awake yesterday, and that Self continued existing during sleep. This means we need good reasons to believe that we ceased to exist during sleep.

There is also the conceptual problem, referred to by Lowe (1991), that no clear idea can be given of the Self ceasing to be. Lowe claims that the capacities for perception and agency are essential to the Self, and that the permanent demise of these capacities would constitute the cessation of the Self, but that the only thing that could constitute the permanent demise of these capacities would be the cessation of the Self. The fact that the capacities are not being exercised at a particular time is not sufficient to prove that the capacities no longer exist, and hence that the Self no longer exists.

This conceptual problem makes it extremely difficult, if not impossible, to prove that the Self ceases to exist during sleep, and that a new Self is generated upon waking. For the sake of argument I will first begin with the argument for the negative claims, (1) that the Self ceases to exist during periods of dreamless sleep, and (2) that a new Self is generated in the process of waking.

The Argument for the Non-existence of the Self During Deep Sleep or Coma

The main argument for the claim that I did not exist during sleep is that of the lack of memory. We do not remember any subjectively experienced mental states in deep sleep or coma, and so parsimoniously we assume that during sleep there is no subjectively experienced mental states at all. If there is no subjective experience, there is no Self existing to be the subject of any experience. Assuming that it is incoherent to speak of a Self having intermittent existence, a new Self is generated in the process of waking. I will offer two replies to this argument.

Reply 1: The fact that I do not remember does not show that there was no mental activity or states.

I have spent many years sitting in schools during my pre-university education. I ought to have a huge stock of memories of school. And yet I have huge gaps in my memory. Perhaps if I struggled to recall each day, each minute, I might be able to recapture them, but they seem to be gone. The fact that I cannot recall the experience of NREM sleep does not prove that the Self did not exist, or even that it did not experience anything at that time.

The psychology of the sixties that I remember included the theory that during sleep the memories of the day are reorganized into long term memory. Assuming memory exists for practical day-to-day purposes, the most important thing would be to arrange memory so that it was easily accessible and appropriately connected with other memories. If this is what is going on during NREM sleep it is not surprising that we have no long term memory of the process of arranging memories in the long term memory. Libraries keep records of where they have put the books, but not records of the appearance, thoughts, or exact moves each library assistant made when putting them there. irrelevant to the essential purpose and running of the library. In the same way the experience of reorganizing memory is not something one would expect to be remembered, especially if it is an automatic process which the Self merely observes.

Reply 2: Is it true that there is no memory? I remember that there was an interruption of normal waking consciousness. If I am certain that I existed during sleep or unconsciousness is this not because I remember existing?

Butler and Reid claimed it was possible for the Self to continue to exist without consciousness or activity, so long as it retained the *capacity* for consciousness and agency. Unger (1990) has two objections to this claim. The first is that while consciousness seems to be all-or-none, the capacity for consciousness is not clearly absolute. It might be a matter of degree.

The second is that it makes the nature of the Self completely mysterious. What is it that exists, in order to provide a ground for this dispositional capacity?

This objection seems to me to have considerable force. A reply that could be offered is that agency is not always exercised, and yet the capacity remains. In the same way the capacity for consciousness can remain even if consciousness is not being present. However, this seems to me to extend the mystery of the persistence of the capacity for action to make an additional mystery of the persistence of the capacity for consciousness. If consciousness persists, it can be offered as a ground for the dispositional capacity for action.

Lowe (1991) refers to the continuity of the capacity for *perception*, which could be interpreted as the continuity of consciousness, but this requires the continuity of consciousness to be shown. Unger's objection is directed at the continuity of consciousness.

Unger claims that we do not really think our continuity requires continuous consciousness. He argues that we would not worry if it were shown that in fact there were none of the brain activities associated with consciousness. Unger suggests the following scenario. A drug is found that affects the brain so that it supports no conscious experience during sleep. All the evidence supports this belief about the effects of the drug. We would not, he claims, regard the taking of the drug as equivalent to taking a fatal poison

For once, Unger is rather brief in his presentation. We have to assume that the persons who take this drug wake afterwards, and seem to be unchanged. Nonetheless, I would want to interview them carefully before being so sanguine about the effects of the drug. If the drug takers do not report the same kind of continuity , and awaken with no idea that they are continuations of a persons who fell asleep, then I would suggest that the drug is too close to fatal poisoning for comfort.

What could be the evidence that supports the belief that the drug has the alleged effect? If it suppresses certain types of brain activity (seen on an EEG, perhaps) that are thought to be those associated with consciousness, and yet the persons taking the drug report the same sense of continuity that is associated with ordinary sleep, this could be taken as evidence that the consciousness that provides the necessary continuity does not require the particular type of brain activity that is suppressed. And if we know (perhaps from experience) that the continuity will not be broken, we are not likely to be worried about the presumed effects of the drug.

If the drug suppresses every brain activity so that there is *no* brain activity during sleep, the drug taker will almost certainly die. Eccles (Popper and Eccles 1977, p. 372) points out that if there is no neuronal discharge for over thirty minutes the condition will probably be irreversible and the brain will be dead.

Unger refers to conscious experience, and not consciousness, so even if the drug suppresses all experience, it need not suppress consciousness as well.

Since I will be concerned to show the continuity of consciousness, I will give no further discussion of the possibility of intermittent existence of the Self. Nor will I discus the suggestion that the Self exists continuously in subjective time.

The Argument for the Existence of the Self During Sleep and Coma

I have argued that the experience of Pure Consciousness is one of consciousness without content. Pure Consciousness is a state in which the attention is firmly controlled, and so it can be remembered. It is therefore possible for consciousness to continue without content during sleep or coma, and without being remembered because the attention is not active during sleep. It is possible that in sleep we do not lose consciousness but only the contents of consciousness. Ideas, thoughts, sense perceptions, emotions, images, all disappear, and only awareness rèmains.

It is easy to confuse losing the contents of consciousness with losing consciousness. "I am aware of no thing, no feeling, no idea, etc.," is, from the first person point of view, almost identical with "I am not aware." I say almost identical because there is one difference. Consciousness cannot be separated from the sense of existence. To be conscious is the fundamental experience of being, and so while consciousness persists the sense of existing will also persist. I will return to this later.

Descartes (1991, p. 196, para. 433, and p. 357, para. 222) suggested that conscious thinking continued unbroken during sleep, but that we did not remember it. This suggestion has been denounced as implausible, but modern studies of sleep provide evidence that supports him, and makes the claim that there is no mental life during sleep seem implausible. Not only do people report dreams from periods of REM sleep, but also thinking of a more conceptual and less pictorial kind from NREM sleep.

Dreams

Dreams are normally regarded as a variety of consciousness with subjectively experienced mental states.

Squires (1973) and Dennett (1976) have argued for the possibility that there is no conscious experience during dreams. They claim that what happens is that the story of the dream is composed unconsciously and then placed in memory. When we wake up, we read off the story, and assume that since we experienced it because we remember it. Dennett admits that it cannot be demonstrated that this is what happens, but suggests that it is at least as possible as the standard view, and prefers it because it fits his general theory of consciousness.

A major problem with this theory is that it makes it difficult to account for lucid dreams, in which the dreamer not only realizes he is dreaming, but sometime can even control the content of the dream. He can think "This is a dream. I will now dream a bottle of beer in my hand." and accordingly he dreams that he is holding a bottle of beer.

Dr. Keith Hearne (1990) reports a remarkable observation he made in the sleep laboratory at the University of Hull. He asked an experimental subject to move his eyes back and forth from left to right if, during a dream, the subject realized he was dreaming. Eventually, during one of that subject's periods of REM sleep, the eye movements suddenly became a simple left-right movement. Subsequently the subject reported that he had been dreaming, realized the fact, and moved his eyes. Dr. Hearne was able to get similar results from other subjects. This strongly suggests that the dreams were actually occurring at the time of eye movements. Since the dreamer claimed that he performed an intentional act the time of the dream, it seems that the dream was a state of consciousness.

It is possible for lucid dreams to be reconciled with Dennett's model, by arguing that the brain includes the realization that it is a dream complete with all the appropriate feelings of insight, the decision to include the bottle of beer, the feeling of mental causation and the resulting image of the bottle of beer, all without any conscious experience or agency occurring. It is even possible that the brain activates the movement of the eyes (with all the appropriate feelings of decision and causation) immediately after the realization and the feelings of insight. However, as far as I am concerned, to be convinced that there is no consciousness involved requires a greater commitment to Dennett's theory of consciousness than I possess.

NREM Sleep

Even REM dreams are usually forgotten, but we are clearly aware of them. Thus, even though we may forget them after we wake, experience can be reported. Similarly experience and mental activity are reported on waking from NREM sleep, and when experience can be reported, it is good evidence that there has been experience and mental activity. Foulkes (1962) discounted the possibility that the phenomenon was an artifact of the waking process. He pointed out that the faster waking occurred, the more likely there was to be a report of thinking, and the reports were longer and more detailed.

This implies that the report is of something retained in echoic memory or short term memory (assuming the two to be different) rather than something that is composed during the waking process.

People wakened from NREM sleep often describe what they have been experiencing as thinking, since it seems to be non-pictorial, more conceptual kind, and less vivid than dreaming. Nonetheless, as Empson (1989, pp. 69 - 70) states, it is "clear that mental life does not cease during sleep".

In dreamless sleep, the mind seems to operate in the way it operates when the attention is not being controlled. An introductory textbook on the psychology and physiology of sleep expresses it thus:

> The impression is that NREM mentation resembles that large portion of our waking thought that wanders in a seemingly disorganized, drifting, non-directional fashion whenever one is not attending to external stimulation or actively working out a problem or a daydream. (Dement, 1974, p. 44)

This does not show that there is no attention, only that the attention is not being controlled and held onto a single item. Thus, even if it is a necessary truth that all consciousness has to be consciousness of something, the reported experience of NREM sleep fits that requirement. The only reason for denying that it is conscious experience is that it is not remembered. The fact that the attention does not fix on any of the contents of consciousness would also explain why there is usually no memory of the NREM thinking. That which is not attended to is not usually remembered very well. Even during normal waking consciousness, if the mind has been drifting, it is usually very difficult to remember everything that passed through the mind. Only the last one or two items can be recalled.

A possible objection: There is no experience during NREM sleep. When someone is woken out of NREM sleep, what they experience is what is left in the echoic memory, which retains a memory of whatever brain events are going on. They then assume that this was experienced at the time it was going on, that is, before waking.

Certainly, unconscious thinking *seems* to occur. I am faced with a problem, but cannot think of a solution. I turn my attention to something else for a while, and then suddenly the solution to my problem presents itself. Apparently the thinking that has reached the solution has been done unconsciously. However, it seems unintrospectible. If, before the solution to my problem comes, I start to consciously think about the problem, I do not detect a chain of thought that has been continuing unconsciously. On the other hand, the thinking done during NREM sleep can be detected and reported on upon waking. This seems to indicate that it is conscious thought.

While I cannot think of a way of disproving the idea that thinking during sleep does not involve consciousness, I cannot think of a reason for believing it either. Many reports of experience are reports of the content of echoic memory. It seems perverse to say that in just this case the report of experience should not be taken as meaning that there was experience.

A final item of evidence was pointed out to me by Michael Proudfoot during a conversation on the matter. If one goes to sleep while expecting a call in the middle of the night, one wakes up very quickly when the phone rings, usually with the idea that this is the expected call. If the phone rings unexpectedly the waking is slower, and the realization that the noise is the telephone ringing comes slowly.

Again, it is possible to devise explanations that do not include consciousness, but accepting the idea of consciousness during sleep provides a single explanation that covers both this phenomenon and a variety of other phenomena.

Coma

Dreams and out-of-the-body-experiences sometimes seem to take place during traumatic and anaesthetic coma. The same consideration apply to them as applies to ordinary dreams. (With the added complication that the reports of out of body experience sometimes include embarrassingly accurate accounts of real events that the person in the coma theoretically has no way of knowing about.) My own recent experience of anaesthesia was comparatively unexciting, being merely a completely blank period followed by a period of intense dreaming. The blank period could have been a period of consciousness without content, or consciousness without remembered content.

So far, I have shown that there is evidence for a continuous mental life, and that the only argument for the belief that this is not conscious, not subjectively experienced, is a weak argument. However, even if all this activity is not conscious, and the blank period I remember was as empty of content as it seemed to be, this does not imply that consciousness had ceased. Consciousness might continue without being conscious of the mental activity.

Silkstone (1973) says that when we wake, we infer our sleeping existence from seeing the hands of the clock, the familiar bed, and the memory of going to bed the previous night. But that is exactly what we do not do. When we wake our in-tray of tacit knowledge/belief has the following three items in it.

(1) Time has passed.
(2) I existed during that time.
(3) I am the continuation of the person that fell asleep.

We start operating on the basis of these straight away. We do not spend our time working out who and what we are. Nor is our experience one of a sudden shift from lying down to waking up. If one Self ceased to exist, and a later one took over, we would expect that the experience would be one of unbroken consciousness with a sudden change in content, or of coming-into-existence. I admit that I am not sure what it would be like to come into existence, but as I wake up my experience of my own continuity extends backwards to the time I was asleep. I certainly do not feel that I have just come into being, but rather the opposite, that I existed before I awoke.

The source of the three beliefs that we wake up with has to be explained. One, that time has passed, is (necessarily) true. The same explanation can be used for all of them, that is, that they are all true. I did exist while I was asleep, and I am a continuation of the Self that went to sleep. That Self continued to experience its own existence, to recognize itself as a being of the sort that could be conscious and act, and to be aware of its own existence during time.

Let us suppose that one Self ceases to exist when sleep starts, and another comes into existence on waking. It is loaded with the memories of the preceding Self, and is constructed after the same pattern. The new Self believes, from the start, (1), (2), and (3). It is odd that it should believe (1) straight away, without any conscious inference. I shall return to this subject later. (1), nonetheless, is true. But (2) and (3) are (under the supposition) false. Either these beliefs are built - in, or they are deduced. Now if they are built-in, that would explain why no-one except philosophers doubts them, and philosophers only *say* they doubt them because their theoretical position commits them to the doubt.

If (2) and (3) are deduced then either consciously, or, more likely, unconsciously the following deductions must occur.

(a) "I have just become conscious, and yet I have apparent memories of normal waking consciousness from a first person point of view, including memories of previous awakenings."

(b) "Therefore I must be continuation of a person who was conscious before."

(c) "Time has passed since I lost consciousness."

(d) "I must have continued to exist in an unconscious state during that time."

It is not immediately apparent that (b) follows from (a). If there were no experienced gap in time between the first and second Selves, so that there was a sudden change in the contents of consciousness, then there would be a greater likelihood of the second Self assuming it was a continuation of the first Self. However, with the time gap, it seems just as likely that the second Self is another of the same kind. Similarly, (d) does not necessarily follow from (a), (b), and (c). Of course, the unconscious mind is under no constraint to be logical, but the fact that the same result is *always* arrived at, and (*ex hypothesi*) is *always* wrong, makes it seem more likely that (2) and (3) are built - in false beliefs. Even the classic amnesiac, who has been hit by a falling safe, asks "Who am I" to find out who he was before the safe and the amnesia struck. He has the sense of being a continuation of a previous person, even though he has no memory of his previous existence, and can make no deduction from that memory.

If a new Self emerges each morning, then our deep seated beliefs about ourselves are false, even though they are supported by the constant experience of continuous existence. It seems rather odd that we should have false beliefs built in to us. We need better reason to doubt them than the argument from lack of memory. Of course, I claim that they are neither false deductions nor false built - in beliefs. They are true beliefs, coming from the immediate recognition of reality.

A Speculation About the Awareness of Time

I am aware that time has passed when I emerge from a period of hard thinking, when I emerge from meditation, from being absorbed in practice of a physical skill, and, as far as I recall, when I emerge from the state of pure consciousness. I am not always aware of how much time has passed, but certainly of the fact that it has. This awareness is just there. Now this is exactly the same as the situation when I wake up. I have the knowledge that time has passed between my last period of normal waking consciousness and the normal waking consciousness that has just begun.

The methods by which we know that time has passed form a large topic in psychology. I do not intend to deal with the issues in detail here, and I lack the necessary expertise. Rather, I shall put forward, tentatively, a speculation which seems compatible with the facts and with my general position. The speculation is that in all the cases above, the knowledge that time has passed comes from the fact that I have been conscious throughout that time.

Explanation for the Belief that Time has Passed

I use my internal clock to compare the present time with the time I went to sleep or started thinking. However, introspectively there is no sense of looking at an internal clock and saying "I started thinking at time x, and it is now time x+z, so time z must have passed."

First, there is no sense of having noted the time I started thinking. Also, how do I note the time I went to sleep? Second, there is no sense of remembering what time I started thinking, or making the calculation. Third, I am not always sure of how much time has passed. Finally, I do not know what the time on my internal clock is *now*, so I could not make any calculation from now.

If comparison on my internal clock has happened, it must have been done unconsciously (by a brain mechanism) and only the conclusion "time z has passed" becomes conscious. But when I stop being absorbed in the thinking, why does this mechanism note the time on my internal clock when I started thinking, and then tell me that time has passed? Similarly, why does it tell me that I have been asleep for a while?

Block (1979) claims that the internal clock theories have become somewhat unfashionable, and assumes a cognitive or information processing approach, in which time is deduced from change, while suggesting that some sort of conciliation with the internal clock theories is necessary. He notes that studies by Noble and Lundie (1974) indicate that people can make fairly accurate judgments of how long a period of NREM sleep lasted. (There was a considerable absolute error, so the results should treated with some caution.) Block (p. 199) concludes that "people make inferences about duration based on other cues" and suggests that both external and internal cues are used.

This seems a little unlikely to me. After the plastic dinner has been served and the equally bland film is over, I have often fallen asleep for a short time on an intercontinental flight. The surroundings are all the same, the lighting is still dim, and the sound of the engines has not changed. Nor are there any easily noticeable internal cues, such as increased pressure on my bladder. Nonetheless, I do know that I have been asleep, and that some time has passed during the sleep, even if I do not know how much time. The knowledge that time has passed, at least, even if not the estimate of its duration, does not seem to depend on cues.

Block also briefly reviews the literature on people who can awaken, without assistance, at a preselected time, and concludes that the ability comes from "the operation of subconscious (dissociated) information-processing mechanisms." (p. 200)

Both these conclusions are based on the assumption that there is no *experienced* duration because there is usually no awareness in NREM sleep. (Block does not believe that the reports of NREM mentation justify the suggestion that it is continuous.) Suppose, though, that there *is* awareness during NREM sleep, even if it is only the awareness of existing. In that case I could experience the passing of time as part of the awareness of existing. This provides a simpler explanation than that of deduction from cues or subconscious information processing.

I suggest that the knowledge that time has passed is there just because I have experienced the passing of that time. Either the experience of existing includes the experience of the passing of time or the experience of the passing of time is a separate experience. If the latter is the case then there are two experiences that continue during sleep.

(I have read in third-hand accounts that trauma and some anaesthetics disrupt this knowledge of time passing After an accident, the victim awakes disorientated, not knowing that time has passed. There seems to be a sudden jump from the events before the accident to the hospital ward without any existence in between. This is not to claim that the patient's consciousness ceased to exist during the operation, only to show that waking from periods of sleep and unconsciousness is usually accompanied by the idea that time has passed during the sleep or unconsciousness. Probably in these cases there is a disturbance of memory so that neither existence nor the passage of time are remembered. Apparently, in these cases the victim nonetheless believes he or she is a continuation of the person who had the accident.)

Explanation for the Belief That I Existed During Sleep

The belief that we have existed during sleep is the result of existing and being continuously aware of our own existence even during sleep. Comans, discussing the Advaita position, wrote as follows.

> Yet there still remains a sense of the continuity of being between the waker and the sleeper for upon waking there is no sense of non-being, but rather there is the sense of a continuity of being, for the waker does not think that he is essentially different from the one who was asleep. Thus the Advaita position is upheld: though the states of waking, dream, and sleep are usually discrepant, the sense of being persists and this is because Consciousness is identical to a person's fundamental self-experience of being. Consciousness neither disappears during sleep nor manifests at the time of waking, but rather Consciousness persists as the unchanging basis of the states of waking, dream, and sleep. (Comans, 1990)

Although I do not commit myself to the Advaita position, this lengthy quotation does form a neat summary of my views. It gathers together several points: first, the sense of the continuity of being between sleeper and waker, second, the persistence of the sense of being, and third, the connection between consciousness and the sense of being. I will discuss these in turn.

On waking the experience of the present includes the "just now" of waking, and the "just past", which includes the experience of just-before-waking. This can be the last rags of a dream, so that for a moment one is confused about whether reality is the dream or not, or it can be the disorganized thinking of NREM sleep, whose content is lost as the "just past" fades, or perhaps even an awareness of "no thing". The "just past" links in turn with the vague memories from earlier in sleep. At the time of waking, we have no doubt that we existed during sleep. Our knowledge of our continuity extends through sleep as well.

This cannot just be the recognition that the body existed during sleep. The sensations of the body might have been continuous, but to be known as continuous they need to have been recognized by consciousness. I felt that I continued to exist during general anaesthesia, when a large number of the sensations of the body were absent.

The awareness of existence, the sense of being, seems to have very little in the way of phenomenal content, but this does not disqualify it from being a psychological item. The knowledge of the position of our own body seems to have no phenomenal content. Nonetheless I am continuously aware of the position of my body and this knowledge is a continuous item of my mental field, even when I am not concentrating on it. The awareness of existence is not the sort of awareness that is easily attended to. Further, the consciousness of existence is constant and unchanging. Unlike the awareness of the position of the body, the consciousness of existence is not used for daily life. Thus it forms an extended background experience in our mental life, and so is easily missed out of our accounting. We consider our mental life to be the changing items. In sleep, the consciousness of existence is, perhaps, the only item in our mental field and so might easily be confused with having no mental life at all. If it is the only item in our mental field when we are asleep, it is not surprising that we cannot clearly remember existing during sleep. There is precious little to remember. We can remember that we existed but not much else.

The claim that consciousness (as distinct from normal waking consciousness) is identical with the fundamental awareness of being is difficult to argue, not least because the notion of the sense of being is a slippery one to catch. I have argued earlier that the experience of Pure Consciousness is an experience without objects, and so can only be an experience of the subject being itself. The Pure Consciousness experience is a waking experience in which the attention is engaged but withheld from the content of the mind, and is different from dreamless sleep. If dreamless sleep or coma are periods of consciousness without objects they must be periods in which the attention is not engaged. My own suspicion is that during dreamless sleep the attention simply does not fixate on any item long enough for it to be remembered. It is also possible that the memory does not function during that state.

Consciousness is the ground of all experience. In order to experience, it must exist, and in order to be consciousness, it must be aware. If there is no content, no objects, it can only be aware of existing. Thus, consciousness is the fundamental experience of being. All other experience is modification of consciousness, but it includes the sense of being.

Explanation for the Belief in Being the Person Who Went to Sleep

This belief is simply an extension of the previous one. The consciousness of existence continues through all my states of being, and so links the various states. The truth of this belief is shown by Foster's proof above, because consciousness of existence is co-conscious with all experience.

It cannot be a result of recognizing the body of today as being the same as the body of yesterday. I recognize the body as being the same because I am the same. If I cannot recognize that the memory of the body is *my* memory from yesterday, I cannot recognize that the person now inhabiting the body that matches that memory is the same as the person who inhabited it yesterday.

The best explanation for the three beliefs is simply that they are true and are based on experience. The Self does not cease to exist during sleep, but goes on experiencing. Thus, there is an unbroken stream of experience, and the sense of continuity of identity that Hazlitt recognized is not actually broken. We have a tacit knowledge of our own continuity. It is important to recognize this knowledge, and make it explicit. Many of the puzzle cases that clutter the literature on personal identity refer to the doubtful person "waking up", and so smuggle continuity in by the back door. I shall point this out in some cases later.

The concept of the intermittent Self is, at best, no more than a bare logical possibility that runs counter to our experience. It is certainly not an equally likely alternative to the hypothesis of a continuant Self. There is no reason whatsoever for believing that the possibility is realized. The claim that the Self ceases to exist during sleep also runs counter to our experience. The only arguments in support of the claim are extremely weak, and all the evidence stands against the claim. Perhaps the above arguments do not fully prove the continuity of the Self, but they place the burden of proof solidly on the claim that the Self ceases to exist during sleep or coma.

A Summary of the Argument

1. There is no real possibility of the Self being a series of Selves during normal waking consciousness.

2. We are aware of our own continuity.

3. It is logically possible for consciousness to continue during deep sleep or coma.

4. The argument against consciousness during deep sleep is weak. It depends on the lack of memory, but that lack can be explained in other ways.

5. There is empirical evidence that indicates that there is mentation, and consciousness associated with it, during sleep, both in dreams and in dreamless sleep.

6. Our deep seated beliefs about our own continuity during sleep are best explained by the continuity of consciousness.

7. Even if the continuity of consciousness during sleep has not been proved, at least the burden of proof has been shifted to those who would deny it.

5 Survival

Recent work on personal identity by Shoemaker (1984), Parfit (1991), and Brennan (1988) has claimed that the basic relation uniting persons over time is not identity but survival. Identity, they claim, is a particular type of survival. It is the survival relation that matters, and identity is of derivative importance. This idea is the result of considering cases of fission, where one person divides into two, as leading to the existence of survivors who are not identical with each other and so not identical with the pre-fission person. Cases of fusion, where two people become one, and of transformation, where a human being slowly changes into some other organism, have also been offered as cases wherein the original person ceases to exist and yet has survivors. I will argue later that fission is probably not possible, and that even if it is possible, it still need not destroy identity. Nonetheless, for the purposes of this chapter, I shall take seriously the possibility that there can be survivors who are not identical with the original.

The debate has been carried out recently in terms of Parfit's claim that survival gives us "what matters" even when identity is lost. Martin (1988) has pointed out that the question is not especially clear. There can be differences between what actually matters and what rationally ought to matter. Rey (1976) claims that what matters in survival and what counts as survival depends on what people think matters and counts. This makes survival a matter of personal or social choice, but also a matter of little philosophical interest. Rather than attempt to formulate the question precisely, I will suggest an answer, and try to show that it is more generally satisfying than others in terms of the way it coincides with our pretheoretical concerns.

A Misguided Approach

Lewis (1976) and Brueckner (1993) claim that the question of whether I will survive a battle is equivalent to the question of whether I will be numerically identical with anyone alive after the battle. They present the situation as "a person B at t2 is a survivor of a person A at t1 iff At1 ≡ Bt2".

This formulation leads, with an awful inevitability, to the question being interpreted backwards, as one of "is B a survivor of A". When it is agreed that there can be survival without identity, survival is regarded as a relationship (symbolized by "→") obtaining between a present person A and a future person B, so that "a person B at t2 is a survivor of a person A at t1 iff At1 → T2". The inquiry than becomes one of the relationship between two items, A and B, which makes it very easy to look for the answer in terms of the characteristics they have in common.

This is to misconceive the situation. The question is not one about the state of affairs at a particular future time, but about the state of affairs during the full extent of time from now. I am not interested in the relation of any future persons to me. I am interested in my continued existence. As I have shown above there is good reason to believe that the subject (or stream of experience) is continuous, even during times of unconsciousness, and that we have tacit knowledge of our own continuity. My question about the battle is whether my existence will cease. I ask "what will happen to me during the battle? Will this stream of consciousness come to a gruesome end?" If it does, I will not survive.

Thinking in terms of a set of characteristics is also misleading. To look at a set of characteristics is to conceive the question in third person terms, and ask of one person whether we would regard him as a survivor of another. This approach only works when we look at other persons. It does not work for me. My concern for the future is not that the future experiences will be accompanied by a particular set of characteristics, but that the future experiences will happen to *me*. Even if all the characteristics change I am still concerned about the experiences, so I am concerned about the experiences happening to something other than the set of characteristics.

The Priority of the First Person Point of View

Some recent theorizing about survival starts from considerations of what counts as survival of physical objects. Much is made of the ship of Theseus, of dismantled and re-assembled watches, of statues and lumps of clay. (Brennan's S-relation, which uses the concepts of structure, matter, and cause, is derived from such cases.) I consider this theorizing to be largely irrelevant to the survival of persons. Persons are not the same as objects.

Persons have, as a necessary condition of being persons, a first person point of view. There is a "what it is like" to be a person. Physical objects which are not persons do not have a first person point of view. If Theseus tells his ship that its planks will be replaced by steel, and that the planks will be gathered together and reconstructed (with that great concern for antiquities the Greeks have shown since they realized the rest of us would pay good money to see them) and then asks "which will be your survivor; the rusty freighter carrying dubious cargoes between disreputable Mediterranean ports, or the tourist trap floating in Piraeus harbour?" he will receive no answer. The ship will have no opinion. It is neither a conscious nor a self conscious entity. It does not have a first person point of view.

A person, when told that he will have all his parts replaced, will have, if not a well-formulated opinion, at least some concern about the prospects for survival. It is, therefore, necessary for any account of survival of persons to include an account from the first person point of view .

Our major interest in persons is interest in them as beings with a first person point of view, as beings who make judgments, have intentions, perform actions, and who act unpredictably and with originality. Of course, sometimes we are not interested in persons as anything other than the performers of certain functions. A ticket clerk at the station can be replaced by a machine as long as there is no problem about the purchase of the ticket. However, when I am in a desperate rush to buy a ticket which costs £7.35, and only have £7.34 and a spare shirt button in my pocket, then I prefer to deal with a functionary who has a first person point of view. I believe that I can convince such a person to have sympathy with *my* first person point of view and sell me the ticket anyway, whereas I could not convince a ticket machine. The point of identifying persons and their survivors is to identify them as *persons*, beings with a first person point of view, who can give an first person account of themselves.

Of course, from the point of view of each person, the account of his own survival that matters is that from the first person point of view. My supervisor has watched *Invasion of the Body Snatchers* too often, and so has a secret fear that one night, while he is asleep, aliens will replace him with a replica. This replica will be able to give his lectures and run the Philosophy Department as well as he can, and yet this is no comfort to him. The replica might seem like a perfect survivor to his colleagues and students, but my supervisor's fear concerns his fate from the first person point of view. The question for him is what it will be like for *him* to be replaced by a replica?

Furthermore, if I consider the question of survival of a *person* from the third person point of view, I must take the first person point of view into account. So long as I consider my supervisor to be nothing more than a device to help me gain a Ph. D., the aliens can replace him with replicas as often as they like. The cessation of one stream of consciousness by another would not affect me so long as the new stream of consciousness retained the memories and functioned in the same way as the previous one. If I think of my supervisor as a person, however, I am at once imputing a first person point of view to him, since this is necessary for him to be a person. Then I must include *his* first person point of view among my calculations, and decide whether it take priority over the third person point of view considerations.

Suppose the aliens destroy my wife and replace my wife with a replica. If I knew it was a replica my feelings towards that replica would not be those I have towards my wife. Nor would I consider that my wife had survived. I would consider the matter first from her first person point of view. Her concern for herself includes the wish that her stream of consciousness should continue. My concern for her is that her wishes be granted. (Also, I consider my wife to be a combination of Self, mind, and body. If the replica does not have the same Self as the original, I do not believe she is the survivor of the original, and so not the same person as the person I married. But that is to anticipate the results of my inquiry.)

Martin (1992) points out that we identify with our survivors, in the sense that we regard them as ourselves. This identification consists in having the same (or very similar) attitudes and dispositions towards the survivors that we have to ourselves. There are cognitive and affective dispositions. The most important of the affective dispositions are "affective anticipation" and "unconditional giving."

Affective anticipation is the way one feels when anticipating one's own experiences. When I anticipate being tortured I feel fear. When I anticipate someone else being tortured, I may feel pity, satisfaction, or a variety of other feelings, but I will not feel fear. When I anticipate me drinking a glass of whisky my feelings about it are considerably different from my feelings when I anticipate you drinking a glass of whisky. Especially if it is my whisky, and a single-still malt at that.

Unconditional giving refers to the fact that if I sacrifice the pleasure of drinking a glass of whisky now in order to achieve the future pleasure of having finished this chapter, I do not feel that my future self should be grateful to my present self. I feel no resentment at my future self for this ingratitude. I do not feel grateful to my past self for having kept away from the whisky long enough for me to get this far in the chapter.

These attitudes are essentially first person attitudes, attitudes we hold to ourselves. Our concern for our survivors is essentially the same as our concern for our present selves.

For these reasons I claim that an account of survival must first be convincing from the first person point of view, and that the account from the first person point of view must take priority over any conflicting account from the third person point of view. No matter how satisfactory an account may be in other ways, if it is not satisfactory from the first person point of view, it must be rejected or changed.

Ordinary Survival

In order to decide what matters in survival I shall first consider what counts as survival in ordinary day to day life, and then extract the key elements from it.

First Person View of Survival

I have survived since this morning. I have continuously been a subject of experience during the day. My body has persisted, I have gained a few more memories, but I have not noticed that I have lost any. My personality has not changed noticeably. My mental or physical skills have shown no dramatic change, save for an improvement in my Tetris score. In all ways I am pretty much the same as I was this morning. I also believe I have survived since yesterday, even though I was asleep last night. I feel that I am continuous with the person of yesterday in that my body, personality, memories etc. are the same as those of the person of yesterday, but that my capacity for consciousness and agency continued during sleep, that I continued to be a subject and an agent even when I was not acting or experiencing very much at all. So long as this continues, I will survive.

Third Person View of Survival

A person normally is regarded as surviving for a day if his body has physical continuity and he shows psychological continuity. That is, his body and mind stay pretty much the same during the day. There are no sudden changes of personality, no amnesia or acquisition of a set of new memories. The question of whether he has continuously been a subject of experience during the day is not normally raised. It is assumed that psychological continuity includes being a continuous subject. The same considerations are used to justify the claim that he survives from day to day. (Hence the plausibility of the arguments of the reductionists.)

What Matters in Survival?

Ordinary survival of a person is not a single relationship. It is the survival of three things. First, the continuing subject. Second, the continuing instantiation of a set of psychological characteristics. Third, the continuance of a physical body. The three things are of different types. The body is a physical object. The survival of a physical object is the survival of a particular individual, whereas the survival of the set of psychological characteristics is the survival of an something that can be instantiated several times. The survival of a subject is the survival of an entity which seems to be an individual. Thus, ordinary survival is a compound of relationships, none of which can be reduced to the other. Ordinary survival consists in a particular body and a particular subject continuing to exist in the same relation to each other and giving a unique instantiation of a particular set of psychological characteristics. While this situation holds there is full and complete survival. It is not problematic either from the first person point of view or the third person point of view. The problems come in cases of extraordinary survival, when the three items are separated, as they are in cases of fission, transformation, teleportation, reincarnation, disembodiment, replication, etc.

What matters in survival? Christopher Cherry and Thomas Paine give similar answers, which I will discuss and expand upon.

First, Cherry's answer:

> What is it that a person wants in wanting to continue indefinitely in existence? Put in the broadest terms, what he wants is to continue indefinitely as a self-conscious subject of experience. (Cherry 1984, p. 444)

I will call this the continuous subject criterion for survival. From any person's first person point of view what matters is for that person to continue being a subject of experience.

(I do not exclude the possibility that other things may be preferred to survival. The sincere Marxist may be willing to give up his life in order to further the revolution, even though he believes that with death his capacity for experience will cease. This is not wishing for another form of survival, it is wishing for something *instead of* survival. The purpose of Cherry's essay is to show that such alternatives cannot be regarded as real surrogates for survival, even if they are preferred to survival. Survival, he claims, is not something that can have substitutes.

> For if what I essentially want is to enjoy certain conscious experiences my want cannot intelligibly be deputed to one which not merely anticipates but presupposes the extinction of any and every conscious experience of mine. (Cherry 1984, p. 444)

Cherry's statement does not have to be interpreted as referring to an irreducible unitary Self as I have described it. Continuing to be a particular subject can simply mean continuing to be whatever has the capacity for experience. If the reductionists are correct, there is no Self of the type I have described, but merely a bundle of experiences, thoughts, etc. If this is the case, Cherry's criterion can be rephrased as "what he wants is the indefinite continuation of the stream of experience of which his present is experience is part"

Ordinary waking experience comes as a stream of consciousness, made up of an enormous variety of mental items. Thoughts, sense perceptions, emotions, the sense of agency, etc. all combine in a single stream. The unity of consciousness at any one time unifies these into a single state. Many of the items persist through time. Sounds, for example, have to be temporally extended to be experienced. Some items begin before others, but for at least part of their extent they are experienced together. The hideous noise of Concorde flying overhead coincides with, and is experienced with, the final bars of the music from the radio, and continues until after the music is over. My thought about what a public nuisance the plane is, and the associated feeling of irritation, begin part way through the noise, and continue long after the noise is over. The visual image of my computer screen is experienced before, during, and after the noise.

The stream of consciousness is *at least* an overlapping chain of mental items. In fact, our experience is not a chain of separate items, but, as the term implies, experienced as a single continuous stream. It is experienced as unified both synchronically and diachronically. Normal survival includes the continuation of this stream. Continuation of the stream means that new items overlap with the old ones, or the old ones persist indefinitely.

Thomas Paine gives a description of survival similar to Cherry's

> But all other arguments apart, the *consciousness of existence* is the only conceivable idea we can have of another life, and the continuance of that consciousness is immortality. The consciousness of existence, or the knowing that we exist, is not necessarily confined to the same form, nor to the same matter, even in this life.
>
> We have not in all cases the same form, nor in any case the same matter that composed our bodies twenty or thirty years ago; and yet we are conscious of being the same persons. Even legs and arms, which make up almost half the human frame, are not necessary to the consciousness of existence. These may be lost or taken away, and the full consciousness of existence remain; and were their place supplied by wings or other appendages, we cannot conceive that it could alter our consciousness of existence. In short, we know not how much, or rather how little, of our composition it is, and how exquisitely fine that little is, that creates in us that consciousness of existence; and all beyond that is like the pulp of a peach, distinct and separate from the vegetative speck in the kernel. (Paine, 1842, p. 69)

Paine gives no further discussion to the concept of the consciousness of existence, but he clearly means our knowledge of our own existence. I am aware of my own existence, and this knowledge persists continuously. I am aware not only of being in a certain mental condition, but also of being a certain kind of thing, of being something that can be conscious, and that can be an agent. (The sense of being something that can be conscious or an agent does not imply that the something is a unitary Self, only that I have the idea of there being something permanent. The reductionist can claim that the something is a physical body.) This awareness can only be interpreted ostensively by reference to what is revealed by introspective awareness. It cannot be conveyed any other way, just as there is no way of explaining "red" to the congenitally blind. I do not always attend to this awareness; indeed, I usually ignore it. Nonetheless it persists as a background mental item, as part of unprojected consciousness. This mental item persists throughout my mental life, and forms a common thread which overlaps with all the other mental items of the stream of consciousness.

I have argued above that this stream of consciousness does not cease with sleep or unconsciousness, so what counts in survival of the subject is the continuous flow of the stream, even if that stream is reduced to the bare minimum of the consciousness of existence.

This gives us a first person criterion for survival of the subject that does not directly imply a unitary Self. I claim that the continued existence and coherence of the stream is the result of the experience being had by a unified persisting Self, but this is not necessary for my argument so far. The point is that this aspect of ordinary survival is what matters (from the first person point of view) in extraordinary survival.

Cherry and Paine regard their version of survival as self evident. Cherry offers no justification, and Paine only argues briefly that it does not necessarily involve the survival of the body. I shall therefore start with a few considerations that seem to me to support Paine and Cherry.

Raymond Martin has claimed that an important source of our concern for our survivors is the anticipation of our survivors having experiences. If (for example) you knew you were going to divide it would be important to know that you could look forward to having the experiences that the fission products would have, and to having them directly in the way you have your experiences now. The same consideration applies to such transformations as slowly changing into an insect or fusing with another person. If this were lacking

> something crucial would be missing, *regardless of how else you and your descendent(s) might be connected* . . .

and if it were present

> something of extraordinary and perhaps overriding importance would have been retained, *regardless of what other connections might be missing.* (Martin 1993, p. 308)

The way I have my experiences now is as part of the present stream of experience. To anticipate having future experiences in the same way is to anticipate those experiences being part of the same stream. That is, the present stream will continue and eventually include those experiences, so that the experiences I am having now will overlap with experiences that overlap with experiences that overlap with experiences, in a chain that has experiences that overlap with the anticipated experiences.

Martin supports his point by contrasting it with Perry's views. Perry (1976) considers anticipating having experiences is important, but he regards it as derivative from the desire to promote certain projects. If I am in pain tomorrow it will interfere with my projects more than someone else's pain would, so I have special concern to avoid pain.

Martin's criticisms are as follows: assume you are told that tomorrow you will suffer thirty minutes of severe pain, pain much worse than anything you have experienced before. Your natural reaction would be dread. If you had no major projects for tomorrow, and you were told that neither the anxiety at the prospect nor the after effects of the pain would interfere with those projects you did have, that might reduce the anxiety a little. It is unlikely that you would accept it with equanimity, or only slight anxiety.

But if your main concern was for the promotion of your projects, the information should not cause such strong fear. The actual cause of the fear is that the pain will hurt you, and you will experience this directly. Having the experience itself is what matters, not its results.

Perry recognizes that generally we not only want our projects to be completed, but also we want to complete them ourselves. What he does not seem to give sufficient consideration to is the fact that we want to experience completing them. The motive Perry offers for our desire to complete our projects ourselves is that we believe that others are unlikely to complete them as reliably or as well.

Now this simply flies in the face of reality. I was about to spend a day laying a carpet. After wrestling with it for a little while, I lost my nerve and called a carpet fitter, who completed the task far faster and more skillfully than I could. I am well aware that there are tasks outside my competence, and that some of my projects (writing great philosophical treatises, for example) might be better carried out by persons more brilliant and more persevering than me.

Martin gives the example of the project (he notes that the terminology is unfortunate in this case) of making love to someone you deeply love. The important thing is not that *someone* makes love to that person, nor even that *you* make love to that person, but that you *experience* making love to that person.

To clarify this point even further, consider the following three possibilities for the honourable and desirable project of punching the Prime Minister on the nose.

First, I punch him while sleepwalking. I did not experience it at the time and have no memory of the incident. Nonetheless my martial arts training ensures that a respectable punch is delivered. The newspapers are full of pictures of the P.M. sprawling on the ground with blood gushing from his nose. I am feted by a grateful nation.

Second: A muscular and athletic Member of Parliament, worried by his declining popularity, on his own initiative punches the Prime Minister and instantly becomes the most adored politician in the country. This MP is both stronger and more expert at punching them I am, and does a better job of it.

Third: In full waking consciousness I deliver the punch, feeling myself to be causally efficacious and experiencing the whole delightful incident. Nonetheless the punch is not as powerful as that which would have been delivered in the second case.

The first possibility is better than nothing. At least the Prime Minister gets punched on the nose. I think, however, that in terms of the project itself (if not in terms of the resulting adulation, which in this case I would miss) I would prefer the second to the first. The project is more thoroughly carried out. Since I do not experience carrying it out in either case, it is less important to me that I am the one who carries out the project, and more important that it be done well.

The third possibility is the one I most desire, for in that I have the experience of carrying out the project. When I do not have the satisfaction of punching the Prime Minister I am much less concerned with who does it. A large part of my concern that I should carry out my projects is that I should have the experience of carrying them out.

Of course, I might regard a project as so overwhelmingly important that I would altruistically sacrifice my experience of carrying it out in order to ensure that it was done properly. I might consider that I am too feeble to punch the Prime Minister effectively, and so, in the public interest, give up my own desires and let the MP punch him instead. But in this case I am very clear that I am giving up the pleasure of the experience, and I feel very noble about the way I sacrifice my own pleasure for the good of humanity.

(Naturally, the most desirable constitutional reform would be an arrangement whereby I and the muscular MP took turns in punching the PM.)

Martin's conclusion seems to support the continuous subject criterion. If the way we have our experiences now is as part of the continuous stream then this means anticipating the future experiences as also being part of the stream.

Martin refers to cases of fission and of transformation as cases in which the *person* does not survive, so that we are anticipating having someone else's (another *person's*) experiences in the way we have our own experience. Nonetheless, the anticipated experience would have to be part of the same stream, and if, as I claim, experience is had by a subject, it would have to be had by the same subject. As I have shown previously (by Foster's argument) a stream of experience cannot shift from subject to subject, so the future experience must be an experience had by the same subject now having the present experience. A subject might (just possibly) share an experience with another subject, but it cannot have another subject's experience. Having the experience constitutes the experience being *that subject's* experience.

I cannot anticipate having the experience of whoever will be the Professor of Philosophy at the University of Reading in 2015 unless my present stream of experience overlaps with the stream of experience of the Professor, and that implies I and the future Professor have the same subject of experience. My survivor must have the same subject of experience as the subject of experience that is having my present experiences. This means that to survive, I must continue to exist as a subject of experience.

This explains both affective anticipation and unconditional giving. The pain that the torture victim will feel is part of the same stream that anticipates it now. The anticipator will also be the sufferer, and so feels fear. Similarly, for unconditional giving, the beneficiary of self restraint will be the same stream as the restrainer. The subject is also the agent, so the agent of self-restraint is the subject of the benefits.

Extraordinary Survival

In ordinary survival the essential feature (from the first person point of view) of survival is the continuity of the subject. It is accompanied by the same mind and body. The question now arises as to whether the mind or body are also necessary for survival. In all the following cases of extraordinary survival I consider that I would survive. In each case I think that only those philosophers who are committed to other theories would disagree. The sequence of cases shows that the continuity of the subject can be sufficient for survival, albeit survival of a very etiolated form.

Personality

Suppose I suffered from a brain disorder that could only be cured in a way that would lead to a total change in personality. Before the treatment I am a taciturn, irascible, fussy, boring introvert, but afterwards I will be a noisy, sport-loving, boring extrovert. This I find to be an unpleasant prospect. I am exceedingly unhappy at the prospect of this change.

Some changes in personality happen to us all as we get older, and so constitute part of ordinary survival, but this is not quite the same. Although I no longer have the interest in Dinky toys that I had when I was a small boy, I can sympathize with, and in effect draw back the feel of, that interest. The situation I am trying to imagine is one in which I have no sympathy or understanding of those earlier interests.

It is true that people like me try to improve their personalities all the time by reading American paperbacks on how to be a new, assertive, non-victimized, calmer, more creative, more open, more self-assured, gentler person. But those are voluntary changes. If I could, I would choose to be a bit more like James Bond, and a lot less like Basil Fawlty, but in this case I have no choice. I am to have a personality foisted on me, and it is one that I don't like the sound of.

In the television series *Red Dwarf* the characters discovered that in the future they were to become people of a type they regarded as revolting. They chose annihilation rather than face the prospect. It was not a decision to merely prevent such people from existing. The revulsion was deeper than that; it was a decision not to become such people. Survival as people of that sort was regarded as a fate worse than death.

The moral here is clearly that I would survive as a subject of experience, and experience myself as having a certain personality. Having the sort of personality I have now means that I would prefer *now* to anticipate experiencing myself in the future as having the same, or preferably (if the techniques described in the American paperbacks actually work) a better personality. I certainly do not regard a change in personality as a threat to my survival, and the point of changing my personality for the better is so that I can experience having that better personality.

Since the slow changes of personality that occur during life, and the faster ones that result from "life changing experiences" do not seem to affect the continuity of the subject, there is no reason to think that very fast changes would have that effect either. It might be claimed that I had become a different person, but from the first person point of view to deny that I survived the change seems absurd.

Memory Loss

The same considerations apply to memory. Loss of memory does not seem to be the sort of thing that could affect the continuity of the subject. If all my memories were to slowly fade away, until I had no memories of my previous life left, the subject of experience would survive the change, and continue to exist. Nor does there seem to be any reason to doubt that the same subject would continue to exits if all the memories were lost at once.

(I am assuming that I can lose my memories without any change in personality, even though I will no longer remember the events that produced it.)

Memory seems to be important in personal identity, but in terms of my survival I find I am much more willing to give it up than other elements of the mind. The idea of having perfect memory of my past, but not being able to form new memories; of losing the mental capacities to organize thought; of living with severe Alzheimer's syndrome; of being totally paralyzed so that I can only remember and perceive, but not think rationally, or act; of having a human mind in a frog's body, are all more horrific.

Loss of Mind

I have good reason to believe that tomorrow I will lose all those capacities that make me a person except for consciousness and agency. I will lose memories, personality traits, the cognitive structure that allows me to reason and think, etc. In short, I will be reduced to an empty subject of experience; as near to a Lockean *tabula rasa* as is possible. My body will then be tortured, and pain will be felt. In this case I fear both the loss of the capacities, and the pain. Clearly I expect to survive even though I will no longer have the mental characteristics I have now. I will not be the same person. I will not even be a *person*. Nonetheless, I expect to feel the pain. To feel the pain I have to be a subject of experience, so I expect that even when all the elements that make up my mind have been lost I will still survive as a subject of experience.

This example is adapted from one given by Nollaig Mackenzie (1982).

Becoming Another Person

Again I have good reason to believe that tomorrow I will lose all my memories, my personality, cognitive structure, and become a *tabula rasa*, just as in the preceding case. Subsequently this amnesiac will undergo a change in personality and acquire a set of ostensible memories. Still later the resulting person (at this stage it is less question begging to say "the person" instead of "I" or "the amnesiac") will have to choose between two courses of action. Action A (say, burning down the orphanage) will lead the person to Hell. Action B (donating a large sum of money to the orphanage) will lead the person to Heaven.

If today, before these changes, I perform act C (put a note on the refrigerator, instructing the person to do B) the person will perform B. If I do not perform C, the person will perform A.

What should be my attitude to performing C? Reductionists would claim that I will not be the person. There are no psychological connections. They have all been wiped out. On the other hand, when during the process would I have ceased to exist? It seems to me (though perhaps not to Parfit) that I will be that person, that I will suffer that pains of Hell if I fail to perform C now. My attitude depends on the anticipation that the future experiences will be mine in the way that my present experiences are mine, even though I will have no memory of my present experiences or characteristics. Again, I anticipate continuing to exist as a subject of experience.

This example is taken from John Knox, 1969. In his reply, Mark Woodhouse (1970) suggested that in this case there are no positive criteria for me to use to make my decision about act C, and so that my decision to perform C was no more than a Pascalian wager.

The ground offered for my performing C is the supposed fact that it is *possible* I will be the person. If it is not possible, then there is no ground for performing C. In that case the argument would be less reasonable than a

Pascalian wager. If the subject's survival of the loss of the mind is logically possible, then it is *as reasonable as* Pascal's wager.

Pascal's wager is based on lack of other reasons for believing in God. In this case, however, we have plausible reasons for believing that I will survive the changes proposed, which make the argument more reasonable than Pascal's wager. Bodily identity is *evidence* for subject identity, and so is mental identity. Bodily identity extends from now (when it is my body) until the death of the person (when the same body is the person's body). By hypothesis in this case, the person survives death, so the mental identity of the person extends from before death to the future existence in Heaven or Hell. This acts as evidence for the continuity of the subject from now to the afterlife. It is plausible to believe, then that the person's experiences in the afterlife will be mine. (Knox 1970)

Are there any reasons for supposing it is not possible that I will become the future person? The only possibilities are that total loss of mind either make me into a different subject of experience or that it destroys the subject of experience.

If I have been made into a different subject of experience, do I fade into the new person's subject of experience? This seems impossible because being a subject of experience is not a matter of degree. Suppose my memories fade and the ostensible memories become more comprehensive in a continuous process. It is still me experiencing the changing memory. The experiences cannot slowly stop being mine. An experience cannot be partly mine and partly someone else's. If an experience is mine, it is wholly mine. Some other subject of experience might have a qualitatively similar experience, but that is all. If there is a series of experiences, each linked to the previous experience, the same subject has all the experiences. This has been shown in a previous chapter.

Can total loss of mind destroy the subject of experience? This would mean that every item of the mind would have to be eliminated before the new items were introduced. However, there is no reason to believe that even if this were done, the subject of experience would cease to exist. Even if there were a period of sleep between the loss of one mind and gaining of another, the subject would continue to exist during the sleep. For destruction of the mind to cause destruction of the subject of experience requires a reductionist theory of the mind that denies the existence of any subject of experience. In this case, the loss of all the items of the mind would mean that the original stream of consciousness would cease to exist. Of course, there would be no mind for the new items to be introduced to. The new mind would be created by putting the new items together. In this case, the reason I do not survive is because the stream of consciousness ceases as a necessary result of all the psychological characteristics being changed.

Out of the Body

This example is taken from Unger, 1986

(Part 1) I collapse onto the floor. Then I find that I seem to be floating up out of my body and hover near the ceiling, looking down on my body, as in the standard accounts of disembodied existence. (I will defend that coherence of disembodied existence later.) The body on the floor begins to move. It gets up and acts. Consciousness is again associated with the body. There are two conscious beings. One, me, floating near the ceiling, and one with a human form.

(Part 2) While floating away from the body I suddenly lose my personal memory and my personality changes. The being in what used to be my body appear to have memories qualitatively similar to the memories I had, and a personality qualitatively similar to the personality I had.

In part 1, I consider my survival as a conscious subject to be independent of my body. I survive as the floating being, not the one that inhabits the body I thought of as mine. If the floating being is the one that faces torture, I will fear the pain. (This is Unger's conclusion as well) In part 2 the being in my body has physical continuity with the person I was, and has greater psychological continuity with the exception of the continuity of conscious experience. Yet in this case also I consider that I survive as the floating being, not the embodied one.

(Unger agrees with this as his dominant response, but notes another response. This is that too much has been given to the embodied being, and that the case is no longer coherent. I suspect that the other response comes partly from regarding the question from the third person point of view, and partly from commitment to Reductionism If such a thing happened to the person next to me I would have no way of knowing it, and would consider that the original person had survived. The case as described sets up a conflict between the third person point of view, that regards a person as a set of psychological characteristics and a body, and the first person point of view, by which I regard myself first and foremost as a subject and an agent. Also, if there is no subject distinct from the combination of memory and personality, the existence of the floating being is impossible.)

These cases show that the unbroken continuity of the stream of experience seems to be a *sine qua non* of survival, and that survival of the subject without survival of the body or mind is conceivable. Clearly it is not sufficient for full, ordinary, survival.

Replicas and Survivors

Theories that regard survival in terms of the characteristics that the survivor has in common with the earlier person cannot easily distinguish between replicas and survivors. However, the continuous subject criterion for survival gives us a satisfactory way of distinguishing between replicas and survivors which can then be used to show why dubious cases of survival are inadequate.

I do not regard the Prime Minister as my survivor in any important sense. Suppose that he is kidnapped by the Psychology Department of this University, and subjected to a complete change in appearance and personality. He is brainwashed to share my memories, personality, ideas, and brought to a state exactly like the one I am in now. Plastic surgery has made him look like me, as well. After these improvements are completed, the Psychology Department then announce to me that they intend to kill me. I do not find the existence of this copy as much comfort as I should if all I wanted was for there to be a future person with my characteristics. I would still prefer the copy to die. I do not regard him as my survivor, but as another person.

To speed up the process, I step into Calvin's replicator. (Watterson 1993) The machine goes "boink", and I and an exact replica of me step out. I do not share consciousness with the replica. As soon as we step out we start thinking slightly different thoughts, and having slightly different experiences. I do not have direct access to his thoughts, nor he to mine. Again, I regard the replica as another person. If he faces torture, I would feel pity, but not fear. If he helps me, I would feel gratitude. If I help him, I would expect gratitude. On the future concern test, my concern for my own future is different from my concern for the future of the replica, because I do not believe that I will experience the experiences of the replica directly in the way I experience my own experiences now. I consider him to be a distinct subject of experience.

My reasons for considering him to be another person include the following:

(1) The lack of shared consciousness.
(2) The lack of a common body.
(3) Neither person can directly control the body of the other.
(4) The causal independence of the persons. Cutting either person does not leave a scar on the other.
(5) The inability of each person to remember the post-creation experiences of the other.

Ehring (1987b) argues that the above reasons are not sufficient for considering time travellers or fission twins to be different persons. If I go back in time and meet my fifteen year old self, it could well be said that there are apparently two persons, but they are in fact the same person. I will discuss the arguments for this later. Here it is sufficient to point out that the arguments are against the sufficiency of the above reasons *in the cases of time travellers or fission twins only*. In the case of time travellers, the stream of consciousness of the older person is a continuation of that of the younger person. In the case of the fission twins they shared their stream of consciousness before fission, and could, perhaps, fuse again to have a single stream of consciousness. The case of the replica is quite different. His stream of consciousness was never continuous with mine. We never shared an stream of consciousness. If we fuse, then we will share a stream of consciousness, but this is also the case with the unreconstructed PM and me. I have no reason to believe that we will fuse, and so no reason to consider that our streams of consciousness will ever be connected.

My reasons for thinking of the replica as another subject of experience are as follows. Since there was no sharing of thoughts or experiences when the replica was created, it seems unlikely that there would ever be overlap or continuity between the two streams of consciousness. Only if we fuse can we have the same stream of consciousness. Now if we assume that a subject can have only one stream of consciousness, or that it cannot have two streams without being aware that it is having two, then there must be a distinct subject for each stream. (If we do not make this assumption, we are on the way to the position that there is only one Self.)

Suppose the replica is created just at the moment of my death. Assuming that the stream of consciousness associated with my body ceases at that moment, will my stream of consciousness be continuous with the stream of consciousness associated with the body of the replica? My stream of consciousness would end. The replica's stream of consciousness would start, perhaps with the belief that it was a continuation of mine, but it would be a distinct stream of consciousness, and a distinct subject. Creation of a replica is not the same as continuation of the stream of consciousness and the continued existence of the subject of experience.

From the first person point of view, then, the replica would not be the same sort of survivor as a continuation of my stream of consciousness would. Clearly, in order to believe I will survive, I need to expect at least the same sort of continuity as I feel between one day and the next, if not that between one moment and the next. Merely for my successor to have my memories, etc., is not sufficient for the survival that matters.

No matter how similar a person is to me, if there is no continuity of subject, no continuity of stream of consciousness, he is a replica, but not a survivor of me.

Fake Survival Exposed

I will now apply this distinction to some cases that have been treated as survival, and show that they fail to be survival on Cherry's criterion, but explain why we are tempted to accept them as survival.

Rimmer

Case: Arnold Rimmer, a character in *Red Dwarf,* was killed in the first episode. The spaceship's computer has a complete record of his memories, personality, appearance, etc. The computer therefore sets up a programme that will simulate Rimmer's mind, and projects a hologram image of Rimmer that acts in association with the simulation programme.

Comment: For the purposes of the story we are prepared to regard this as being a continuation of the original Rimmer, but in fact there is no reason to regard it as anything but a replica.

Although the computer simulation of Rimmer's mind may include a stream of consciousness, there is no continuity between that stream of consciousness and the stream of consciousness of the original Rimmer.

Death and Resurrection

Case: When I die, I stop. All my feelings, experiences, etc., just stop. At the end of time God will re-create my body and reinfuse it with life, with my memories, my personality, my ideas, etc. The resurrected person thinks he is me who has started again.

Comment: The first problem is that of the body being recreated. Aquinas faced the question of whether the person who was resurrected was the same person as the one who died. His answer was, roughly, that the soul was immortal, and was reunited with the same body. Although the body had been dispersed after death, God gathered the bits together and reconstructed it. Because each soul is the form of a particular body, the body it informs must be the same body.

A standard objection here is that the matter in the body is constantly changing, and so the matter in the body at fifteen may be completely different from that at fifty. Thus, it is possible to reconstruct two bodies, one the fifteen year old body, and the other the fifty year old body. (Church fathers speculated about the case of a person who had been eaten by cannibals, so that their bodies had become intermingled.) However, for the sake of simplicity I will assume that God manages to get all the bits and reconstructs them to produce a version of my body as it was just before my death. The set of psychological characteristics (psychological identity) is also recreated as it was at the moment just before death.

It is not immediately apparent to me that this reconstruction is a continuation of me. If such a person were created while I was still alive, perhaps out of matter that was part of my body most recently (so that the atom I just scraped off my nose is used for that part of my nose) and with a psychological identity that matches that I have now, I would regard him as nothing more than a replica of me. I do not think I would be a continuous subject of experience with him. He would seem to be a separate subject of experience. And in the same way I can see no reason for regarding him as anything more than a replica if he is created after I am dead. It seems that he is just a new subject of experience with a copy of my memories, personality, body, etc., and so from the first person point of view this is not survival of a continuous subject of experience. On the contrary, *ex hypothesi* my stream of consciousness has stopped. The subject of experience no longer exists, and the resurrected body has a new subject of experience.

Brain State Recording

Case: I am suffering from a brain disorder. The only known cure is an operation. The doctors have to copy all my memories, ideas, personality traits, and thoughts on tape (just as they did with Lister in *Red Dwarf*) and then stop my brain, de-coke it, flush out the cooling fluid and antifreeze, replace them, and then start my brain again and put in all the information from the tape.

Comment: Even though the brain and body used are mine, and the memories used are mine (transferred through another medium), I fear it will be the same for me as dying, because there is no guarantee of continuing to be a subject of consciousness during the operation. The process seems essentially no different from creating a replica.

Teleporting

Case: I get into a machine that instantly scans and records the position of every particle of my body. It destroys my body in the process. The information about my body is then sent to another machine that instantly creates a living copy of my body.

Comment: If, when the machine destroys my body, my stream of consciousness stops, then I have ceased to be a subject, and the case is no different from replication. I would not regard the new person as my survivor.

Default Assumptions and Implicit Dualism

What are the factors that make these cases seem like survival? The first factor is default assumptions in general, and the second is the specific default assumptions made on the basis of the dualism implied in the cases. "In understanding the stories ... we adopt assumptions that are not strictly given in the stories themselves..." (White 1989) In the absence of cues that show that we cannot adopt the assumptions, we assume that everything will be as it usually is, and our interpretations of the stories will follow accordingly.

We are accustomed to the idea that memory, etc., and continuity of subject go together. Thus we assume that they will go together, unless it is made clear that they do not. Now in the cases given above it is not usually spelt out that they do not go together, and so the case is treated as if they did.

Default assumptions are also made on the basis of the dualism implicit in the cases. In each of these cases, it is *possible* that they are cases of survival. If, in each case, a Cartesian soul left the person in the first stage, and then entered the person in the second stage, continuity of subject would be assured, because it would be the same subject. If Rimmer's soul entered the computer, or my soul entered the resurrected or replicated body, or my soul left my body and then re-entered it, continuity of subject would be maintained. It is our automatic belief in Cartesian dualism that makes these cases seem plausible ways of surviving.

As Baillie (1990) pointed out, in the recording cases, substance dualism has been replaced by a dualism of matter and information. When the Cartesian soul is replaced by the information that describes the mind, the default assumption is that it will ensure continuity in the same way. But this assumption is invalid. Information is not the same as a soul. Even if we hold a computer model of the person, in which a conscious brain is a computer processing information, the programme and the information it is processing are not the same as the actual activity of the brain, and it is (in the computer model) the continuous activity of the brain that provides the continuity of the stream of consciousness.

Often the cases are described in language that implies the default assumptions. In the teleportation case, we frequently read something of the style of "the person wakes up on Mars". The use of "wakes up" implies the same sort of continuity exists between the person who stepped into the teleporter and the person who steps out on Mars as exists between a person who goes to sleep and wakes up in the ordinary way. But it is by no means clear that this is the case. In ordinary sleep the body and brain of the person do not cease to exist and do not cease to function. It is quite reasonable to suggest that this continuity is the foundation for the continuity we feel between the person who went to sleep and the person who wakes up.

Taking a third person point of view also leads to assumptions being made. Usually, if we cannot discern a change in someone, the relevant continuities have been maintained, and so if we cannot discern the difference between the person who stepped into the teleporter and the person who steps out on Mars, we are inclined to think that they are the same person.

When our attention is drawn to the possibility that the normal continuity has not been maintained, then these cases become much less convincing.

Other Criteria: Parfit's Relation R

An alternative criterion which is frequently given is the Relation R type of criterion. This type is used by Lewis (1976), Parfit (1991), and Perry (1976) although Lewis at least seems to think it is equivalent to the continuous subject criterion. The essence of this criterion is that a person survives if there is a future person with the memories, personality, desires, intentions, etc., of the original. It is frequently regarded as possible for these to be transmitted in the form of a signal or tape recording.

Parfit (1991) claims that the survival relation is his relation R. Relation R is defined in terms of memory, desire, and intention. A future person is R-related to me if he has my memories, my desires, and my intentions. A replica of me created at some time in the future is R-related, and is a Parfitian survivor. There need be no continuous stream of experience between me and a Parfitian survivor. Parfit makes this clear in his example of the Branch-line case. The replica is created on Mars while the original remains on Earth. The original regrets that his stream of consciousness will cease forever, but the Martian replica still should be counted as a survivor.

Parfit's argument for his claim has two steps. The aim of the first part is to show that identity is not the survival relation, and the aim of the second part is to show that relation R is the survival relation. (p. 262 ff.)

First Part: That Identity is Not What Matters

Suppose a person divides. The fission products are not identical with each other, so they cannot both be identical with the original person. There is no good reason for claiming that either one of them is identical with the original person and the other is not identical, so

(a) The correct description of this case is that the original person has ceased to exist.
(b) Nonetheless, it seems irrational to regard this as being the same as death or extinction.
(c) Therefore identity does not matter for survival.

Criticism of the First Part of the Argument

First, the argument depends on a particular view of the possibility and results of fission. Later I will argue that fission is not possible, and so Parfit's argument fails to get off the ground. I will also discuss views of fission cases which support the conclusion that no one ceases to exist, either because there were two persons there to begin with, or because both fission products are identical with each other. On these analyzes identity may well matter because it is retained.

Second, accepting that the original *person* does not survive fission does not automatically mean that the original *subject* does not survive. The case as envisioned does not include the idea of the original stream of consciousness ceasing, but of dividing, in the way it does in Parfit's thought experiment about doing algebra with one half of his brain and geometry with the other. Thus, the case does not exclude wanting to continue being a subject of consciousness. By dividing we expect to become *two* subjects of consciousness, but consciousness continues, so this is survival under Cherry's criterion.

The plausibility of the argument comes from a confusion of two ideas. The first is that there is survival where there is continuity of consciousness, and the second is that there is survival where there is continuity of memory, desire, intention, etc.

Fission is apparently survival without identity, but with psychological continuity in the sense of a continuous stream of consciousness as well as continuity of memory, desire, intention, etc. Relation R is a relation of psychological continuity in the sense of continuity of memory, desire, intention, etc. which does not preserve identity and which holds between the original and the fission products. Because I am usually R-related to the person I was yesterday, I am inclined to think that a future person who is R-related to me will be a continuation of me in the way that I am a continuation of the person I was yesterday. It is therefore easy to conclude that it is Relation R that *makes* the fission products the survivors. But, as the Branch-line case shows, this is not necessarily so.

Second Part: What Matters is that the Survivors are R-related to Me

(d) Personal identity (PI) is non-branching (U) relation R. (PI =R + U)

(e) PI has value.

(f) If I will be R-related to a future person (survival = R) the presence or absence of U makes no difference to the intrinsic nature of my relation to this person.

(g) What matters most will be the intrinsic nature of the relation.

(h) So R without U will still have most of its value.

(i) So R is what fundamentally matters. Relation R is the relation of survival.

Criticism of the Second Part of the Argument

The second part of the argument depends on Parfit's claim that the normal connection between one stage of me and another is non-branching Relation R. (PI =R + U) The relation between me this morning and my survivor this afternoon will be simply that of non-branching relation R.

If we interpret "what matters" in the sense that "nothing is missing" (Parfit 1991, p. 261) then the relation between the original and any fully R related survivor is the same as that between me this morning and my survivor this afternoon, with the possibility that there is another survivor who is as strongly R related. If "nothing is missing" in relation R then we would expect our concern for the R-related to be the same as our concern for ordinary survivors. An ordinary survivor just is a Parfitian survivor (Noonan's term) who has come into being in the ordinary way. But in fact, in some cases, we have greater concern for one survivor than another. We think something is missing.

Noonan (1989) adapts the following argument from Nozick.

If our basic concern is that there be a Parfitian Survivor, that is, that there be a future person who is R-related to us, then our concern for our own future existence is derived from this. (In Cherry's terms, the claim amounts to saying that we derive the desire to continue as a self-conscious subject of experience from the desire to have an R-related survivor.) The claim that our basic concern is that there be a future person who is R-related to us is strongly counter intuitive, and needs strong arguments to support it.

Parfit's argument relies on a group of intuitions about fission, but his theory is not in accordance with others which are as worthy of attention. These intuitions are that some aspects of our self-concern cannot be explained if that concern is taken to be just derived from concern to have Parfitian survivors.

Parfit holds a "best-candidate" theory of personal identity. In the T1 teleportation case he holds that the Martian Replica is identical with the original, but in the Branch line case the Replica is not identical with the original because the original continues to exist on Earth. In both cases the degree of psychological connection is the same, so, Noonan suggests, the concern he has for the Martian Replica in the first case should be equal to the concern he has for the Martian Replica in the second case. But Noonan suspects that in the second case his, Noonan's, greatest concern would be for the original on Earth, whereas in the first case it would be for the Martian Replica. This suggests that what concerns him (and others who share his response) is not just the degree of psychological connection, and so his concern is not just to have a Parfitian survivor. Indeed, it seems that Parfit himself shares this response to that case. Parfit says "Dying when I know that I shall have a Replica is not quite as bad as, simply, dying. Even so, I shall soon lose consciousness, forever." (Parfit 1991, p. 201)

Parfit's position cannot provide a comprehensive account of our intuitions.

Garrett (1992) claims that Noonan misinterprets Parfit. What Parfit is claiming, Garrett says, is not that we will have the same concern for a Parfitian survivor as we have for the ordinary survivor, but that we rationally should have the same concern. When we fully understand relation R, our concern for our Parfitian survivor and for our ordinary survivor should be the same. This seems implausible.

Why should we rationally have any concern for any survivor whatsoever? The sort of "rationally should" Parfit means is the concern an Egoist has for himself. "What is the relation that would justify egoistic concern about this resulting person?" (Parfit 1991, p. 283)

But an Egoist"s concern for himself is to have good experiences and not to suffer bad experiences. His only interest in a survivor comes from the expectation that he will have the experiences of the survivor directly. If the Egoist does not expect to directly experience the good or bad things that will happen to his survivor, he will not worry about the survivor at all. But in order for the Egoist to expect to have the experiences directly the relation between the Egoist and the survivor must be that of continuity of stream of consciousness, that is, the Parfitian survivor must be a continuous subject survivor. Relation R then has to be the relation of continuous stream of consciousness. But it isn't. It is described in terms of memory, desires, personality, none of which are necessary to the continuity of the stream of consciousness.

This explains our reactions to the following case adapted from Johnston 1992, p. 606. Replicas of living people are made in order for them to be sent on a dangerous mission to Jupiter. There is little chance of returning from Jupiter alive, and it is certain that everyone who goes on the mission will suffer great pain. Parfit would claim it would be a mistake for the original to prefer the replica to go on the mission rather than for the original to go. The replicas are R-related to the original, and so there is no good reason to prefer that he be sent rather than the other.

Before the copying process the original is told that the copying process causes some loss of memory in the original. The replica retains those memories, and so the replica is *more strongly* R-related to the original than the original after the replica has been made. In such a case Parfit's claim requires that the original should, before copying, prefer the original to go on the dangerous mission. If the original did not, he would, according to Parfit, be open to the accusation of being irrational.

However, if Relation R is not the relation of the continuity of the stream of consciousness, that is, continuity of subject, it is perfectly rational to prefer the replica to go to Jupiter.

Perhaps Parfit thinks that the *etcetera* of the definition of Relation R include the relation of the continuity of the stream of consciousness. (His Martian examples discourage such a reading.) We have seen from the cases above that the relation of the continuity of the stream of consciousness can be separated out from the other elements of Relation R. The "becoming a new person" case from Knox is one in which all memory, intention, personality, desires, etc., are lost, and the only continuity is that of stream of consciousness.

So either Relation R is not the relation of survival, or it is a fuller relation which can, but need not, include the relation which is necessary for survival.

A Further Argument Against Relation R

Parfit claims that what matters is how many of your beliefs, desires, intentions, memories etc. are preserved in the alleged survivor.

What is the difference to me between my ideas A, B, and C being recreated (after my death) in one person (a Parfitian survivor), and A being in person a, B in person b, and C in person c? Why should my beliefs, desires, intentions, memories, etc. surviving in one person be preferable to them surviving in different people, so long as the total number that survives is the same?

The difference would seem to be that the ideas come together in a single structure. This seems at odds with Parfit"s treatment of psychological connections as simply cumulative. If Parfit wants the ideas to survive in a single person, it is not merely the number of items, but also the interrelation between the items that is important.

Relation R as a Survival Surrogate

Diotima, in the Symposium, gives as one survival surrogate, the desire for "immortal renown and glorious reputation." (Plato 1985, p. 90) Cherry points out that this is, in effect, to be remembered in a special way. He damns this sort of survival surrogate as "bogus and falsely seductive" because "it is shot through with idle references to the self". (Cherry 1984, p. 454) Cherry claims out that this is appealing because it seems to most people to be less remote from what they really want than the alternative. What a person really wants is continued consciousness, whereas the alternative is that after the person dies other people will live on with concerns in which dead person has no part.

It seems to me that Cherry's criticisms can be applied to Parfitian survival as well. Relation R is essentially the way a future person thinks about a person who preceded him. For a present person to want a future person to be R-related to him is not just to want the present person"s intentions to be continued and carried out by a future person and the present person's desires to be shared by a future person, but also to be remembered in a special way. That is, to be remembered "from the inside".

Parfitian survival is actually a survival surrogate of the same type as the desire for posthumous fame. It can be confused with a form of real survival for similar reasons to those that give posthumous fame its appeal.

(Not only is Parfitian survival unsatisfactory as survival, it also seems unreasonable to me. While it is reasonable that a person could want a future person to desire and intend to bring about the revolution, it seems unreasonable for the present person to want that future person to remember the present person "from the inside".)

Thus, Parfit fails to establish his claim. His argument from fission does not show that our concern for the future is or should be the existence of a Parfitian survivor. Also, the very concept of a Parfitian survivor does not seem to be sufficient for the concept of survival.

Parfit and Causation

Eli Hirsch (1982), Daniel Kolak and Raymond Martin (1987), Robert Elliot (1991) and Douglas Ehring (1987a) have all suggested that causation is not a necessary requirement for survival. Parfit, however, includes a causal requirement in his account of survival. Parfit's version of the causal requirement is simple. Any causal connection will do. It need not be the usual cause or a dependable cause. Parfit agues by analogy: If I am ill, and am cured by an unreliable treatment that only works in a few cases, I would be indifferent to the fact that the cause of my cure was unreliable. It is the effect that counts. In the same way, if Relation R is the result, I would not be concerned with the cause. Relation R with any cause is adequate for survival.

If this is the case, then anything that resulted in a future person being related to me by Relation R would count as survival. After my death, a fanatical admirer of my work could study everything about me until he came to be psychologically continuous with me. By Parfit's theory he would be my survivor.

However, as soon as Parfit admits that any cause which has the requires effect is admissible, he implies that what matters is the effect, regardless of how it is caused. If my cure had no assignable cause, and was a mysterious, random, spontaneous remission , I would still be indifferent. What matters is the cure. Similarly, I would be indifferent whether the Relation R had any causal link to my original psychological states. (Noonan 1989, p. 208) *Any* cause becomes indistinguishable from *no* cause.

Elliot argues that if psychological continuity (of the Relation R type) with a causal connection is sufficient for survival, then psychological continuity alone, without any cause, is sufficient. He offers two pairs of cases in which the original person is destroyed and a replica made. In the first of each pair, the replica is made as a copy of the original. In the second, the replica appears accidentally, and has no causal connection with the original. Elliot argues that in each case the replica would regard himself, and be regarded by others, as a survivor. But in half the cases there would be no causal connection.

(I give a more detailed account of Elliot's argument in the appendix to this chapter.)

Certainly it seems that if a replica is survivor, there is no need for there to be a causal connection. This means that if Relation R is the relation of survival, Parfit's causal requirement is unnecessary.

Other Criteria: Brennan's S-relation

Brennan (1988) sets up a general relation for all kinds of survival, which he call the S-relation. The S relation depends on three conditions, the structure condition, the causal condition, and the matter condition.

Structure condition: x and y must share the same structure. Their component parts must be of the same relative size, shape, and positions to each other.

Causal condition: x must play a significant and direct role in the production of y; specifically, x must be the 'prototype' for y - a copying process takes place in which x is the model on which y is based.

These two conditions are necessary.

Matter Condition: x survives as y if, alongside the satisfaction of the other two conditions, x and y are constructed of the same kind of matter.

The S-relation is obviously designed to accommodate compound physical objects. Brennan and Baillie seem to believe it can also be used for survival of persons. In respect of minds, they point out that a person's psychological make-up can be regarded as a structured set, and so survival requires the survival of this cognitive structure.

Baillie (1990) applies Brennan's analysis to Parfit's teleportation cases and to some others.

T1. The teleport scanner records the exact state of all my cells while destroying my body. The information is sent to a replicator on Mars which makes an exact copy of my body. When I enter the machine I lose consciousness and wake up in the new body. All my psychological attributes are unchanged. (This assumes a materialist view of the mind.)

T2. (Branch line case) The scanner does not destroy my body. It merely damages my heart so that I will die within a few days. Otherwise it functions as in T1. In this case I remain on earth, and my replica is on Mars. (But my replica will become less and less like me - physically and psychologically - as time goes on. If I did not die, in time he would be at most like a brother.)

T3. I have been injured, and I am going to die soon. On the planet Zarf there are intelligent beings who look and act like humans, although their genetic structure is very different. A scanner will record my brains states (and therefore, presumably, all mu memories, personality traits, etc.) and send them to Zarf where a Zarfian body will be made and have my memories, personality traits, etc. programmed into it. I will awaken in the Zarfian body.

T4. Similar to T3, except that this time, the planet is Zerg, and the Zergian body I awaken in is nothing like a human body.

Brundlefly: In the film "The Fly" a scientist, Seth Brundle, slowly transforms into a giant insect. He changes psychologically too, but slowly, retaining his memories, so the psychological continuity is maintained.

Baillie claims that all these cases are cases of survival, and that they fulfil Brennan's conditions for S-relation. "What matters" in future survival is that the S-relation holds.

T1 and T2 clearly fulfil the conditions. In T2 I "S - survive" twice over. In T3 and T4 the psychological structure is carried on, but the matter condition is less closely fulfilled. Baillie points out that there are varying degrees of accuracy of copies, but that our priorities will decide which copy we prefer. The fact that we can imagine surviving in a new body that we prefer to the original shows that we do not necessarily require the copy to be exact. He also says that we seem to regard the survival of the psychological structure to be the of the utmost importance. Baillie sees this as support for Parfit's thesis on relation R, but I claim that it is support for Cherry's claims, since we tend to regard the maintenance of the psychological structure as being part of what is involved in being a continuous subject.

Brundlefly shows a continuous casual connection between the human and insect stages, and maintains psychological continuity. Again, the necessary conditions for S-relation are fulfilled.

Criticisms

First: In the light of the previous discussion of survival and relation R, it does not seem that the teleportation cases are cases of survival. Baillie begs the question when he says "*I* wake up on Mars." Someone wakes up on Mars, but this person can be regarded as just a replica of me, and not me myself. Indeed, in the Branch line case I would claim that I survive as the original, and the Martian replica is another person. To accept this as survival is to accept that relation R is sufficient for survival.

Second: In the Brundlefly case the psychological continuity is uninterrupted. It can be just as well construed as continuity as a self-conscious subject of experience. While it fits the S-relation, it also fits Cherry's version.

Third: The presence of the causal condition in Brennan's scheme is questionable. Elliot's argument applies here as well. If destruction and replication by a teleport machine counts as survival, why should it make a difference if the replication is accidental rather than a direct copying of the original? It is certain that the replica would not worry about the difference.

If a Self is a simple entity, it is not clear how its ordinary, moment to moment survival would fulfil Brennan's causal condition. A simple entity, having no structure, would presumably fulfil the structure condition. It is rather more difficult to see how the existence of such an entity at one time plays a direct role in the existence of the entity at another time.

Consider again the Epicurean Atom. First, it is created by God. God's creative power causes it to exist at t1. However, it then continues to exist. It survives, and exists at t2. What is the cause of the existence at t2? One possibility is that God's creative power is also sustaining power. Nothing could exist without God's constantly willing its existence. God constantly looks at the atom and makes a copy of it in its place. This is clearly the copying process of the causal condition.

But suppose that, having created it, God forgets about it completely and busies himself with smiting evildoers with plagues and thunderbolts. The atom, nonetheless, continues to exist. Once created, atoms can exist without Divine maintenance. What *then* explains its existing at t2? Its existence at t1. However, there is no apparent copying process. To claim that existence at t1 causes existence at t2 seems to be extending the notion of cause beyond intelligibility. It certainly does not fit the notion of cause as explaining change. It becomes cause to explain persistence, or lack of change. The idea that the atom, by existing, causes itself to exist further, seems absurd. That it recreates itself moment by moment may (or may not) be sound Whiteheadian metaphysics, but I would first need to have that metaphysics justified before I accepted it.

Finally, consider survival as the continuity of the stream of consciousness. The continuity of the stream of consciousness consists in the various mental states that are part of the stream overlapping with each other. Suppose, now, the Epiphenomenalists are correct. The relation between mental states is not casual. Mental states are causally ineffective. My previous mental state played no role in the production of my present mental states. All the mental states in the stream are casually unconnected, even though they overlap. By Brennan's conditions I do not survive as a mental entity. Nonetheless, if the stream of consciousness continues, I am likely to consider this to be survival. (This argument is adapted from Kolak and Martin, 1987)

Thus, Brennan's causal condition excludes cases which seem to be survival.

The Appeal of Psychological Connection

Since there are such obvious faults with the psychological continuity accounts of survival, such as relation R, why are they so widely held by philosophers?

First, Commitment to Reductionism. By Reductionist theory the connection between my present mental state and my previous mental states is that of Relation R with normal (fairly reliable) cause. There is nothing else to connect them.

Second, Reductionists usually do not recognize the continuity of the stream of experience through periods of unconsciousness. They consider that the connection between one period of waking consciousness and the next is Relation R. This leads Reductionists to the position that if there are two periods of consciousness connected by Relation R and some sort of causal connection (the limitations on acceptable causes varies from theory to theory) then they are connected in the way one period of waking consciousness is connected to another.

Third, this viewpoint is bolstered by a tendency to think of the third person view as being privileged. The psychological properties of people are regarded as characteristics, so if one entity and a later entity have the same characteristics, from the third person point of view there is no difference between them. Since the Reductionists deny the existence of anything but psychological characteristics to being a person, they see no logical reason for denying the S-relation.

Survival and Identity

The stream of experience, of awareness of existing, has continued unbroken throughout our lives, and we are tacitly aware of this. We have direct awareness of our own continuous existence, and our own continuous existence is the continued existence of the Self. We expect to continue existing, and to awaken to full consciousness from time to time. This expectation is deeply entrenched, being based on our knowledge of our own continuous existence. Our concern for our own survival is the desire to continue as a Self conscious subject of experience. When this is taken as the staring point, a lot of confusion and puzzles can be clarified.

Many of the confusions and puzzles arise from clashes between the intuitions derived from our deep beliefs, which are based on our experience, and the ideas derived from philosophical theory. Explaining intuitions has a whiff of speculative psychology about it. However, I will show that our intuitions are reasonable ideas derived from our basic knowledge of ourselves, and our rational expectations.

One set of confusions comes from the failure to distinguish between logical identity and personal survival.

In spite of the separation between identity and survival, it is still not sufficiently appreciated that they are different types of relation. Logical identity contrasts with resemblance. It denies that two apparently distinct entities are distinct. Identity can be synchronic or diachronic. Survival contrasts with cessation. It asserts continuity of existence, and can only be diachronic.

Martin (1992) tells us that philosophers have been exercised by cases in which people have "*self-interested* reasons to cease to exist" as "an expression of their desire to survive". These allegedly paradoxical cases are those in which, for example, to avoid death you can either undergo a very risky operation or risk free fission. The alleged paradox comes from the fact that choosing fission will mean that you cease to exist.

The confusion is that of thinking that logically ceasing to exist is the same as extinction of the subject, when it is only a change in logical status. Changes in logical status can be psychologically trivial, and certainly seem to be no threat to survival. If it could be shown that when I finish this sentence I will not be logically identical with the person I was when I began to write this sentence, I would feel no dismay at all. When I got married the bachelor Robin Harwood ceased to exist, but I did not feel that logical change affected my survival. King George the Sixth was Emperor of India, until India gained its independence in 1948. The Emperor of India ceased to exist, but King George die not die until 1952. I remember coming home from school, and seeing his funeral on television.

When we face fission, we might well consider that we would logically cease to exist. Nonetheless, we are not too worried about the possibility as long as we consider the survivors would be continuations of our stream of experience. While the stream of experience continues, the subject I regard myself to be continues. Even if it splits I expect that direct experience will continue, and that means I will continue. The logical status of the subject may have changed, but that does not affect my attitude towards continued experience.

A second set of confusions come from the failure to distinguish between survival of the subject and survival of the person.

Survival of the Self is the continuity of existence of the subject of experience. Survival of the person is the continuity of the whole person, or at least of the subject and the set of psychological characteristics as described as ordinary survival above.

Since the basis of our knowledge of our own continuous existence is obscure, we may well believe the basis of continuity is psychological connections of the type described by Parfit *et al.*, and that while these connections hold there will be our continuous stream of direct experience. When faced with cases in which the stream of experience does not seem to be clearly continuous, but the psychological connections hold, we will tend to believe that these will guarantee the continuity, and that where our memories and personality go, our sense of being a continuing subject will also go. The clashes come when we find cases in which the psychological connections and the continuity of the subject clearly diverge.

Since I am used to my body, memories and personality accompanying the sense of being a continuing subject, I am inclined to get confused when they are separated.

Thus, in the case of Methuselah, at the respectable age of 900, it is quite possible that every part and characteristic of Methuselah's body, memory, and personality is quite different from those of his callow youth at the age of 200. Methuselah at 900 is not the same person as he was at 200. Philosophical theory leads to the conclusion that Methuselah at 200 has not survived. Nonetheless, we imagine that his Self has continued to exist, and so conclude that he has survived after all. When the basis of the judgments is made clear, there is no puzzle to the case.

The same is true of Williams' (1973) famous puzzle of two descriptions of what is essentially the same case.

Case 1. A is told that he will have his mind transferred to B's body, and B's mind will be transferred to A's body. B is told the same. The A and B have to choose which body will be tortured and which will be given £5,000,000. A chooses that A's body be tortured, secure in the knowledge that he will be in B's body.

Case 2. A person is told that he will have his memory and personality erased and replaced with another personality and set of memories. Then he will be tortured. He objects, suspecting that it will still be him that feels the pain.

Williams claims that these are the same case differently described, and that they show that the idea of personal identity is disjunctive.

But they are in fact underdescribed. From the first person point of view, in case 1 we assume that the mind transfer includes transfer of the Self. This is because we are used to the Self accompanying memory and personality. Therefore our intuitions tell us that we, like A, would expect to be in B's body.

In case 2 our focus of attention has shifted. We are also used to memories and personality being slightly impermanent, but the Self remaining attached to the same body. Therefore from the first person point of view we assume that the same Self will feel the pain of the torture.

Before we can regard the two cases as the same we need to be told what happens to A's Self in case 1. If it stays with A's body, then case 1 and case 2 are the same case, and we will give the same response to them. If in case 1 the Self is transferred to B's body then the two cases are different, and will get different responses.

Again, the puzzle vanishes when the basis of the judgments is made apparent.

Conclusion

Cherry's criterion for survival has proved to match our concerns, to explain our intuitions, and to clarify some of the famous puzzle cases. It seems to be the most satisfactory criterion of those offered. When we think about survival, what we want is for our current subject of experience to continue to exist.

Appendix

Elliot offers a set of cases *Aa, Ab, Ba,* and *Bb*. In the *a* cases the causal condition is met, and in the *b* cases it is not met. The point of these is to show that if psychological continuity with any cause is sufficient for survival (which I do not believe) then psychological continuity *alone* is sufficient. Psychological continuity does not need to be causally connected continuity. (The ultimate aim of Elliot's paper is to show that psychological continuity is inadequate.)

Case *Aa*.

i/	Person X dies at t1
ii/	Y comes into existence at a later time
iii/	X and Y are psychologically very similar
iv/	Superbeing created Y because it wants to resurrect X. Creation of Y is causally guided by the beings knowledge of X
v/	X and Y believe i - iv.

There is no physical continuity between X and Y. The psychological continuity includes causal continuity. In Brennan's terms it is reasonable for X to anticipate surviving as Y, and for Y to believe he is the same person as X, because X and Y are similar and the similarity is explained by causal connection. The Causal connection entails that the past psychological states gave rise to some of the present psychological states, and so leads to the idea that X and Y are the same person. Also, in ordinary life the materialist thinks that the causal connection of a continuous brain makes psychological continuity.

Case *Ab*.

i/	Person X dies at t1
ii/	Y comes into existence at a later time
iii/	X and Y are psychologically very similar
iv!/	There is no causal connection between X's ceasing to exist and Y's coming to exist.
v!/	X and Y believe i - iv!

Accepting that in *Aa* it is rational for X to anticipate surviving as Y, and for Y to believe he is same person as X, is it irrational for X to anticipate surviving as Y? Is it irrational for Y to believe he is X's survivor?

X knows that Y will come to exist, and it Y will be psychologically similar to X. In *Aa* the psychological similarity was such as to make Y psychologically connected with X. In *Ab* the similarity s the same, but there is no causal connection. What X thinks will happen in fact happens. Y will say that what X expected did happen. X anticipated surviving as Y, and Y will believe that X's anticipation was fulfilled, that he is indeed X's survivor. It is difficult to see how the causal connection, the intention of the superbeing, is necessary to make *Aa* a case of survival, and its absence is sufficient to make *Ab* a case of only apparent survival.

Case *Ba*. X travels to a distant planet by teleporter. This process is that of making a complete record of the biochemical constitution of X's body, destroying the body, and sending the complete description of the body to the receiver on the destination planet, where a replica body, Y, is built from stock chemicals.

Y is physically and psychologically exactly similar to X. There is a causal chain which explains the similarity. Again, In Brennan's terms it is reasonable for X to anticipate surviving as Y, and for Y to believe he is same person as X.

Case *Bb*. In this case the teleporter transmitter malfunctions. It destroys X's body, but does not transmit the information. On the destination planet, the receiver also malfunctions. It accidentally produces a replica of X without receiving the information.

Once again, Y is physically and psychologically exactly similar to X. The final situation seems to be the same as in *Ba*. Y would not know of the malfunction, and would regard himself as X. Again it seems just as reasonable for Y to be regarded as the survivor of X in this case as in the previous case, even though there is no casual connection.

The *a* cases have psychological continuity that involves causal connection. The *b* cases have psychological continuity that involves psychological factors only, without any causal connection. In each *b* case the non-causal psychological connection seems to provide as good a support for personal identity as the causal psychological connection in the *a* cases. This suggests that the causal connection is superfluous.

6 Fission and Fusion

The possibility of personal fission has been a constant theme in recent literature on personal identity. Various arguments have been based on the possibility of fission, and more have been constructed to refute them. Parfit and Shoemaker have argued from fission cases to the separation of personal identity and survival, and Martin (1987) claims that this separation has led to a crisis in the personal identity question, in that it is no longer clear that identity is important to survival. The basis of the argument is that the fission products cannot be identical with each other, and so cannot be identical with the original. Nonetheless, they are clearly survivors of the original and so survival must be a different, and more basic relation, than personal identity. Personal identity must be non-branching survival. Since this view requires rejection of the only x and y rule, other writers have tried to provide accounts of fission that do not lead to this conclusion. The "only x and y" principle is the principle that the only things that are relevant to identity between two entities are the entities themselves. Parfit *et al.* describe identity as a non-branching relationship, or a relationship between an entity and its closest continuer.

In order to retain the "only x and y" principle, Lewis (1983), Perry (1972), and Noonan (1989) claim that before fission there were two persons sharing a single body, a single mind, and a single stream of consciousness. Madell (1981), Ehring (1987b) and Dainton (1992) suggest that the fission products are in fact identical. Sprigge (1988) offers the possibility that synchronic identity is not transitive with diachronic identity. Dainton points out that all theories but his own are revisionist, in the sense that they revise either the concepts of identity, or of what counts as being a distinct person. His own theory also seems revisionist to me, in that it requires us to disregard objective time when counting persons.

Rather than accept any revision, I shall show that it has not been properly established that fission is a genuine metaphysical possibility. Since the possibility of fission has not been shown, we should reject it rather than make the drastic revision that otherwise seem necessary. Wiggins (1967) claimed that it was not possible, basing his argument on his conception of persons as being essentially animals. Garrett (1988) summarized various objections to Wiggins' claims, and showed that they are not convincing. My arguments will be based on the idea that a person is a combination of a body, a mind, and a Self. The division of bodies is not especially contentious for the division of persons, so I shall concentrate on the division of minds and Selves. I will argue that there is no coherent account of how a Self, a mind, or a stream of consciousness could divide. Since the existence of Selves is widely denied, I will concentrate on the division of minds and streams of consciousness, and show that even using a reductionist model of the person, there is no coherent account of fission.

I also shall argue that the concept of one person dividing and becoming two persons creates such a "conceptual quagmire" (Robinson 1988) that we have good reason to rule out the concept as incoherent.

Finally I shall argue that if a person were to divide, there would still only be one person. The conceptual difficulties with this seem no greater than those resulting from the rejection of the only x and y rule. I will show that when fusion is taken into account, this line of argument leads to similar possible worlds as that of the Multiple Occupancy theories of Lewis, Perry, and Noonan.

From all this I conclude that until we have good reason to accept the metaphysical possibility of fission, we can ignore it, but that if we do have to accept it, we are still not bound to accept that fission separates identity from survival.

Fission - a Metaphysical Possibility?

What are the criteria we use to establish whether or not something is a genuine metaphysical possibility? The most common criterion used is that of conceivability. If it can be clearly and distinctly conceived, it is possible. However, there is the problem of judging when we have conceived the situation sufficiently clearly. These judgments are themselves fallible. Thus, although "apparent conceivability … may count in favour of … possibility, it does not establish it…" (Mills 1993) and so other considerations should also be taken into account. I suggest the following conditions are sufficient to at least cast strong doubt on alleged metaphysical possibilities.

(1) There are no reasons aside from the alleged conceivability for accepting the possibility.
(2) The situation cannot be clearly conceived.
(3) There are arguments against the possibility.
(4) Accepting the possibility leads to a "conceptual quagmire"

None of these are sufficient by itself to rule out an alleged possibility. The second depends on the power of imagination and the judgment of the conception. The fourth depends on how easily we give in to conceptual difficulties before we judge them to be a quagmire. Nonetheless, if all four conditions are at least partly met, their combined force gives us good reason for doubting the alleged possibility.

Reasons for Accepting the Possibility of Fission

Parfit claims that the results of experiments on commissurotomy show that fission has in fact happened, and is therefore, possible. I have established that the alleged empirical evidence for division of streams of consciousness actually having happened fails to convince, and so rejected the Parfitian interpretation of commissurotomy. Garrett's claim that fission is nomologically possible depends on the same misinterpretation of commissurotomy. There is no other reason, aside from the alleged conceivability, for accepting the possibility of fission, so the first condition is met.

Specific Arguments Against the Possibility of Fission

The main arguments against the possibility of fission are the problems it creates with the logic of identity, the incoherence of fission from a first person point of view, the related incoherence of fusion from a first person point of view, and the moral conflict. I will consider the first three in the context of the attempt to give an account of division of a substantial Self.

Here I will give the moral argument against the possibility of division set out by Mills (1993). I give this important argument here because, first, the general principle of rejecting the possibility of fission on the grounds of theoretical conservatism is the same general strategy as that of my whole argument, and second, it introduces the important idea of dual occupancy.

The Moral Conflict

Mills sets up a conflict between, on the one hand, pre-theoretical prudential and moral intuitions, and, on the other hand, the possibility of fission. He argues from this to the view that there is no good reason for believing that fission is possible, and that if apparent fission happened, it would show that there were two streams of consciousness before the fission.

Suppose a murderer, A, embodied in the A-body, undergoes fission into two exactly similar persons B and C. B and C each seem to themselves and others continuous with and indistinguishable from the original A. We then can make the following claims.

(1) B and C are different persons.

(This is our immediate, pre-theoretical view. I will give arguments for the possibility that they are not different later.)

(2) Band C are both responsible for the murder.

(To deny this requires us to accept either that A has ceased to exist or a revolution in moral concepts. But the basis for the revolution - that fission is possible - must first be established. By "A has ceased to exist" we must mean that the stream of consciousness that was associated with the A-body has ceased, not merely that A no longer stands in some logical relation or other.)

(3) B is responsible for the murder iff B committed the murder.
C is responsible for the murder iff C committed the murder.

(U) A is a unique single person.

U+1+2+3 form an inconsistent set.

Parfit's position is that 3 is not true. Since 1+2+3 are by themselves a consistent set, Mill's position is that U cannot be true.

(4) Only the A-body committed the murder.

It follows from 4 that B and C were both associated with the A-body. (The phrase "associated with" is designed to avoid any judgment on the mind-body problem.) This is a multiple occupancy theory, but Mills' version is different from the Lewis/Perry/Noonan version, so I shall call it the Dual occupancy theory. The Lewis/Perry/Noonan version includes the claim

> (S) That there is a single stream of consciousness before division.

This claim is vulnerable to various objections against two persons having a single stream of consciousness (see below). Accepting these objections leads to

> (5) If (S) there was only a single stream of consciousness associated with the A-body before fission then (U) there was only a single person associated with the A-body before fission.

The set 1+2+3+4+5+S is an inconsistent set. It makes B and C each identical with the same pre-fission person, and so identical with each other. This contradicts 1.

Mills rejects S and concludes that, since U is false, there must have been two distinct minds (B-mind and C-mind) each with an associated stream of consciousness prior to fission. These are the minds that subsequently became the minds of persons B and C. B-mind and C-mind are not aware of each other. They are two minds with two thoughts. Before the fission, their sensations, feelings, thoughts, etc. were exactly similar but distinct. The day before the murder C-mind thinks "I'll be in prison in a week." At the same time B-mind also thinks "I'll be in prison in a week." After a week B is in prison, but C is still on the run. B-mind thinks "My previous thought was right" C-mind thinks "My previous thought was wrong"

B-mind's thought on the day before the murder was true and C-mind's was false, so they cannot have been the same thought. There were *two* token thoughts on the day before the murder.

Mills' position is that *if* apparent fission were to happen, it would mean that there were two persons associated with the original body.

The argument leads to the position that fission is not possible. Mills rejects the uniqueness assumption U. Accepting it means accepting the following thesis is metaphysically possible.

(7) The A-body underwent successful fission, resulting in fission descendants B and C, and there was only a single stream of consciousness associated with the A-body before fission.

The set 1+2+3+4+5+7 is an inconsistent set. If 7 is possible then at least one of the other members of the set must be abandoned. If 7 is impossible then the others can be retained. We have a pre-theoretical commitment to 1 – 5. There is no obvious pre-theoretical commitment to 7. If there is no independent reason for believing 7, why should it be believed at the expense of 1–5?

The main, perhaps only, argument for 7 being true is that it seems clearly conceivable. Conceivability is not an infallible guide to truth, and does not establish the truth of 7, whereas 1 – 5 count against it. It is less radical to reject 7 than 1 – 5, and so on the basis of epistemic conservatism rejecting 7 is preferable.

Mills' Replies to Possible Objections

(a) What is the truth value of the statement "A underwent a fission operation"?

The reply is that there was no unique person A. A was two persons in one body. When A said "I" it was actually B and C saying "I" simultaneously. "I am hungry" was B expressing B's hunger, and C expressing C's hunger.

(b) Suppose A were to divide into six thousand persons. This would imply that there had been six thousand persons, and six thousand streams of consciousness, associated with the A body.

Mills agrees with this bizarre implication, but points out that it follows from a bizarre supposition. He only accepts the metaphysical possibility of dual (or, in this case, semimilial) occupancy, not its truth. The metaphysical possibility of undergoing successful fission only entails the metaphysical *possibility* of a body being dually inhabited. It does not entail that any body *actually is* inhabited by two minds.

Mental Continuity and Personal Identity

Mills' version makes both mental continuity and identity matter in survival. B before fission is identical with and has full mental continuity and connectedness with B after fission. Similarly for C. Since B and C have exactly similar mental states before fission the Parfitian description of Relation R would make B's post fission states R-related to those of C. However, since I have shown that Relation R is not the relation of survival, this does not affect Mill's position.

The Conceivability of Fission

A lot of popular accounts, no doubt influenced by commissurotomy operations, use the idea of a brain being cut in half and transplanted. Since we have seen that this does not seem possible with a real human brain, there seems to be no reason why we should keep this account. Indeed, it should be rejected. The images of bright lights, skilled surgeons, nurses with beautiful eyes shining over their masks, flashing scalpels, and life support machines going *pocketa pocketa pocketa* (Thurber 1953) in the background make a compelling vision, and lends the whole idea a totally spurious scientific respectability.

To avoid the seductions of this deceptive image I shall go for straight unabashed fantasy, imagining people with non-human brains. I shall have to imagine that these people can split like amoebae, and become two people. As such a person I eat a lot, get fatter, lie down, lose my shape and split into two. The two halves take up shapes similar to my previous shape, though slimmer. Each has my memories, desires, personality, etc. One says "I'm Robin Harwood." The other says "so am I." They then agree to use different names.

Although this seems coherent so far, we need to be clear about how this is imagining "division" of my Self/mind, and not merely imagining that my Self/mind has been duplicated. We cannot directly observe someone else's Self/mind, so we cannot see it split. We merely see that there was one person, and then there were two, with, perhaps, a rather confused person intervening. In order to claim that we can conceive personal fission we need to be able to give a detailed account of the fission of a substantive Self, if we hold a theory of persons that includes Selves, and the fission of a mind, regardless of whether we believe in Selves or not. We need a detailed third person account and a detailed first person account of what it is like for a Self/mind to divide

For an account of fission of the Self and/or mind, we need to lay down some conditions that the account of division of the Self must meet. The situation we imagine is that at t1 there is a Self/mind S1, and at t2 there are S2 and S3. S2 and S3 are exactly similar to each other and to S1.

There are four possibilities.

(i) S1 ceased to exist during the splitting. S2 and S3 are new Selves/minds which came into existence during the splitting.
(ii) S1 = S2. S3 is a new Self/mind that came into existence during the splitting.
(iii) S1 divided and became S2 and S3. S1=S2. and S1 = S3.
(iv) S1 never existed. S2 and S3 shared the same body. (Dual occupancy)

Clearly only (iii) gives us the fission problem. In the other situations, (i), (ii), and (iv), there is no problem of identity. In order to exclude those situations the account needs to fulfil three conditions.

First, to avoid situation (i) it must not be possible to interpret the account as being one in which the original Self/mind is destroyed.

Second, to avoid situations (i) and (ii) it must not be possible to interpret the case as being one in which a copy or copies are made of the original Self/mind.

Third, to avoid situation (iv) it must not be possible to interpret the case as being one in which there were two independent minds to begin with.

The problem in situations (i) and (ii) is whether the new Selves/minds could be regarded as satisfactory survivors of the old Self/mind. Even if both Selves/minds look at their memories and say "the Self/mind in that memory is me" this does not show that both or neither is me. We could say simply that one is mistaken. If what has happened is that my Self/mind has been duplicated, then the new Self/mind may believe it is my survivor, but it is not my survivor. The Self/mind is deluded. Nor, in situation (ii) has my sense of self continuation split. It continues along one line, so the existence of the duplicate Self/mind is not a form of survival for me. If my Self/mind has produced a duplicate, that is in fact a new person, not a survivor.

It may be argued that a copy which has the memories, desires, etc. of the original should count as a survivor of the original, or even as being identical with the original. However, this presupposes the psychological criterion of survival and identity, something like Parfit's Relation R. A version of survival that is contentious cannot be used to support the claim for the possibility of fission. The claim becomes weakened by the weakness of the survival relation.

For the purposes of this argument I do not wish to maintain my alternative criterion of continued existence of a Self. In order to make the argument independent of contentious issues of what constitutes survival, I will use a generalized common-sense notion of survival. I consider that I have survived since this morning, with an unbroken stream of consciousness. This notion of strong survival excludes neither Relation R nor the concept of a continuing Self. It is strong enough to satisfy the dualist claim that survival is the survival of an immaterial soul.

If we consider that the person retains waking consciousness while he divides, and has an unbroken stream of consciousness during the process, the two conditions given above can be fulfilled. If the process of fission occurs while the person is unconscious, and unconsciousness means that all mental activity has ceased, the case can be interpreted as one in which the original ceases to exist and two copies are made.

It may be objected here that when a normal human sleeps or is unconscious, we do not consider him to have ceased to exist. We regard the sleeper as a person, and the waker as a genuine continuation and survivor of the person who fell asleep, because of our own first person knowledge of our own continued existence over sleep.

However, amoebic persons are not normal human beings. They might lose consciousness during division, but we, who do not divide into two while we are asleep, have no experience of continuity during the unconscious state of the dividing person. We cannot assume that it would be analogous to our state while we are asleep, and so we cannot apply our normal conception of continuity over sleep to that state. If an amoebic person loses consciousness and then divides, our conception of human continuity over human sleep is not sufficient to establish that the amoebic person has not ceased to be a person, and is becoming two new persons.

Nonetheless, I will consider cases of persons dividing while they are unconscious.

The famous duplicator machine (Perry 1972) will not do. This only makes a copy. The original continues to exist, so we have situation (ii). Accounts based on persons being transmitted as signals, or of brain states being recorded on tape also have to be excluded. In these the original person is destroyed, and two new persons come into being.

Division of the "Substantive" Self

Can the type of "substantive" Self I have been arguing for divide? Traditionally, it has been widely regarded that it cannot, and it is very difficult to try get any sort of mental grasp on the concept of a Self dividing. Actual division of amoebic Selves has not been observed, so to stimulate my imagination I shall try to find analogies for such division, and see if they can be used to develop a model of division.

Analogy 1. Division of a Composite Substance

The concept "divide" comes from division of physical substances. Can we extend the concept of division to the Self? Every physical substance that we recognize division in has parts, down to the level of subatomic particles at least. When such a substance divides, some parts move away from others through space. Since the Self is not composite in that way, we cannot provide an analogous account of the process of division. This analogy fails.

Analogy 2. Division of a Continuous Substance

We have a concept of continuous substance (derived from intensive Plasticene work in nursery school) even though no physical substance may be continuous in that way. Amoebic division seems like blob1 of wilful Plasticene dividing itself into blob2 and blob3. We see some bits of the physical substance go to one side and some bits go to the other side. Each of the resulting new amoebae then has only part of the original substance. The internal organs are duplicated, but smaller.
Can this concept be extended to the Self to give an analogous account? The Self does not seem to be atomic, but it is not clearly a continuous substance. Continuity in substances implies extension. Although the visual field seems extended, and various perceptions have spatial location and extension (e.g. a pain shooting up the arm) the centre of consciousness and agency does not seem to be extended. Nonetheless, I shall continue with the analogy.

The first difficulty is that blob2 and blob3 are smaller than blob1. How can S2 and S3 be (analogously) smaller than S1?

The second difficulty is that blob2 and blob3 are smaller than blob1 because each has only part of the original substance. What would be "having only part of the original substance" of S1? Each part would have self consciousness and will. How can these be part of the originals? Again, the analogy collapses.

Analogy 3. The Light of Consciousness

I have used the spotlight analogy in my discussion of consciousness, so I will try to use that analogy to give a model for fission. Two spotlights are focused on the same part of the wall. Then they are moved so that the patches of light move apart. At the same time the power is increased to maintain the same luminosity of each patch of light. This is intelligible, and avoids the problem of the first two analogies, but it is, of course, a Multiple Occupancy theory. There are two patches of light to begin with, each coming from a different spotlight. If we take into account the concept of the Self as 'self-illuminating" and imagine a patch of light which then divides into two equally bright patches without considering the source of the light, we have fallen back into a pointless description. It gives no account of how one patch of light can become two. It is no longer (I cannot forbear from saying) an illuminating analogy.

Analogy 4. The Hologram

A hologram slide can be cut in half, and yet the complete picture can still be projected from each half. The picture is not destroyed. If the Self is "hologrammatically" distributed throughout the brain, it would be possible to cut the brain in half and still have a complete Self in each half. However, this promising analogy does not need to be pursued very far to become unworkable. The physical arrangement on a hologram acts as a token of a specific type, the type being the picture. When the hologram is divided, it becomes two tokens of the same type. By analogy, Selves would be tokens of the type "self". A substantial Self does not seem to be the sort of thing that can be a token. Pursuing this line of thought seems to lead to Zuboff's idea of the Self as a universal instantiated in each person, or perhaps Clark's Plotinian Self, "refracted" through the individuals.

Furthermore, it is not at all clear to me that I can actually conceive of a unitary Self as being analogous to a hologram. The picture on a hologram slide is static information, from which the picture can be recovered. The Self is not information, but an active entity in its own right. There seem to be no points of similarity between the hologram picture and the Self from which an analogy can begin. The hologram analogy also fails.

A Formal Argument Against Fission of the Self

The difficulty of conceiving division of the Self comes from the fact that it is an attempt to conceive a logical contradiction. If I simply assume it happens *bila kayf* (without asking how) as the Ash'arite theologians put it, and claim that the situation S1 = S2 and S1 = S3 occurs when my body splits into two bodies, then S2 and S3 must be identical. However, they are embodied in different bodies and have access to different experience. It seems perverse to say that they are identical (but see below). We might think that there is one Self which is embodied in two bodies. The idea of one Self having two bodies *and two different sets of experience* is counter-intuitive (though only if one requires a Self to have full unity of consciousness) but it is not surprising that I get a counter-intuitive result from a situation which is *designed* to be logically contradictory. (If we concede the possibility of one Self having two sets of experience, we are again on the way to the One Self theories of Zuboff and Clark.)

By stipulating the situation S1 divided and became S2 and S3, and that S1 =S2 and S1 = S3, I am logically constrained to claim S2 = S3. At the same time I want to claim S2 ≠ S3. I have put myself into the position of trying to give an account of a logical impossibility.

If a continuant Self can divide into two parts each of which is identical with the original, so can any other continuant. If this is possible, the whole concept of identity through time needs revision. The transitivity of synchronic identity with diachronic identity comes into question. (Sprigge 1988) We need strong reasons to make such a major revision of our logic.

Division of the Mind

Here I will ignore the existence of the Self, and consider a series of models for division of the mind. I will show the difficulties that arise when the matter is considered in detail. Although these difficulties do not prove that fission is impossible, they do show that giving a convincing account of division of the mind is a formidable task.

Dividing the Bundle

If we take the reductionist line and start from the idea that the mind consists of a bundle of mental items, it seems quite possible that it can be divided into two bundles. A mind that consists of items

A,B,C,D,E,F

can, perhaps, be divided into the bundles A,B,C and D,E,F. This seems to be a version of situation (i), since the original bundle has been destroyed, and the two resulting bundles are dissimilar. On the other hand, if there were continuity of stream of consciousness between the original bundles and the fission products, they would be survivors of the original bundle, and so would show that there could be survival (in the strong sense) without identity. The belief in the bundle theory of the mind supports the idea that the mind is divisible.

However, it is not clear that a bundle of items that can be divided in this way would constitute a mind, or have or be a stream of consciousness. A mind is, or at least seems to be, a holistic system of items in relationship with each other. (A very simple example is that of one belief supporting another.) It is difficult to imagine the system of the mind separating into two systems while continuing to function. It might be suggested that the mind consists of subsystems each of which is sufficient to be counted as a person's mind, but which can each function independently, and which can continue to function while the mind is dividing. In such a case the original mind would be destroyed, but the subsystems could count as survivors. However, they could only count as survivors if the stream of consciousness of the original mind were to continue. From the first person point of view the dividing person would have to have continuous experience during the process. It is not clear that the stream of consciousness would continue. The stream of consciousness is an integrated collection of items, most of which are, at any time, background items, but which seem to be a seamless whole. The stream of consciousness is not just a stream of perceptions, but also of thoughts, memories, imaginings, judgments, etc., all related to the mind. It is equally difficult to imagine that these items could be separated from each other while still remaining a stream of consciousness. A full, detailed account of the process would be necessary to establish the possibility of this sort of fission.

The Duplicated Bundle

To divide into two similar bundles, the bundles must contain two copies of each item, or each item must split into two.

From the first person point of view, it seems impossible for there to be a mind with two copies of each item, or for each item to split into two. The duplicated items will either be experienced as a single stream, or they will be experienced as separate bundles, as distinct streams of consciousness.

In a single stream of consciousness, it is impossible to experience two qualitatively indistinguishable sensations, or to have two qualitatively indistinguishable memories, or feel two qualitatively indistinguishable desires at one time. If the items are experienced as a single stream that stream will be qualitatively identical to a stream with only one copy. Since the items are mental items, their only characteristics are those of how they are experienced and the relations they have with other items in the mind. If they are qualitatively indistinguishable there is no way they can be experienced as two items. Being qualitatively indistinguishable also makes it likely that they will have the same relations with the other items. This means the duplicated items will have the same characteristics. It seems difficult to regard them a being in any way numerically distinct. In short, if they are experienced as part of a single stream, it seems impossible for mental items to be duplicated.

If the copies are experienced as separate bundles, it seems there will be two minds, two streams of consciousness present before division. Division will be merely the physical separation of the inhuman brains they are associated with. This is situation (iv), dual occupancy.

If each mental item splits into two, the result will be a bundle with two copies, with the results given above. For a mind to divide into two separate bundles there has to be some way of preventing the items from being experienced together. In other words, this is the problem of assigning them to different bundles as they divide. For the Reductionist, this means finding a way that the division of the mental items can take place simultaneously with, and perhaps as a result of, the physical division of the inhuman brain, so that the division is division of the physical arrangement that each mental item is associated with. If a belief is to divide into two qualitatively indistinguishable beliefs, the physical substrate that the belief is associated with or supervenient upon must undergo physical separation. This sort of division has problems. If the division process consists of a copy being made of each physical arrangement/mental item, then the original mind continues to exist. It has been copied, and the copy is a new mind.

The physical arrangement must divide in some way. If, during division, it ceases to be the sort of physical arrangement that has that specific mental item associated with it, the mental item will cease to exist. If all the mental items cease to exist during division the original mind will cease to exist. New minds will be formed at the end of the division process. A mind is not just a set of mental items, it is a set of mental items with particular relations between them. These relations must also be retained during division for the mind to continue to exist. Again, a detailed account of how this is achieved is required if this model is to be used to support the possibility of fission.

The Double Brain

The double brain model has the physical arrangements separated from the beginning, in a brain with two parts, each of which parts has a copy of the total psychology of the person associated with it. It is equivalent to two brains ruling in parallel. The halves of the brain are joined by a neural link. When the person divides, this link breaks. Before division there was a mental item A, associated with the whole brain. After division the mental item A” (qualitatively indistinguishable from A) is associated with a particular physical arrangement W, and this physical arrangement is in one half of the brain. Similarly, A" (qualitatively indistinguishable from A and A') is associated with a particular physical arrangement Y in the other half of the brain.

This model raises a problem of unity of consciousness. If each half of the brain is sufficient for a mind and a stream of consciousness before division, it seems that there would be two minds present before division, even if the neural link ensures that they run in parallel. Two streams of consciousness running in parallel are not the same as a single mind with a single stream of consciousness. When the halves of the brain separate, there is no division of a single mind, and so there is no real personal fission. We are back in situation (iv) again.

If the link in some way suppresses one half, so that only the other half has an active mind associated with it, then the breaking of the link leads to a new mind arising in association with the suppressed half. The original mind does not divide. This is situation (ii).

Some unifying principle is required to make the two minds into one mind and one stream of consciousness. It cannot be a Self, since this is ruled out *ex hypothesi*. It cannot be that the link between the halves creates a mind of "higher order thoughts" out of the streams. If that were the case, when the link breaks during fission that mind of "higher order thoughts" it has created goes out of existence, and two new minds appear.

If the mind is regarded as the system of beliefs, desires, etc., that can persist during unconsciousness, then the two minds must be combined into a unified cooperating mind that generates a unified stream of consciousness. A mind is a system of items with a set of relations between them. To make the two minds into one a set of relations between the items of the two minds is needed. But this means that when the mind divides, some of those relations cease to exist. In such a case the single mind cease to exist.

To claim that fission has occurred, when the two halves are separated, there must be no room for the counter claim that the unified mind has ceased to exist, and been replaced by two new minds generating two new streams of consciousness. To exclude this possibility, a minimum requirement is that it should be evident from the model that each half would experience this as continued existence, as an unbroken stream of consciousness from the first person point of view, during the process.

However, it is not evident from the model as it is usually given. A much more detailed version is required before the model becomes satisfactory.

The double-brain model gives special problems for Parfit's Combined Spectrum Argument, which I discuss below.

The Hologram

The hologram model can be applied to the bundle theory of the mind. If all the mental states are "hologrammatically" distributed throughout the inhuman brain, it would be possible for the brain to divide into halves and retain the whole mental structure. Again, this model raises the problem of the fact that it leads me to imagine the mind as a type, realized in two tokens in the two halves. There are three tokens, S1, S2, and S3, each of which is a token of the same type. The three tokens are different tokens, and so there is no question of identity between them. There is only one type, so there is no question of identity.

Furthermore, the picture on a hologram is static, whereas the mind is active. It seems probable that the mental states would be associated with patterns of activity in the brain rather than physical structures. These brain processes would have to continue during the other processes which caused the brain to divide. Naturally, it has not been established that a hologram mind is metaphysically possible.

This model is not available to Parfit, since it makes the Combined Spectrum argument impossible. The parts of the pattern in a hologram cannot be separated from each other.

Unger's Incremental Fission

Unger has suggested that fission can be achieved by incremental duplication of the brain. Using his "zippering" procedure, a very small portion (A) of the brain is removed. A is so small that its removal will not have any appreciable affect on the working of the brain. Nonetheless, it remains in radio contact with the rest of the brain. Two qualitatively similar copies of A are then created and also make radio contact with the brain. These are A' and A''. The position is represented diagrammatically below.

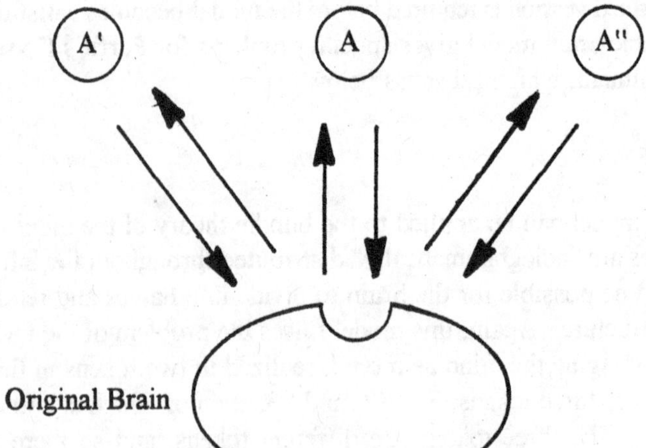

A is then destroyed. Another piece, B, is removed. While B is in radio contact with the brain, qualitatively similar pieces B' and B'' are attached to A' and A'' respectively, and are also in radio contact with the rest of the brain.

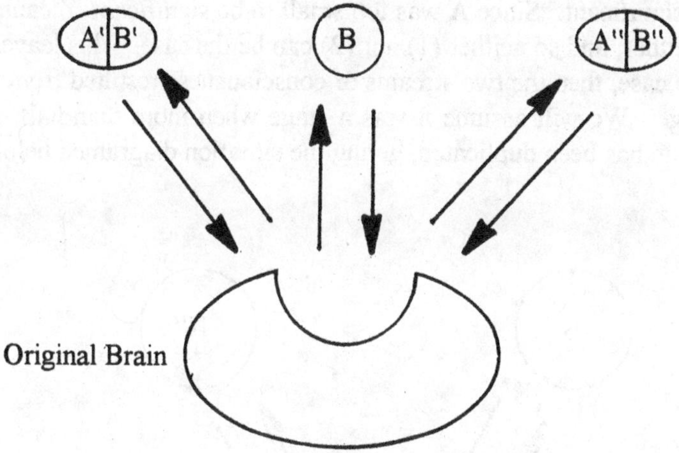

B is then destroyed. The process continues until all of the original brain has been replaced by two copies. Since the brain has remained functioning throughout, the stream of consciousness associated with the original brain has continued, and, by being associated with the dividing brain, has also divided into two streams of consciousness.

Like Unger's other incremental thought experiments, the fact that we have no satisfactory account of the relation between consciousness, conscious experience, brain activity, and information flow makes it impossible for us to arrive at any conclusions about what would happen if the experiment were tried.

In the first place, the removal of A may not affect the stream of consciousness, but the addition of A' and A'' may well do so. B would be indirectly linked with A' B' and A'' B''. We have no idea what effect this would have.

Second, in the final stage of the operation, the two duplicate brains would be in radio contact with the remaining piece, Z, of the original brain. At this stage, there are three possibilities.

(1) There is still only one stream of consciousness.
(2) There is neither clearly one nor two streams of consciousness.
(3) There are two distinct streams of consciousness.

If (1) or (2) are the case, then Z must be significant in preventing two streams from emerging. But Z is no bigger than A. If Z is significant, A must have been significant. Since A was too small to be significant, Z cannot be significant either, and so neither (1) nor (2) can be the case. This leaves (3). If (3) is the case, then the two streams of consciousness resulted from some earlier stage. We will assume it was a stage when more than half of the original brain has been duplicated, giving the situation diagramed below.

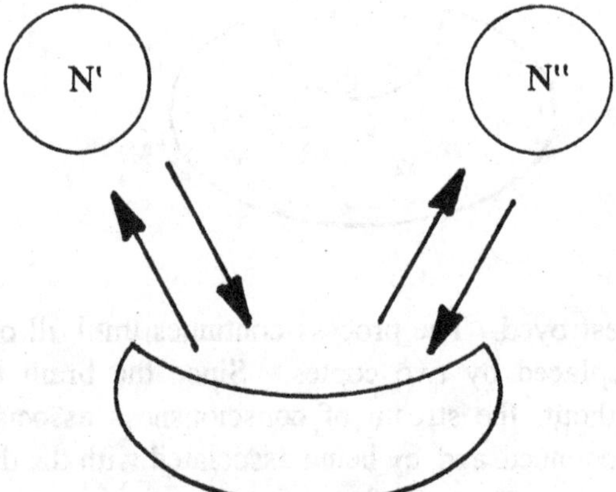

Original Brain

Again, we have no idea what would happen to the stream of consciousness in this situation. Unger would suggest that at this or some similar stage the stream of consciousness is neither clearly a single stream nor two streams, but in some indeterminate condition. However, it seems equally possible that there would come a stage wherein two new streams of consciousness would come into being, perhaps with the original stream of consciousness simply ceasing.

Unger's incremental duplication has too many areas of uncertainly to be accepted as a plausible account of fission.

The Causal Chain

This is little more than an analogy. Dominoes are arranged on a Y shape. The domino at the bottom of the leg of the Y is pushed over, and of course it pushes over the next. The causal chain splits at the junction of the arms of the Y and becomes two causal chains each of which can continue to operate independently.

To use this analogy requires imagining an inhuman brain in which the mental items are supported by physical processes rather than states, and which fulfils the following conditions during fission.

(A) Each process that has a specific mental item associated with it must, during fission, retain that aspect of its nature that ensures that mental item is associated with it.

(B) Each process must, during fission, retain the relationships with other process that ensures that the mental items remain linked in the way that constitutes the specific mind.

(C) The processes must fulfil conditions A and B while coming under the influence of some other cause which leads the processes to propagate in two distinct streams.

I have made no progress in devising such a model.

The Weakness of the Claim that we can Conceive Fission

I have drawn out some of the difficulties that an account of fission would have to overcome, and laid down some of the conditions that an account would have to meet. These arguments do not prove that such an account is impossible, but they do show that an account seems to be exceedingly difficult to produce. The account would have to be more detailed and subtle than any so far offered in the literature. However, the more detailed and subtle the account is, the more difficult it becomes to establish whether the account actually is a successful account of fission. Thus, we would be uncertain whether an account actually was a clear conception of fission.

The strong claim that fission is metaphysically possible because we can clearly conceive it is reduced to the weak claim that, if reductionism is true, fission might be possible because it might be possible to conceive it, though we would not be sure that we had succeeded in conceiving it.

Division and the God's Eye View

If reductionism is correct, the question of the possibility of fission remains open. Nonetheless, the reductionist does not need to claim that fission is possible, since the possibility of fission cannot be used as and argument for the truth of reductionism, whereas in accepting fission the reductionist is open to the God's Eye View argument against his position, and the problems associated with rejecting the "only x and y" principle.

Parfit criticizes the Featureless Cartesian View on the basis that if it were true there would be no way to distinguish between persistence of a Cartesian Ego and its sudden, undetectable replacement by another Ego. There are no "publicly observable or privately introspectible facts" (Parfit 1991 p228) which can indicate the replacement. This leads to scepticism about personal identity in cases where we have no other reason for scepticism, and so by epistemic conservatism it should be rejected.

The same objection can be applied to the Reductionist view. In a case of apparent fission, what basis would there be for deciding between the possibility that two exactly similar streams were separated, and the possibility that a single stream of consciousness divided into two streams? In the first case, since each stream is unaware of the existence of the other, from the first person point of view it would seem to each fission twin that a perfect copy had appeared. (Having two separate streams of consciousness is, of course, compatible with Reductionism.) However, if a single stream divided it would still seem to each fission twin that a perfect copy had appeared. From both the third person point of view and the first person point of view the two cases would be indistinguishable. Thus, the Reductionist has no way of distinguishing between psychological branching and cohabitation. This puts the Reductionist in the same position as the Featureless Cartesian, in that in both cases the facts about personal identity go beyond all the evidential criteria. If Reductionists claim that fission is possible, then they can be accused of making our knowledge of personal identity wholly inexplicable. (Mills 1993)

Presupposing Reductionism

If fission is logically possible only if Reductionism is true, then the truth of Reductionism must be established before the logical possibility of fission.

Reductionists cannot, therefore, use the *logical possibility of fission* as an argument for reductionism. I have already shown that the evidence does not support the claim that fission has actually happened. Even if there were a case of apparent fission that could not be accounted for in the ways given above, Mills' arguments show that there would be no way of distinguishing between Millsian Dual Occupancy and reductionist fission. Therefore such a case would not be adequate evidence for the Reductionist position.

The Reductionist cannot use either the logical possibility of fission or an actual case of apparent fission as evidence for the Reductionist claims. Thus, although there are models which the reductionist might be able to make workable, success carries a high price, and the Reductionist is not bound to assume that fission is possible.

A Standard Argument Against the Possibility of Fission

A first person account of splitting acts as an argument against fission. The moment at which the centre splits is cannot be experienced except as an experience of a single centre. Thus, I might experience strange emotions, a sense of being in two places at once, but the sensation of becoming two Selves at once is unimaginable. I can only imagine experience as the experiences of a single Self. I cannot imagine simultaneous experiences as the experiences of two Selves, because all experience is imagined as united by a single Self. Therefore, it is impossible for me to imagine, from the first person point of view, the continuous experience of having my centre of consciousness cut into two and becoming two points of view which are both mine, but which are inaccessible to each other. If I know that after the division the left hand stream will be starved and tortured in a noisome dungeon, while the right hand one will be given a life of Sybaritic luxury, I simply do not know what to anticipate. I can imagine having both experiences at once, through different bodies, in the way I can imagine my left hand feeling hot and my right hand feeling cold. I can imagine *having had* both experiences (after, say, my two halves have come together again) but before the division it is impossible for me to imagine that I will have both experiences as two separate Selves, each unaware of the experience of the other.

There is, therefore, no useful first person account that would help us to understand what becoming two beings would be like.

Dainton's Division

Dainton (1989) offers the following, related, argument against fission, and then attempts to show how it can be circumvented.

Experiences are not momentary but extended in time. Thus at the moment of division, a total experience A would be extended over the moment of division. The later part of the experience would be co-conscious with the earlier part. A would also overlap with, and be co-conscious with, the following experience. But after the moment of division there would be two following experiences. B and B'. A overlaps with B and with B', so A is co-conscious with both of them even though they are not co-conscious with each other. How can A be shared in this way? First it belongs to one centre of experience, and then to two centres of experience.

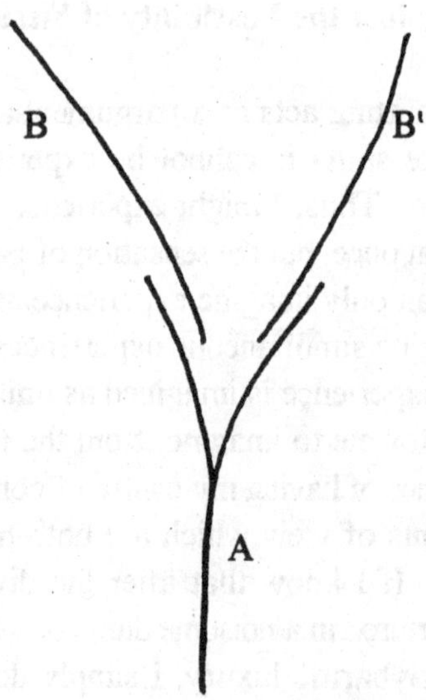

Dainton's answer makes use of the notion of experience in the specious present. In order for a series of experiences to be experienced as a succession, they have to make up a total experience in the specious present. If experience A is followed by experience B, and B is followed by experience C, the three experiences are co-conscious in the specious present. That means that the total experience A is co-conscious with B, and B is co-conscious with C, but A is not co-conscious with C.

Now if there is a division of the stream of consciousness, as in the diagram below, both F and F' are co-conscious with E, while F is not co-conscious with F'. Thus, Dainton claims, there is no obstacle to the division of the specious present and the stream of consciousness.

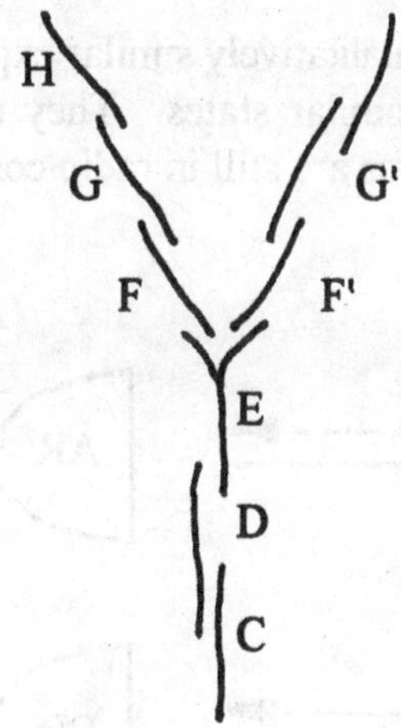

I am not convinced of this. In the specious present, there is a "just now", a "just past", and a "just future". When the current experience, the "just now" experience, is D, the "just past" experience is C and the "just future" experience is E. When experience E is the "just now" experience, the "just future" experience would be both F and F'. This would mean that the single centre of experience that is experiencing E is also experiencing the onset of F and F', that is, a single centre of experience is experiencing the experiences of two centres of experience.

Fusion

If it is metaphysically possible for persons or Selves to split, it seems that it should also be metaphysically possible for them to fuse with another person or Self by a reversal of the process. On what principle can fission be admitted and fusion be excluded? The argument against fusion given below suggests that the process cannot be reversed, but if it is irreversible, some account of fission which makes it irreversible must be given. If no such account can be given, then the argument against fusion suggests that fission is impossible.

I will look at two accounts, Unger's brain combination and Parfit's Combined Spectrum.

Unger's Combination

Two brains, A and B are having qualitatively similar experience (e.g. the blue field) and are in qualitatively similar states. They are divided using the zippering process, so that the halves are still in radio contact with each other.

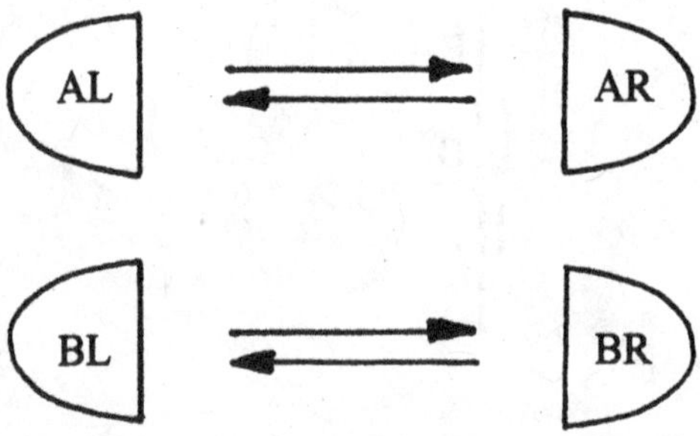

Then the right half of brain A (AR) is put into radio contact with the left half of brain B (BL) without breaking its contact with left half of A (AL). Similarly, the right half of B (BR) is put into radio contact with AL, without breaking its contact with BL.

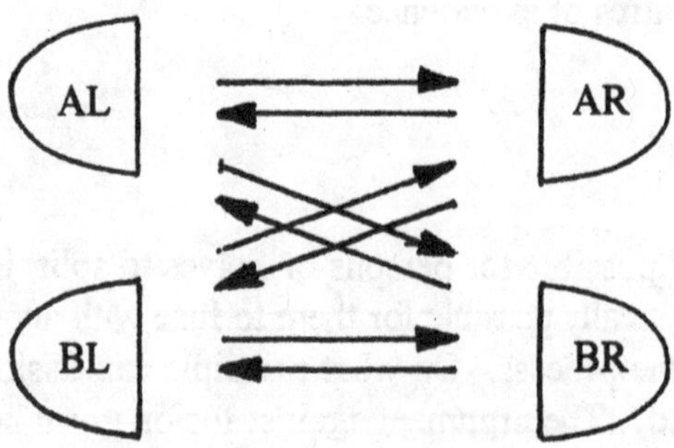

AL and BR are destroyed instantly and simultaneously.

The two halves AR and BL are brought together and put into the same body. The two streams of consciousness realized in brain A and brain B have become one stream of consciousness realized in the combined AR-BL brain.

Again, Unger's account fails on the question of the relation between the transfer of information and the stream of consciousness. It is perfectly feasible that in this case one subject and stream of consciousness is associated with the combination AR-AL, another subject and stream of consciousness is associated with the combination BR-BL, and when combinations AR-BL and BR-AL are formed, two new subjects and streams come into being. All the subjects except the one associated with AR-BL are subsequently destroyed.

The Combined Spectrum

In *Reasons and Persons* (Parfit 1991) Parfit offers the Combined Spectrum argument to support Reductionism about personal identity. The Combined Spectrum is a thought experiment giving a range of cases in which, at one end of the range, there is person who is 100% Derek Parfit, and at the other end 100% Greta Garbo. Throughout the range, more and more pieces of Derek Parfit have been replaced by pieces of Greta Garbo. Since (according to Parfit) our psychological features depend on brain states, this is replacement of psychological features as well as of physical features. By making this a physical as well as a psychological spectrum Parfit blocks the hope of grounding personal identity in physical continuity.

The Combined Spectrum argument is a fusion argument. As with fission, the fusion must take place while the persons being fused are awake. If neither of the pieces of brain to be joined are supporting a stream of consciousness, it can be claimed that the original persons have been destroyed, and so if a joint person is created that has characteristics of both (or perhaps, by some alchemy of the combination, neither) the originals, it can be claimed that this is not a survivor of the originals, but a new person with a determinate identity.

If only one of the pieces of brain is supporting normal waking consciousness at the time of the transplant, then (as Unger (1990)pointed out) the resulting person will be the person whose brain part continued to support the stream of consciousness. Thus, if Derek Parfit has part of his brain removed, but the rest is still supporting his stream of consciousness before the piece of brain from Greta Garbo is added, the result is Parfit with a few of Greta Garbo's characteristics. In this case Derek Parfit has survived. The fact that he has changed a bit does not stop him from being Derek Parfit.

Madell (1985) offers a first person account of what this would be like. When I try to imagine it, I imagine that as the mad surgeons do their evil work I lose my interest in beer and develop an interest in Buddhism. But then what I am imagining is *me* changed a bit, rather than a new person. It is *my* consciousness that I imagine to be different. I cannot imagine "there is a present state of consciousness that is only partly mine", and I cannot consider that my identity has become indeterminate.

The fusion Parfit envisages depends on two principles.

Principle (a) All the mental states, such as memories, intentions, dispositions, etc., which make up the person, can be transferred from one person to another by transplanting a piece of brain in which that state has its physical realization.

Principle (b) The mere fact of being linked together with the recipient brain makes the transferred state(s) part of the bundle of states of the brain, and hence part of the bundle of mental states of the person.

Principle (a) seems highly implausible. Parfit believes psychological features are states of parts of the brain, and so by transplanting a lump of Greta Garbo's brain into Derek Parfit, he also transplants some of Greta Garbo's psychological features. Even a physicalist need not support Parfit's view that psychological states are extractable in the form of lumps of brain. Madell and Stone have pointed out that

> there is no reason to suppose that the brain is composed of organic modules, each determining a particular feature which could replace those of other people. (Stone 1988, p. 522)

and we have no reason to suppose

> it is in principle possible to take out a chunk from one person's mind and replace it with a chunk from someone else's mind. (Madell 1985, pp. 106 - 107)

Principle (b) is also dubious. Simply putting bits of brain together is not likely to result in psychological features being combined to form a single functioning mind. If the transplanted pieces of brain are functioning, there is the real possibility that their activities would clash with those of the receiving brain, and one or both sets of activity would be destroyed. In the middle range of the stage interpretation, the most plausible outcome seems to be that the activity would become chaotic, and the combined brain would cease to work.

Furthermore, as Stone (1988) pointed out, minds are psychological structures, in which the various elements (memories, personality traits, values, beliefs, etc.) are causally intertwined and interdependent. Therefore the replacement of elements of the mind (as distinct from the brain) would lead to a stage at which the new elements would not operate with the old ones, and the structure would collapse. Beck (1991) notes that these considerations apply also to putative non-human persons. Any person must have at least some beliefs, desires, fears, and so on.. Beliefs and desire operate within a network of other beliefs and desires, and so are not the sort of items which can "be separated out of or replaced in a particular person's system without extensive repercussion." (Beck 1991, p. 4)

If both pieces of brain are each supporting a stream of consciousness at the time of transplanting, then it is likely that the result will be a brain with two streams of consciousness. If the piece of Derek Parfit's brain can support a stream of consciousness by itself, and the piece of Greta Garbo's brain can support a stream of consciousness by itself, there is no obvious reason why the streams should not continue to exist after the two pieces of brain have been joined together. On the other hand, since it is unlikely that the two minds could combine without collapsing, there is reason to suppose that, if they continued, it would be as independent streams. The bits of Greta Garbo go on being Greta Garbo, while those of Derek Parfit go on being Derek Parfit.

As Madell says, this is at least as natural and plausible a supposition as that of mixed persons. If there remain two distinct personalities within the one skin, there is no person who is identical with neither. (Madell 1985)

Stone (1988) suggests that Parfit's argument can be saved by assuming a numerically distinct but otherwise physically and psychologically identical copy of Parfit, who I will call *Parfit,* and considering the spectrum between them both. On this version it is less obvious that the objections raised to the Derek Parfit/Greta Garbo spectrum apply. There will be no clashes of physical or psychological structure. From the point of view of the subject nothing will have changed.

Nonetheless, if both pieces of brain are supporting normal waking consciousness, then they are not likely to combine their functioning to form a single mind. The stream of consciousness supported by (say) the left half of

Parfit's brain will be different from the stream supported by the right half of *Parfit's* brain simply because the halves of the brain will be different. The situation is the same as for Greta Garbo and Parfit.

To be clear that we have avoided this difficulties, we have to fall back on the non-human double brain discussed above. We make a duplicate of such a brain, trim away half of each brain so that the remaining half supports a stream of consciousness, then try to join the half of the duplicate with the half of the original.

Even in this case, it seems that principle (b) is not sufficient to ensure that the two streams of consciousness fuse into a single stream. As I showed in my original discussion of the double brain, if each half is capable of supporting a stream of consciousness by itself, there is no apparent reason why these streams should fuse when the brain halves are joined together. The combination of the two halves would be two minds. Some other principle than principle (b) is necessary to fuse the streams of consciousness.

We have come a long way from Parfit's original Combined Spectrum argument, and yet we have not been able to adapt it to give a satisfactory account of fusion of persons, minds, or streams of consciousness.

An Argument against Fusion Adapted from Swinburne

If two people fuse, then Primus would be experiencing at least his own continued existence, as well as, perhaps, other experiences, at the time of fusion. Similarly, Secundus would be experiencing *his* own continued existence. At the time of fusion Coniunctus would then experience Primus" experiences in a continuing stream, with the sudden addition of Secundus" experience subsequent to fusing. He would also experience Secundus" experiences in a continuing stream, with the sudden addition of Primus" experience subsequent to fusing. This means simultaneously being aware of Primus" experience while coming to know Secundus" experience, and being aware of Secundus" experience while coming to know Primus" experience. This seems logically impossible, and makes the idea of fusion seem incoherent. (Adapted from Swinburne, 1984)

If this argument goes through, then the standard first person argument against fission also goes through, since they depend on the same principles. Both fission and fusion are impossible. If the argument fails, the possibility of fission seems to imply the possibility of fusion, and all the moral and logical complications that fusion entails.

Dipping a Toe into the Conceptual Quagmire

I began this chapter with a sketch of some of the solutions offered to the fission problem. I will examine four of them in a little more detail below, but here I will merely note the drastic and implausible revisions they each require

(a) Parfit's claim that survival does not entail identity. This requires revision of the concept of personal identity and survival, and our moral and prudential beliefs. We have to abandon the "only x and y" principle.

(b) The multiple occupancy position of Lewis, Perry, and Noonan. To accept this we have to revise our basis for counting items, our conceptions of our selves, and our conceptions about possibilities.

(c) Madell, Ehring and Dainton suggest that fission twins are identical with each other and with the original person. This requires revisions of our ideas of what makes a person separate from others, and of concepts of time, especially simultaneity

(d) Sprigge suggests the possibility that synchronic identity is not transitive with diachronic identity. This requires radical revisions of the logic of identity.

Thus, we see that accepting the possibility of fission leads to the necessity of making radical revision in concepts which serve us well in other contexts. The arguments over the revisions are complex and convoluted. (To show this, I examine some in more detail below.) If we deny the possibility of fission, the revisions, and the "conceptual quagmire" they create, are not necessary.

A Summary of the Argument

1. The evidence from commissurotomy gives inadequate support for the claim that fission is possible, and includes sufficient evidence against the possibility to leave the question at least open.

2. The only reason for believing fission is possible is that it is conceivable.

However, it is only conceivable on a Reductionist model of the mind. *The possibility of fission cannot, therefore, be used as an argument for Reductionism, since that would involve assuming that which was to be shown.*

3. Arguments *against* Reductionism thus act as positive arguments against the possibility of fission. Arguments *for* Reductionism merely leave the question of the possibility of fission open.

4. The possibility of fission enables the "God's Eye View" argument to be brought against Reductionism. The Reductionist who wishes to use this argument against the featureless Cartesian view must reject the possibility of fission. *By this argument, even an actual case of apparent fission is not sufficient to prove Reductionism*

5. The possibility of fission conflicts with moral and prudential concepts to which we have greater commitment.

6. Attempts to account for the possibility of fission set up strains in concepts of identity and survival, persons, and time.

7. The possibility of fission seems to imply the possibility of fusion which opens up a further can of very wriggly and slippery worms.

8. All these considerations combine to suggest that the concept of fission is incoherent and that fission is logically impossible.

The Balance of Implausibilities

I have argued above that fission is a metaphysical impossibility. In this section I will show that we are not bound to accept Parfit's conclusions about personal identity and survival even if we suppose, contrary to the arguments given above, that fission is in fact possible. In order to show this, I will defend the Ehring-Dainton thesis that the fission twins are identical with each other and with the original person, and try to show that although the thesis is revisionary, it is at least marginally more plausible than such alternatives as the multiple occupancy thesis.

Parfit's Thesis

Parfit uses the fission problem to drive a wedge between the concept of personal survival and the concept of personal identity. This places him in the position of asserting that the identity of a survivor depends on the existence of other survivors. If there are other survivors, then none of them are identical with the original person. Thus, after successful fission, neither of the fission twins can claim to be the original, but if one of the fission twins dies during the fission, then the remaining fission twin *can* claim to be the original.

In terms of the logic of identity, this is a rejection of the "only x and y" principle. Parfit attempts to dispense with the *only x and y* principle by claiming that we find it plausible only because we believe that identity is necessary for survival. Noonan points out (1) that this is question begging, since the issue is whether identity is the relation that matters, and (2) this only applies to personal identity, and yet we apply the *only x and y* principle to other identity questions, even where we are only interested in the continuance of useful characteristics rather than survival.

Oderberg, in defence of the "only x and y" principle, argues that, if the "only x and y" principle were rejected, we could not make decisions about the identity of objects even if we had observed them continuously without taking into account apparently causally unrelated objects. (Oderberg 1993)

Thus, Parfit's rejection of the "only x and y" principle requires considerable conceptual revision.

Destruction of the Original

Oderberg (1993) argues that in fission the original person is destroyed, and two new qualitatively similar persons are created. He starts from the position that the fission products cannot be identical with each other. If they are not identical with each other, they cannot be both be identical with the original. However, each of them has equal right to be regarded as identical with the original, and so neither of them can be. Since neither of the fission products are identical with the original, original person does not survive. Two new people are created.

The problem with this claim is that it is either trivial or a denial that fission occurred. If by "the original does not survive" Oderberg means that the stream of consciousness of the original ceased, and two new streams started, then he is denying that the original stream divided into two streams.

I have already ruled this out, since it is situation (i) rather than genuine fission.

If Oderberg admits that the original stream continued as the two streams of the fission products, then the claim that the original person ceased to exist becomes trivial. It is merely a "Cambridge change", as the logical status of the stream changes. To say that a person ceases to exist in this sense is rather less dramatic than to say that a bachelor ceases to exist when he gets married. I discussed this in the section 'survival and Identity".

If the one stream of consciousness can divide and become two qualitatively similar streams, the real problems remain, even if the term 'same person" is omitted.

Multiple Occupancy

Lewis (1983), Perry (1972), and Noonan (1989) say that persons are four dimensional entities, consisting of aggregates of three dimensional stages. This means that S1 is a series of person stages which are temporarily shared by the two person S2 and S3. There are always two persons involved, so that when the fission occurs it is merely the separation of the persons, not a single person dividing. This position is not the same as Mills" Dual Occupancy. Dual Occupancy is the condition of there being two minds, two streams of consciousness at any one time. Multiple occupancy is the condition of there being one stream of consciousness which is shared by two persons.

Dainton (1992) points out that this requires drastic changes in our thinking. First, a single body and stream of consciousness is ordinarily counted as one person, and yet the multiple occupancy theory requires us to count it as two persons. Second, we normally think of ourselves, and other persons, as being wholly present at any one time. Multiple occupancy theory requires us to accept that the present self we are each aware of is only a (temporal) part of us Thirdly, if we think of a person's whole life as being the person, we lose the ability to make the claim that a person's life could have turned out differently. We have to revise our basis for counting items, our conceptions of our selves, and our conceptions about possibilities.

Noonan (1989, pp. 167 - 168) has argued, in defence of the theory, that our normal way of counting items is not by identity, but by spatio-temporal contiguity. Thus, if two persons are at one place at one time, our common sense way of counting is that there is one item there. If we were to count by identity, which is a four-dimensional concept, we would count them as two persons.

He points out (1989, pp. 141 - 148) that the second objection is simply a denial of the claim that we are four dimensional entities. His answer to the third objection is complex and technical. It amounts to justification for the claim that modal predicates of the type "could have been a contender" do not have a constant denotation. The denotation is dependent on the meaning of the singular term to which it is attached. Thus, if "A" stands for "the summation of person states which is me if I perdure", both,

"I could have been a contender"

and

"It is not true that A have been a contender"

can be true due to the differences in meaning between "I" and "A". Noonan admits (1989, p. 239) that this answer is less compelling for those who do not accept the four dimensional ontology.

I shall not discuss whether these arguments work. Rather, I wish to draw attention to the fact that their purpose is to support the four dimensional multiple occupancy theory. If we can give a plausible account of personal fission that does not require such radical conceptual revision as the four dimensional metaphysic, then the arguments become irrelevant. It is to such an account I shall now turn.

Identity after Division

One way of avoiding the problems outlined above would be to claim that after division the fission twins are still one person.

Madell (1981), Ehring (1987b), and Dainton (1992) have all claimed that after division we would still have one person. They have to give an account of how two apparently distinct person can be the same person. We have the general principle that one person cannot be in two places or two totally different mental and physical states at the same time, and so it must be shown that there are cases where this principle does not apply. Ehring and Dainton appeal to similar considerations, and in so doing show that their thesis depend more on an extension of our current concepts than on rejection of those concepts. Here I have combined their main points to make a single case.

Ehring (1987) cites the following reasons for considering the two fission twins to be different persons.

(1) The lack of shared consciousness.
(2) The lack of a common body.
(3) The causal independence of the fission twins.
(4) The inability of one of the fission twins to remember the post-fission experiences of the other.

(I referred to these reasons in the section on Replicas and Survivors)

To defuse these reasons, Ehring first imagines a case of time travel, in which a thirty-four year old man (Jones34) goes back in time to talk to the four year old person stage Jones4. In this situation it seems natural to regard Jones34 as being a later stage of Jones4. He can remember the conversation as it was experienced by Jones4. There is no point in the sequence of stages between Jones4 and Jones34 at which we can say one person ended and the other began. By using the concept of stages we can overcome the difficulty of saying that Jones has no beard and Jones has a brown beard at the same time.

Jones4 and Jones34 lack shared consciousness and a common body. If they are regarded as the same person then (1) and (2) are not separately or jointly sufficient reasons for denying personal identity.

Of course, in this case (3) and (4) do not hold. There are chains of physical causation between Jones4 and Jones34. If Jones4 has his appendix removed, Jones34 will have no appendix. It is this that maintains the intuition that Jones4 and Jones34 are the same person.

In the case of fission, (3) and (4) do hold.

To show that (3) is not a good reason for denying that fission twins are the same person, Ehring tries to show that physical causal connection between person stages is not necessary. He uses an argument involving division of an artificially created brain, and the embodiment of each half in a separate body. Each half of the brain has both perfect memory and perfect precognition. One half of the brain (B) goes back in time to a time before it is created. B then dies, dying before it is created. The other (C) lives a normal life Since, before division, the two halves shared their memory and precognition, each half knows all the life of the other. C will know the "future" mental life of B, which will in fact have happened in the past, by remembering B's precognition of its future mental life. C will, in effect, "remember" the experiences had by B. B can make plans for C to remember and carry out. B and C are thus related to each other in two of the ways the stages of our own earlier and later lives are related. Thus, says Ehring, we can regard them as stages of the same person even though there is no physical causal connection between the events which happen to B's body Physical causal connection is not necessary.

This seems to me unsatisfactory. I am not convinced that I should regard the two halves of the Brain as being one person. We can say that there were two persons with perfect communication created when the original brain was created, and that they were subsequently separated. It might be possible to use the concept of a hologram brain to make the argument work. However, I think that Ehring's point can be argued from the case of the man with two bodies.

I will describe this case in more detail later. For the moment it is sufficient to state that one mind controls two bodies. One body is called Henry, and the other is called George. Henry was lynched, but the mind took over another body, so that it again had two bodies to control. Later, George was lynched, but again the mind took over another body.

Shaving Henry does not affect George's beard. If Henry was tattooed before he was lynched no tattoo will appear on the new body when it is acquired. This, I think shows that (3) is not a sufficient reason for denying personal identity. Indeed, the man with two bodies shows that (2) and (3) are not jointly sufficient reason for denying personal identity.

If (2)+(3) are not jointly sufficient, and (1)+(2) are not jointly sufficient, can (1)+(2)+(3) be jointly sufficient?

Consider the case in which the man with two bodies has acquired two new bodies, so that neither of the original two exist any more. He then goes back in time to meet his earlier self, still embodied in the old bodies. Here conditions (1), (2) and (3) are all satisfied, and yet I would not be prepared to say that the old-bodies George-Henry and the new-bodies George-Henry are different people.

Can (4) be included? Suppose, then, that George Henry bangs his head as he is getting out of the time machine. He had a memory of himself embodied in the old bodies going to the time machine and meeting himself, in the new bodies, getting out of the time machine. He now loses this memory, though he remembers events from the childhood of the old bodies, up to the age of fifteen.

This is exactly the same sort of case as that which Perry (1975, p. 19) described. To deal with such cases Perry's formulation of the mental relation (R_G) that stages of the same person must bear to one another "allows us, in effect, to change directions and thus ignore time order when linking person stages" (Perry 1975, p. 20)

> R_G: There is a sequence of person-stages (not necessarily in the order they occur in time, and not excluding repetitions), the first of which is A and the last of which is B, such that each person-stage in the sequence either (i) contains, or could contain, a memory of an experience contained in the next, or (ii) contains an experience of which the next person-stage contains a memory, or could contain a memory. (Perry 1975, p. 19)

This relation holds between the old-bodies George-Henry and the new-bodies George-Henry. Although George-Henry has not undergone fission the mental relation between them is similar to that between fission twins. The old-bodies George-Henry and the new-bodies George-Henry can both remember a common childhood, but the old-bodies George-Henry cannot remember the later activities of the new-bodies George-Henry, and the new-bodies George-Henry cannot remember the activities of old-bodies George-Henry (past the age of fifteen.)

Thus, conditions (1), (2) and (3) are all satisfied, along with a condition very similar to (4), and yet they are not jointly sufficient to deny that the two George-Henrys are stages of different persons.

Ehring shows that the mental relation between fission twins is R_G. Between the fission twins there is a series of person stages satisfying the conditions of R_G, leading back from one twin, through the pre-fission stage, and then forward to the other twin.

Fission twins thus satisfy condition (1), (2), (3) and (4), and yet are still stages of the same person.

> Indeed, on a Perry-like memory theory the duplicates stand to each other in just the relation thought to be important to personal identity. (Ehring 1987b, p. 433)

All of Ehring's argument has, however, been about *person-stages*. Can it be applied to persons? It seems to me that it can. Those of us who regard persons as continuants rather than stages will claim that Jones4 and Jones34 are the same person just before Jones34 goes back in time, and so I would make the same claim about them after time travel. Now it may be the case that Perry's memory relation R_G cannot apply to whole persons as distinct from stages, but the memory problem can be solved in another way. Lefty cannot remember the experience Righty had after the split, and vice versa. If they are the same person, this is equivalent to a two periods of amnesia.

Suppose a man of 20 bangs his head and thus loses his memory of his life after the age of 15. Then five years later he bangs his head again, losing the memory of his life from 20 to 25 but at the same time regaining the memory of his life from 15 to 20. To allow that the man of 21 is the same person as the man of 26 in spite of the difference in memory requires a version of memory very similar to Perry's.

Suppose we know that a third bang will restore all the memory. We would be even more inclined to agree that man21 and man26 are the same person, because although they do not share the same memory, the potential for sharing exists.

But the same is true of fission twins. The potential for sharing the same memory exist in fusion. After fusion the reunited person gains a unified consciousness and access to the memories of both parts of the life.

Lack of common memory, therefore, does not present an obstacle to them being the same person.

Simultaneity and the Concept of Personal Time

Dainton deals with the problem of how one person can be in two places or two totally different mental and physical states at the same time by drawing a distinction between personal time and external time, and then claiming that although the fission twins co-exist in external time, they are not simultaneous in personal time. Thus, the same person does not exist in two places at the same time. In order to make this claim he has to show that personal time is a legitimate temporal system, and that for considerations of personal identity, personal time takes priority over external time.

Dainton adapts the idea of personal time from Lewis. He says that Lewis defines personal time as an ordering relation between person stages. Since Dainton rejects the idea of person stages, he reinterprets personal time as the ordering of life-stages.

Personal time is time as it is experienced. In our lives we find that some events are experienced before others, and some are experienced simultaneously. The same goes for ideas, actions, feelings, and, indeed, almost all the elements of life. Life seems to be a linear ordering of experience and action.

This ordering usually matches the ordering of the events in the world. The cat comes in before it jumps on my knee. I see the cat come in before I feel the weight of it. In time travel personal ordering does not necessarily match the ordering of events in the world. The tree is standing before it falls. I see the fallen tree, go back in time, and see the tree standing. My personal experience of the fallen tree comes before the experience of the standing tree.

If I travel back in time and meet myself when 26, I exist twice in objective time, but in my personal time, I47 is now, and I26 is my past. There is a succession of experienced stages between us. My personal time retains a linear ordering. I26 do not, of course, remember these stages. For me26 they are in the future. I26 expect that I will experience this meeting at some time in my personal future. I26 expect that when I am I47, experiencing the meeting, I will experience it as coming *after* my experience as I26. Thus, although I exist twice in the external time system, I only exist once in my personal time system.

In fission cases, personal time divides into two branches, and the fission twins each live in a branch of that time. For each twin events in their own branch are linearly ordered with respect to each other.

Thus, as far as personal time is concerned, the person does not exist twice at one time.

To show that personal time is a genuine temporal system, Dainton argues that kinds of events that make up personal time are suitable for the basis of a relational temporal system. We accept that relative motion is a basis for a temporal system, so it seems reasonable to accept personal continuities. There is no reason to believe that the conception of temporality is restricted to physical theory. A world consisting only of minds would only have personal time. Personal time can be regarded as a legitimate temporal system.

Our response to time travel shows that we *do* give priority to personal time. This is because personal time is the time we know from the first person point of view. We are persons, and we regard our lives as being in personal time. The problem of personal identity requires solutions in the form of continuities between life stages. These can be physical continuities, mental continuities, or the continuity of a Self. Life stages are ordered in personal time, so the continuities are those which hold across personal time. Thus, diachronic personal identity is identity across personal time.

An Objection

Again, the difficulty with Dainton's idea is that the twins do not have direct access to each other's life histories. But the same considerations that applied to Ehring can be applied here. Again, the potential for fusion exists. There is nothing in the concept of personal time that prevents this. A dividing and rejoining temporal system seems to be possible.

Dainton describes a simply linear temporal system as one in which every event is either before or after every other event, that is they are "strongly connected". In branching time the events in each branch are strongly connected to each other and to the events before the branching, but not to the events in the other branch. The events in one branch are not before, after, or simultaneous with those in the other branch, and so are not strongly connected. None the less events in each branch are temporally connected to the events in the other branch by being related to the events before fission. If the branches rejoin the events of the branches will be strongly connected to the events after fusion. Thus any event in either branch can be placed within the system as being after fission and before fusion, and as before one set of events in the branch, and after another set, but it would not be possible to relate it to the events in the other branch except by relating it to the external time stream. If I divide and fuse I find I can remember two sequences of events between the fission and the fusion. I cannot combine the events of each sequence into a single order, but can I regard the sequences as wholes to be simultaneous? They both happened after I divided and before I fused. But to be simultaneous means that they happened in the same time stream. They are simultaneous in the external time stream, but not simultaneous in the personal time streams. To decide whether any event in one stream was simultaneous with an event in the other stream, I would have to connect them both with an external event. Thus, to decide whether the time one stream dropped the coffee pot was simultaneous with the time the other stream burnt the toast I would have to decide whether dropping the coffee pot and burning the toast both happened at the time the Prime Minister was deposed. Alternatively, I would have to remember seeing the toast burning at the same time I remembered dropping the coffee pot, and remember burning the toast at the same time as I saw the coffee pot being dropped.

Thus, in personal time, the lives of the fission twins are not simultaneous.

By Ehring's and Dainton's arguments, then, we can claim that the fission twins are not two different persons, but identical with each other as well as being identical with the original.

A Comparison of Multiple Occupancy and the Ehring/Dainton Theory

Noonan's (1989) multiple occupancy theory has some interesting parallels with the combined Ehring/Dainton theory. They both suggest that our normal way of counting persons is a convention, and they both suggest revision of our normal view of time.

Our normal way of counting is that when there is one body and one stream of consciousness there is one person, and where there are two bodies and two streams of consciousness there are two persons. Noonan says there must have been two persons before fission because they are separate after fission. Spatio-temporal contiguity does not make two persons into one. Ehring and Dainton say that there is one person after fission because there was only one person before fission. Spatio-temporal separation (in objective time) does not make one person into two. Noonan views persons as four dimensional entities, extended in time as well as in space. Dainton views persons as each existing, as a subject of experience, in personal time, as well as existing as physical objects in objective time.

It seems more plausible that there is only one person present when there is only one stream of consciousness, and it seems more plausible that a person is wholly present at any one time, so the Ehring/Dainton theory seems marginally more plausible than the multiple occupancy theory.

(A mystical note. There is a set of possibilities that both multiple occupancy and the Ehring/Dainton theory seem to open up. If one person divides and then recombines, or two persons separate and then come together again, there is still the situation of one stream of consciousness becoming two, and then one. It seems that one stream of consciousness can become many streams of consciousness, and then they can all fuse into a single stream again. In the four dimensional metaphysic, all these streams of consciousness can be counted as a single entity or a set of connected entities. In personal time one person, one Self exists along many branches, each of which seems to be separate from the others, but which had the same origin and which then recombine into the same person. In this regard, the multiple occupancy theory and the Ehring Dainton theory seem to come to the same thing. We seem to have stumbled onto a way of understanding the claims of the Ancients, that the process of emanation for souls from the One, and their return to the One, is not a temporal process as we usually understand it, and yet we experience our lives as separate temporal beings. Of course, those who accept the possibility of fission and fusion are not automatically committed to accepting these mystical interpretations.)

In Ehring's version, there is strain on the idea of what constitutes a separate person. In Dainton's version, there is strain on the idea of temporal system. I can think of no way of showing that these strains are greater than the those set up by interpretations which conclude that the fission twins are separate persons. Since Dainton's account of fission uses the concept of the specious present, which is the present in personal time, to make fission possible at all, his account of fission leads naturally to his account of the identity of fission twins. If his account of fission is acceptable, it strengthens the plausibility of the Ehring/Dainton theory.

Two Conclusions

In sum, then, the problem of fission leads to two conclusions. The strong conclusion, and the one I favour, is that fission is simply not possible and if fission is not possible, we no longer have good reason for believing that there can be survival without identity.

The second, weaker, conclusion is that even if we allow fission to be possible, the most plausible and coherent account makes the fission twins identical with each other and the original. Again, we have no good reason for believing that there can be survival without identity.

7 The Physical Criterion for Personal Identity

So far I have argued that the core of personal survival and personal identity is the survival and identity of the Self. However, since it has been argued that personal identity just is the identity of the person's body, I have to show that physical identity is not a sufficient condition for full personal identity, and is not a necessary condition for psychological or self identity. I shall do this by showing that it fails to give an acceptable account from the first person point of view, and is inadequate from the third person point of view.

According to the physical criterion, personal identity is logically constituted by bodily identity. It gains its force from looking at persons from the third person point of view, as though they were nothing more than physical objects in the world.

Giles expresses it as follows:

> What determines whether two paintings are the same is whether there exists a continuous path in space and time which connects the earlier painting with the later one. What determines whether the two persons are the same is whether there likewise exists a path in space and time which connects the earlier person's body with the later one. (Giles, 1991)

Of course, this is not identity in the "proper philosophical sense" (Butler) but is the sort of identity that other living things have. There is a flow of parts through the body. The body slowly changes, but the same form is retained, or changes slowly, with the replacement of the matter it consists of. The identity is the identity of form, not of matter.

The normal way of checking the identity of a person for everyday activities in Berkshire is through the physical criterion, because in our ordinary lives personal identity and bodily identity go together. Flew considers that present practice of using bodily continuity as *evidence* for personal identity supports the *constitutive* physical criterion of personal identity. He writes that:

> the truth is that in all ordinary and everyday cases – all the cases, that is, which actually do arise, as opposed to those merely conceivable cases so joyously excogitated by philosophers – physical continuity is not only the necessary but also, for all practical purposes, the sufficient condition of personal identity. (Flew 1987, p. 132)

Flew rather unfortunately conflates the normal with the actual, apparently forgetting that what is considered weird and bizarre in Normal, Illinois may be mundane in Eerie, Indiana. The actual includes cases which may not be regarded as normal by some people in some places, and even cases which are not regarded as normal by anyone anywhere. It certainly includes cases wherein reidentification is made in the known absence of bodily continuity.

For example, after the death of a Dalai Lama, his successor is chosen by finding the boy into whom the soul of the Dalai Lama has been reborn. This requires reidentifying the soul of the Dalai Lama. The evidence used for this reidentification is the fact that the boy apparently has memories from the life of the previous Dalai Lama. Before China seized Tibet, this reidentification was of maximum legal importance, since it was the method for choosing the ruler of the country. The cases of the Dalai Lama and the Panchen Lama (who is chosen in the same way) are actual cases in which physical continuity is not regarded as a necessary condition of personal identity.

Flew may say that the monks are wrong in supposing that there is a reincarnating soul, but he cannot argue this from "present practice."

When we deal with persons, we are interested in persons as beings with minds, and, as I have shown in a previous chapter, our concern for personal survival is concern for psychological survival. This is why, even in Berkshire, nonphysical evidence as well as physical evidence is used to make judgments of personal identity. If we meet an old friend whom we last saw when we were in high school thirty years ago, it may well be impossible to detect the lineaments of that slim spotty youth in the balding, bewhiskered, fat, wrinkly middle-aged man peering at us through his bifocals. However, after a few minutes conversation, we are assured of his identity by his tricks of speech, his memories, and his personality.

Since psychological continuity and identity are associated with the continuity and identity of the brain in humans, the physical criterion is sometimes reduced to the (part) brain criterion.

If the brain of one person is transplanted (while still functioning) into the body of another, the psychological identity is deemed to follow the brain. This leads to a limitation of the bodily criterion to the brain criterion, which is that a person at t1 is the same person as the person at t2 if both persons have the same brain. But persons can survive with incomplete brains, so the criterion has to be further limited to the part brain criterion, that is, a person at t1 is the same person as the person at t2 if the person at t2 has enough of the brain of the person at t1 for it to be the brain of a living person.

However, suppose we go to the planet Jell, and discover that the Jellians seem remarkably similar to ourselves. They are bipedal humanoids (with, admittedly, stripy skin and a few too many eyes) who have similar cultural patterns to ours. We are generally disposed to regard them as persons, particularly since their philosophers worry over problems of personal identity. When visiting their medical schools, we discover that they have no internal organs. Inside their skin is a pale grey jelly. They assure us that this jelly is undifferentiated, and performs all the functions that our own organs, bones, muscles, and nervous systems perform. The jelly in the arm can move the arm and think at the same time. There is no particular part of their bodies that acts as a brain. We cannot use the (part) brain criterion for these beings. This leaves us with three possibilities. First, there are different criteria for different beings. Second, we must reject the (part) brain criterion. Third, it is not logically possible for the Jellians to exist.

Rather than argue that the Jellians are logically possible, I will sidestep the question by suggesting that a more general physical criterion can cover such cases. The more general version will be more along the lines of "a person at t1 is the same person as the person at t2 if the person at t2 has enough of the physical carrier of psychological identity of the person at t1 for it to maintain the psychological identity of a living person".

I shall argue that the physical criterion is inadequate as an account of full personal identity. First, I shall recount an argument from Giles to show that the view of the body as a physical object does not apply to my own body, and, therefore, I cannot use the physical criterion to give an account of my own personal identity. Second, I shall show psychological identity can be logically separated from bodily identity. I shall argue this by using the case of the prince and the cobbler and the case of the man with two bodies to show that psychological identity can (logically) move from one body to another, and then by defending the logical possibility of disembodied existence. Finally, I shall comment on bodily continuity as a necessary precondition for memory.

Why I Cannot Use the Bodily Criterion for an Account of My Own Identity

Giles (1991) claims that I can apply the bodily criterion - spatio-temporal continuity - to other bodies, but not to my own, and that therefore it should be rejected. His argument is that although all paintings are experienced in essentially similar ways, my own body is experienced differently from other bodies. From the first person point of view my body is not a physical object but a point of view. The physical criterion does not apply to a point of view

Giles starts his argument by setting out features of the body from the first person point of view (attributed to Hospers) and combining them to form a coherent theory. The essential features are

(1) I cannot get away from my own body (but there are some parts, such as the back of my head, which are never there as direct visual experience)
(2) I can only see it from certain perspectives
(3) It is the only body of which I can have kinaesthetic and somatic sense experiences
(4) It is the only body over which I have direct control
(5) It is the only body through which I can experience the world.

The importance of (5) is that the sense organs cannot experience themselves directly. The eye cannot see itself, the finger tip does not feel itself, but what it is touching. Of course, one finger tip can feel another, and if my eyes were on stalks, one of my eyes would be able to see another, but they do not perceive themselves. This is just as well, since if they could they would be permanently sensing themselves and this sensation would interfere with their perception of other things. The result of this is that there are two phenomenologies of the body: the third person perspective, and the first person perspective. The third person perspective is that of the body as an item in the world, whether it be part of my own body or another person"s body. When I look at my hand, or at the Queen"s hand, I have a third person perspective. The hand is an item in my perception of the world. The hand with which I perceive the dry roughness of sandpaper is not an item in my perception of the world, it is the manual-tactile perception of the world

From the first person point of view my body is an arrangement of centres of perception, and this arrangement constitutes my phenomenological point of view on the world. My body is a point of view on something other than itself.

Giles considers the possible objection that somatic and kinaesthetic sensations are experiences of the body which are not from a third person point of view. I cannot have these experiences of another person's body, I do not direct a specific sense organ on any part of my body, and the sensations are usually not clear. It seems here that in fact my body is a point of view on itself.

Somatic sensations, such as the pain in my ankle or the vague queasiness in my stomach, seem to be merely sensations from the body. Nonetheless, when we attend to these sensations, we find that we "we contemplate from a distance, so to speak" (Giles 1991, p. 343). The manner in which we attend to them is the same as the way that we contemplate our hand when we look at it, or the back of our head when we touch it, in that we still take a point of view from the third person. Of course, somatic experiences of my ankle are different from visual experiences of my ankle, but so are tactile experiences. Tactile experiences and visual experiences are both "third person point of view" experiences of the body even though they are qualitatively different. The qualitatively difference between somatic experiences and visual or tactile experiences cannot be used as a reason for denying that somatic experiences are a kind of third person perspective of the body.

Kinaesthetic experiences are different. These are experiences of the position and the change of position (that is, movement) of the body. This is not a sensation at all. It is just an awareness of the spatial arrangement of the points of view that constitute my body. "That is, I am aware that the arm of the chair which my hand senses is above the floor which my foot senses." (Giles 1991, p. 342) When I move I am aware of the change in spatial arrangement of these points of view. (Giles does not note that movement can be accompanied by somatic sensations of joint and muscle movement, especially in the more arthritic of us, but his basic point remains.) Kinaesthesia is not first person awareness of my body as a physical object but as a (shifting) spatial distribution of points of view.

> Having thus arrived at a theory of the body we can now see why the bodily theory of identity must fail. For the bodily theory construes the body as a physical object that persists through time and space; that is as a body from the third person perspective. But the body from this perspective is the body I examine from the point of view of the body in which I live. But ... to live

a body is just to undergo the world from a particular point of view. And here the notion of physical object identity can get no foothold; for a point of view is not a physical object. (Giles 1991, p. 347)

(Flew (1992) presumes (without explaining why) that Giles is assuming his own incorporeality; an assumption which Giles denies. (Giles 1994) Flew admits that "we do not usually require direct evidence of spatio-temporal continuity ... in order to know whether it was to us that it happened or we who did it," but claims that in cases of memory failure we may need such evidence. It seems to me that here Flew is confusing evidence for identity with the criterion for identity. A photograph of me punching the Prime Minister on the nose might convince me that I did in fact do it when I was drunk last week, since it shows that the body I currently inhabit was the one involved. It is certainly evidence that I punched him. However, the fact that it was the same body does not of itself mean that the same person was involved. My will might have been temporarily disconnected from my muscles, with my muscles being operated by a spirit more personal than whisky.)

Psychological Separability: the Body Switching Case

If it is logically possible for psychological identity to be transferred from one physical carrier to another, or for psychological identity to exist without the body, then even the revised physical criterion fails, since it demonstrates that psychological identity is logically separable from the body. I will turn my attention to cases intended to show this psychological separability.

In the standard form of the body switching case, as derived from Locke, the prince wakes up to find himself in the body of the cobbler. A difficulty is that it can be claimed that this is no different from the prince finding that his body has undergone a strange metamorphosis, but is continuously the body of the prince, or that the cobbler has had a strange mental aberration in that he wakes up with the memories of the prince, and the belief that he is the prince. I shall elaborate the case to make it more resistant to these objections.

I am the prince, sitting on my throne, looking at the cobbler in front of me. I have a sudden dizzying sense of seeing from two points of view at once, the two being confusingly superimposed, and then find I am seeing from the cobbler's point of view. I am looking at the throne, and there, seated upon it, is a figure in princely robes which exactly resembles that which I saw mirrored in my long mirror this morning when I looked at myself. The hands on the ends of its arms are those which I was wont to call mine, and the hands on the ends of the arms I now have are those of the cobbler I was just looking at. The figure on the throne reports the same sort of story, that is, he was a cobbler looking at the prince and who now finds that he is the position of the prince looking at the cobbler. It seems that I have swapped bodies with the person opposite. My body has not undergone strange changes while I was asleep, so the bodily metamorphosis objection cannot be used.

It could still be claimed that both the prince and the cobbler simultaneously had strange delusions. The cobbler had a delusion that he had been a prince, developed a set of delusory memories that precisely matched those of the prince, lost all his own memories, and hallucinated seeing from two points of view at once. The prince had the corresponding delusion of having been a cobbler.

This interpretation saves the bodily continuity criterion, but at the cost of suggesting that we cannot trust our own continuous experience. However, if we cannot trust our own continuous experience, we cannot be sure whether a particular body has persisted unchanged. I will pursue this point further below, in the comment on memory.

Green and Wikler (1980) claim

(a) that this case requires an account of how the person switched bodies,
(b) that this account must be different from an account of personality change or brainwashing, and
(c) body transfer occurs iff the sort of explanation of the continuity of the person's psychological properties is the same as that which explains continuity in ordinary life histories.

In the case as described they consider the account would be that of a Cartesian soul moving from the prince to the cobbler. However, an alternative account would be that the transfer is done by using a physical intermediate carrier of psychological continuity.

An imaginary method Williams (1973) gives is that of using the Wonderful Brain Recording Machine to record all the memories and personality from the brain, and then to replace it into the same or another brain. If the same brain is used then, Williams says, the person remembers and would count him as same man. But if the man is given a new brain with the information transferred into it, Williams suggests he would still count as the same man.

This case is based on two dubious assumptions. The first is that a person's psychological identity consists of brain states which can be recorded in another medium. Thus, as long as this information is recorded, the states can be re-created. The second assumption is that if a total brain state is destroyed and then recreated, this gives personal survival and identity. If, as I claimed earlier, survival requires continuity, this process would not provide survival and identity. However, this objection does not seem insuperable. All that is necessary is that psychological identity be in some way transferred from one brain to another while the brains are still functioning. A fantasy of this is as follows.

I am the cobbler. My brain is connected, by thousands of connections, to the Even More Wonderful Total Brain Prosthesis. I learn to use the prosthesis to perform the functions that I use my brain for. For example, I learn to use the prosthetic visual cortex to do what I previously did with my natural visual cortex. (The idea of learning to use sensory equipment is not incoherent. Blind people who have had their sight restored have to learn to use the new sense that is available. When I am connected to the Total Brain Prosthesis I have immediate access to the prosthetic visual cortex, and learn to direct my attention to that cortex rather than the natural cortex.) I learn to transfer all my memories to the Prosthesis, to think with the prosthesis, to feel irritated by the government with the prosthesis, to dream with the prosthesis. As each function is taken over by the prosthesis, the appropriate system in my brain is rendered inoperable in some way that will not affect the rest of the system. (It might be the case that all the systems in the brain would have to be left operable until I could use the prosthesis for every function.) Eventually I am using the prosthesis for my entire mental life, and my brain has gone. My Self is associated with the prosthesis. The prosthesis is then disconnected from the cobbler's brain and connected to the brain in the princely body. The prince has been through a similar process, and his prosthesis is connected to the brain in the baser body. I and the prince then start the process of learning to use these brains.

This account satisfies Green and Wikler's criteria.

Since the point of the thought experiment is to show that psychological identity is logically distinct from brain identity, (a) seems an unnecessary requirement. The point of (a) is to show (d)that the case cannot be classed as one of personality change or brainwashing. But if (d) can be shown in another way, (a) and (b) become unnecessary.

Swinburne (1984 and 1986) gives a version of body switching that cannot be classed as one of personality change or brainwashing. Swinburne imagines the case as being gradual, perhaps spread over a few hours. First I find that I cannot control the right side of my body. When I try to move it, my wife's right side moves. She, on the other hand, finds that she cannot control the right side of her body, but can control the right side of mine. Next, I lose vision from my right eye. My visual experience comes, confusingly, from my left eye and my wife's right eye. Her visual sensations are similarly confused. Then I find that I cannot control any part of my body, but can control my wife's body. and she can control mine. Finally, my visual sensation comes from both her eyes. We have changed bodies.

Of course, the whole process has taken place in front of a group of psychologists who have been constantly checking to see that my wife's right hand can obey command whispered into my left ear, that I can see things placed in front of her right eye, and so forth.

In this version, the claim that I am undergoing a delusion that I am able to control my wife's right hand is unconvincing. I can detect no difference between the experience of moving my own hand before the process started and moving hers afterwards. In each case, I just move it, and it moves. The vision I have from her right eye gives information as veridical as that from my own right eye used to be. To claim this is a veridical hallucination seems to be clutching at straws.

This is a case wherein my experience is that of losing control of my own body and gaining control of my wife's. In order to distrust that experience I would need some explanation of my experience that was more convincing than the immediate experience. What could that explanation be?

Does the case satisfy (c)? From the first person point of view, there is no explanation given, but there is no first person explanation for the continuity of ordinary life history aside from the explanation that the experiences all happen to *me*. From the first person point of view, to claim that I know a set of experiences are part of my psychological continuity because they are all connected to the same brain is ridiculous.

This description of my psychological continuity and identity moving from my body/brain to my wife's body/brain is coherent, and shows that psychological identity is logically distinct from brain identity.

Psychological Separability: Publicly Traceable Reincarnation

A further argument is that of cases of reincarnation. Suppose a living person claims to be the continuation of a person who died before the living person was born, and presents memory evidence of this. It can be claimed that this is logically equivalent to a person gaining a set of "memories" of the previous person's life, without there being any traceable connection between the persons. However, the case I describe below provides a way for a person to change bodies completely and yet remain traceable.

George-Henry: the Man with Two Bodies (Part One)

George-Henry has two bodies, one called George (tall, dark haired, well muscled, running to fat) and the other called, unsurprisingly, Henry (shorter, fair haired but balding, slim). George-Henry is a surgeon and a musician. Sometimes George operates while Henry conducts, and sometimes *vice versa*. Musicians cannot hear any difference between George's conducting and Henry's.

Naturally George-Henry's claim to be one person with two bodies met with some scepticism. The bodies were given a large number of tests in which George and Henry were separated, given lists of questions, and Henry then answered George's questions, and *vice versa*, or George carried out instructions given to Henry, etc. George and Henry both displayed the same personality. They told and laughed at the same jokes. Only the fact of having two bodies could lead anyone to suggest that they were two persons, and not one. George-Henry gave a first person account:

> I am one centre of consciousness, with one set of memories, ideas, emotions, etc. Everything is the same as with a single bodied person except that I am skilled at manipulating and handling the senses of two bodies. Just as a musician can do two totally different things with his left and right hands, I can conduct with one body and operate with the other. An experienced English teacher can, while correcting the pronunciation of a student in front of him, hear and note the mispronunciation of a student behind him. In the same way I can listen to the orchestra and the conversation in the operating theatre. My visual field is divided into halves. On the left I see what is in front of George, and on the right I see what is in front of Henry.

(This split-screen effect seems to be the simplest way of dealing with vision. Alternatives are superimposition, as one gets with two different pictures in a stereoscope, or having two different visual fields. It is a long time since I tried the experiment with the stereoscope, so I can"t remember how difficult it is to handle the two images, and I cannot easily imagine having two visual fields.)

I do not think there is anything logically impossible or incoherent in this account. Clearly there is only one person from the point of view of self identity and psychological identity. To deny that George-Henry should be counted as only one person is simply to assert a one body, one person criterion

In this case, if we class George and Henry as parts of the same person, as my right hand and my left are parts of the same person, then we are saying that a person can be embodied in two living human bodies. If we say that, we have to set a criterion for deciding between when two bodies are one person, and when they are two persons. But that criterion cannot be a bodily criterion. It has to involve psychological connection between the bodies.

If, on the other hand, we say George is psychologically identical with Henry then we are saying that the psychological aspect of one person can be in two places at once, which suggests that the psychological aspect is not the same as a physical object, but is the sort of entity that, either, cannot be located spatially, or can be located in several places at once.

In neither of these cases can a person be a body. Both of these conclusions are uncomfortable for the bodily criterion of persons.

George-Henry (Part Two)

A group of outraged philosophers lynched George. For a little while George-Henry was handicapped, and could not carry out all his duties. With only one body, he could not operate and conduct at the same time, though he could do them both at separate times.

"I can no longer be in two places at once," he said wistfully.

Shortly, however, a patient in a mental hospital, who had been declared little more than a vegetable, sat up and declared himself to be George-Henry's new other body. Henry made the same declaration. The new George looked different from the old one, but otherwise everything was as before.

The philosophers lynched Henry. A new Henry emerged.

When George was lynched, George-Henry continued to exist. When the new George came, George-Henry continued to exist. When the new Henry came, George-Henry continued to exist. But by now George-Henry had got a completely different pair of bodies, and acquired them in an unusual way. The gradual replacement of parts may be regarded as preserving identity, but there is no spatio-temporal continuity whatsoever between George-Henry's old bodies and his new ones. Thus we can imagine a case of publicly checkable reincarnation which does not presuppose that George-Henry lives as a disembodied spirit. Indeed, the spirit is doubly embodied. Of course, it may be claimed that for the case to be possible there has to be a nonphysical connection between the two bodies, but this is not required. If we suppose that George-Henry's bodies are connected by something analogous to radio that provides a physical means of transmitting information and co-ordinating brain activities, then the case can be accepted even by materialists. This case cannot be easily redescribed as one of personality change or brainwashing.

Is it logically possible for George-Henry to take over another body? The possible emergence of others *ad infinitum* does not mean that none of them are George-Henry. All of them could be him, assuming that he can handle them all.

Thus far George-Henry's transfers from body to body have been easily traceable, and sufficient to show that the physical criterion is inadequate. In the next stage, it is less clear that the transfer is publicly observable.

George-Henry (Part Three)

The philosophers then lynched George and Henry at the same time, but two other such patients took over. They exhibited all George-Henry's characteristics, skills, memories, etc., and claimed to be George-Henry.

It seems difficult to maintain the bodily criterion of identity in this case. One has to claim that the continued existence of Henry after the death of old George validates the identity of the new George, and that when both George and Henry were strung up together the chain of identity was broken, so that the new claimant was not George-Henry, but merely someone like George-Henry. But why should we deny that the new claimant was George-Henry? We have seen that he can take over a new body when one of his old ones is killed, so we need good reason to deny the possibility that he can take over a new pair if both the old ones are killed together.

The only reason I can think of is as follows. When George is killed, George-Henry is still embodied in Henry, but when they are both killed together, there is no embodiment of George-Henry. If he is to take over new bodies it must be at the moment of death, or he must exist as a disembodied spirit between the death of the old bodies and the take-over of the new ones.

The first alternative is certainly possible. Philosophers are notorious for their incompetence at hanging people, and so George-Henry would certainly die slowly enough for him to be able to take over two new bodies just as the old ones died. To show that the second alternative is possible, we have to show that it is logically possible for a person to exist as a disembodied spirit.

Psychological Separability: Disembodiment

Something has happened. I can"t feel my body. I can"t feel any tactile, kinaesthetic or somatic sensations. I have no feelings of warmth or cold. I can see, but that is all. I try to move my hands, but I feel no hands. I don"t even feel the sensation of trying. I remember hands, and what I did and what it was like when I moved them, but now I can only form the intention of moving them. That seems to be the case for everything. No! I can move my vision! When I want to see to the left, I look left without difficulty. When I want to see something more closely, my vision moves closer to it. Are my brain and eyes just floating in vat, just like the character in *En Levande Själ?* But he had ears as well, and used them as flippers to swim in his vat. (Jersild, 1982) I am not doing that. I get no feeling of using any muscles at all. And I can see up, and go up to the ceiling and look down around the room. All I can see is an ordinary room. No machines. No vat. No body, no camera boom, no cables. Now I suspect the truth. The first test is the wall. I move my vision to it, into it (brick walls are not very interesting seen from the inside) and through. Another room. This one has a mirror. I go to the mirror and look into it. Of course I see the room reflected, but only the room. There is no visible person reflected in the mirror.

This is an old philosophical fantasy, designed to show that disembodied existence is logically possible. It has been criticized in a variety of ways, all of which are intended the show that the fantasy is incoherent, either directly or by the fact that it depends on the idea of an immaterial soul that can survive independently of the body. I will show that none of these criticisms work.

First, it is important to note that my memories, personality, etc., were all formed while I was embodied, and my current disembodied state is the result of an administrative error. I am not attempting to show that I could develop into a full person without being embodied at some stage.

The ghost can have at least two senses, vision and hearing. Nielsen (1987) asks how there can be a visual field when there is no spatial entity to have a viewpoint. However, my ghost is in space. The visual field has the same angle of view as would come from a pair of eyes at a particular place. The direction of view, and location of the place can be chosen by the ghost. That location can be regarded as the location of the ghost.

How can the ghost move its visual field just by trying? When in my current embodied state I peer myopically at something, I simply try to see it better, and discover I have moved my head forward. I am not trying to move my head, but that is the way my visual field gets moved. All I wanted and tried to do was move the visual field. After disembodiment I am differently constituted (critics may say I am not constituted at all, which is true as far as physical matter is concerned) and so have a different repertoire of basic actions (after I wrote this I discovered Penelhum (1970) uses exactly the same phrase) which are those for adjusting the visual field. I discover that I can alter my visual field in such a way as to give the effect that moving my head had on the field.

There is nothing logically impossible about having visual images without eyes. People have visual images in dreams, without using their eyes. In the case of the ghost they are veridical. They are images of things that are really happening. The strongest single objection to this version of disembodied existence is the question of how it happens that the images are veridical. (Price, of course, avoids this question by admitting that they are not veridical in the sense of being images of physical objects, and that the disembodied spirit lives in a sort of dream, in which he can control some of the events in the dream. Price 1972)

The same argument can be used for hearing.

Geach (1969) attempts to show that this is incoherent by claiming that concepts such as "see" are connected with ideas such as "I can't see, it's too far off", and "don't look round", and that when the concept is disconnected from these less obviously psychological concepts the concept of seeing collapses. I am not convinced that it does, but even so my ghost has a moving visual field that can be too far off, and can look round, so this sort of objection does not hold.

Flew has produced a series of arguments against the possibility of disembodied persons, based on the principle that the possibility of disembodied person requires that persons be made up of a body and a Cartesian or Platonic immaterial soul. Thus, some of his arguments are against the coherence of the fantasy of disembodiment, and some are against the immaterial soul.

First, Flew suggests that the fantasy of disembodiment is not what it seems to be, in that there is no difference between imaging myself being a disembodied soul floating around the world and imagining the world without me in it (Flew 1976)

The difference lies in the fact that when I imagine being a disembodied ghost, I am imagining not merely what the world looks like when seen from various viewpoints, but also:

(a) that I change the viewpoint by act of will.
(b) that I think comments about the things I see at the same time as I observe them.
(c) that I can connect the comments and the observations with my memories.
(d) that I can control my thoughts.

Even in my disembodied state, I have agency, inasmuch as I can control my viewpoint and my thoughts. If I were imagining the world without me in it, I would not be imagining the agency, the comments, or the coordination between them. Even if I did not remember, from my time as an embodied being, learning the distinction between self and not-self, it is quite possible for me to recognize that distinction. The perception and the agency are limited. I cannot see some things unless I move my point of view, and that involves the use of agency. Some things (my thoughts and the position of my point of view) can be changed by my will, but most things cannot.

Second, Flew (1987) suggests that there is no characteristic we can give to a disembodied soul that will differentiate it from non-existence, and so there is no way we can differentiate a world with disembodied persons from a world without disembodied persons.

From a third person point of view there may be no characteristic to the disembodied soul, but from the first person point of view the difference between existing and not existing is obvious. Being a ghost such as I have described is very different from not existing at all. The difference between a ghost and nothing is that the ghost has a first person point of view. The ghost knows that it exists, even if no-one else does.

If another ghost has exactly the same contents of visual field and consciousness, how can we individuate the two ghosts, rather than saying there is just one? This can be answered in two ways. First, from the first person point of view, one of them is me, and the other is not. Second, one ghost has a set of memories and attitudes, etc., that the other ghost, coming from a different life, does not have.

Flew (1987) claims that if we cannot give an indication of how we can identify or re-identify a disembodied immaterial soul, we cannot give a meaning to the term, and that identification and reidentification is based on bodily continuity. The question of identifying I take as being epistemological, as asking how we could *tell* the difference (as distinct from what would *make* the difference) between "there is a disembodied soul in this room" and "there is no disembodied soul in this room". I cannot see any reason why something could not be both true and in principle unknowable (Goldbach's conjecture, perhaps, or the completeness and consistency of mathematics) but I will not pursue the point, because in the case of a disembodied soul its existence must be known by the disembodied soul itself. Even if it is impossible for us to know there is a disembodied soul in this room, the disembodied soul would know.

If the identification has to be made by a third party, then it will be on the basis of evidence. All third person judgments of personal identity are made by considering evidence. Usually the evidence is that of the behaviour and appearance of a person's body.

However, I will combine and adapt arguments from Gillett (1986b) and Brooks (1994) to show that it is logically possible for us to identify and reidentify a disembodied person.

Suppose that two of us (embodied persons) are in a room, and find that when we close our eyes, cross our fingers, and put our thumbs in our ears, we get visual images of the room we are in as seen from a third point of view. We see the room as if we were floating near the lamp shade. Also, we find we have a series of thoughts, perhaps something of the style of "Who are these two idiots? Why have they got their fingers crossed? The one with the moustache reminds me of someone I met in Liverpool a couple of years ago. (Brief memory of Liverpool)" The centre of the visual images moves (though we have no sensation of agency) until it is viewing the car park outside the building we are in. We see visual images of someone stealing my car.

Of course, we both check with each other, and find the same images and thoughts came to each. We find that when we open our eyes, uncross our fingers, or pull our thumbs out, the thoughts and images cease. (Subsequently, we find out that the car has been stolen.) Suppose further that we find this phenomenon continues, and that the thoughts reveal a consistent and coherent personality. The phenomenon would be a good reason for us to think we had made contact with a disembodied person. Of course, we are making a deduction that there is a disembodied person from the evidence of the thoughts and images, but out judgment that embodied persons exist is based on the evidence of our senses. It should be noted that the mental events of the disembodied soul are in some way causing qualitatively similar mental events in us. We do not have numerically the same mental events as the disembodied soul.

Such a case would be one in which we identify an immaterial disembodied soul. Furthermore, if this happened on several occasions, with apparently the same personality being contacted on each occasion, we would have reason to believe we were reidentifying the disembodied soul. This is reidentification on evidence, which is also the way we reidentify embodied persons. Thus, it is logically possible to identify and reidentify immaterial souls.

Geach (1969) and Flew (1987) both argue, in roughly that same way, that the concept is incoherent because I am using concepts rooted in person language that is based on our experience of persons who are corporeal beings.

Flew's argument seems to be, in part at least, that "person" means "an embodied human being" and so to talk of disembodied persons is self contradictory, as self contradictory as a the idea of a square circle. But "circle" and 'square" are technical terms in geometry, defined in such a way as to be mutually exclusive, and so defined in order to make formal geometry possible.

Flew claims that our whole vocabulary of person words is and has to be, explained by reference to physical beings, and that native speakers of English know this. He says that we teach person words to children by reference to actual human beings, as though we taught the words by ostensive definition. (Flew 1985)

But there are more ways of learning the meanings of words than by ostensive definition. The meanings of many words are learnt by hearing them used in a variety of contexts, and extracting the meaning from the context. Children learn very few person words and phrases by being taken round to paradigm cases and being told "This is a philosopher. This is a departmental secretary. This is a man who goes down sewers in big rubber boots." They learn person words for themselves by hearing adults apply the terms to living, dead, and imaginary human beings, fairies, teddy bears, cats, invisible and intangible spirits, even more immaterial gods, cartoon characters, animals, Daleks, ghosts, cars and other machines (especially when they don't work, for then they get sworn at) cakes which fail to rise satisfactorily ("As soon as it saw me open the oven the silly thing decided to fall") and even plants.

Children also hear person words applied to themselves in ways that makes it clear that the speaker makes a distinction between the child's mental state (which the word applies to) and the bodily state which expresses the mental state. The difference between feeling angry and looking angry is learnt quite early in life.

From all these examples children then have to extract the meaning of person words, and will conclude that person words are applied to anything, corporeal or incorporeal, which is deemed to be capable of some sort of consciousness.

A possible reply to this is that the child first learns the words in reference to such undeniably embodied persons as elder brothers, teddy bears, and cats, and only later learns to use them metaphorically about ghosts and gods. This reply implies that there is strict sequencing of the language children hear and learn, so that the embodied uses of the words come first. It also begs the question. The uses of person words about gods and ghosts can only be regarded as metaphorical if we assume that gods and ghosts are in some way disqualified from having the words applied literally. But this disqualification cannot be shown by appeal to usage. In short, neither logically nor chronologically are meanings of person words essentially about embodied human beings.

Even if we concede that Flew is right about the *original* meanings of person words, his argument still does not hold. It depends on the assumption that words and concepts cannot be extended beyond the original use. This is to confine the limits of our understanding within the limits of our language, when in fact what we do is to extend our language to fit our new understanding. This principle holds both for our language learning as children, and for the socially agreed uses of language. When I was a small child I thought "material" meant only "woven textile", and "matter" meant "dried discharge from the corners of the eyes of children or cats suffering from severe colds". Subsequently I have learnt more general meanings for both words. In the English speaking world generally, "condenser" originally meant a device for converting vapour to liquid, but later also came to mean an electronic device.

Flew wants us to make our theory of persons fit the use of words, rather than allow us to adapt our use of words to fit our theory of persons.

Anyway, as Ayer (1991) pointed out, the person who becomes a ghost won't care if philosophers won't call him a person.

Memory and Bodily Continuity

It is often claimed that bodily survival is needed to authenticate memory, and so only bodily continuity can authenticate a survivor. However, as Madell (1981) points out, this leads to a circularity. To trace X's psychological continuity, and so to authenticate X's memory of and event, I have to know that I saw X at the event. This assumes I am continuous. To check my own continuity I have to check that my seeing of X and my memory of seeing X are attached to the same body. How cam I check this? If I get someone else to do the checking, can I be sure of the continuity of the checker?

Madell's argument aside, I will offer an argument (from Wei, 1990) for authentication of memory in absence of bodily continuity.

In life some memory is relied on without any check for maintenance of personal identity. There are two reasons for this.

(1) Each experience is a continuum involving some of the past, therefore present thinking involves memory.
(2) Also, major past events are part of the present context of experience. E.g. the memory of flying to America is part of the present context of sitting in Temple University library. The irritation I currently feel includes the memory of the discovery that the unbound journals are arranged alphabetically rather than by subject.

(I wrote the forgoing while in that library.)

I cannot deny my current experience, and so I cannot deny the majority of the memories that render my current experience coherent and possible. Indeed, my ongoing consciousness involves self consciousness which in turn involves a sufficient majority of memories crucial for self identity.

This or that memory can be doubted, but not the majority. Therefore bodily continuity is not necessary for authentication of memories, and so it is not necessary for post-mortem self recognition.

Conclusion

The arguments above have shown, first, that the bodily criterion cannot provide an account of my own identity. Since I stress the importance of the first person point of view, this is a major weakness. Second, that it is logically possible for me to switch bodies, and it is logically possible for me to survive as a disembodied being. This shows that psychological identity is logically distinct from bodily identity. Therefore bodily identity cannot be a sufficient criterion for total identity, and it is not a necessary condition for psychological identity. It is only necessary for total personal identity.

8 Memory and Self Knowledge

A final topic to discuss is that of memory and personal identity. This discussion will lead on naturally to the final conclusion of my book.

Memory has been a central issue in the debate on personal identity since the debate was started by Locke. The position normally labelled the Lockean position (which may not have been the position Locke himself held) is that memory is a constitutive criterion of personal identity.

The circularity objection (attributed variously to Samuel Clark and to Butler) has been recognized as a powerful argument against the Lockean position. Various attempts have been made to meet this objection. Since these attempts have not been very successful, I will only note, briefly, a few of the attempts here.

Perry (1975) offers an analysis of memory that includes M-relation. M-relation is the relation between a past experience and a present representation of that experience when this relation is the characteristic causal process that explains memory in human beings. Ehring (1985) drew attention to the fact that this version is too species-specific, and will not provide a suitable account of memory for non-human beings, and is even less capable of accounting for persistence of memory in cases of metamorphosis from human to (say) Jellian. Oaklander (1984) shows that the M-relation cannot be identified other than by stating that it is the relation that obtains when we really remember, which reintroduces the circularity.

Other attempts to meet the circularity objection use the notion of Q-memory (quasi - memory) which is a faculty that gives knowledge of the past in the same way that memory does, but does not entail that the person who q - remembers is necessarily the same person as the person who experienced the event remembered. Various versions of q-memory have been devised by Shoemaker, Parfit, Noonan, and others. Most of these forms of q-memory have been subjected to damaging criticism. Noonan has shown that Shoemaker's version of q-memory (which also uses M-relation) cannot be used to give a non-circular account of personal identity. Schechtman (1990) shows that q-memory must either (a) presuppose identity, or (b) remove so much content from memory that it is no longer plausible to say that q-memory preserves that which is relevant to personal identity in genuine memory. Oderberg (1993) attacks the logical coherence of the concept of q - memory.

Neither M - relation nor q - memory are satisfactory ways of coping with the circularity objection.

The Argument from Self Recognition

Both Butler and Reid use a second argument against the Lockean position. This is the argument that memory cannot constitute identity, since memory reveals Self identity. When I remember experiences or actions, I recognize the subject/agent of the remembered experiences and actions to be the same subject/agent I am now. This argument is both directly powerful against the Lockean position, and against the possibility of q-memory. It shows, first, that if I can recognize the Self of the past as being the same Self as the present Self, then the Self cannot be either a collection of mental states, since they would all have changed, or a body, since that also would have changed. Second, it shows that memory is marked as "mine" by the presence in it of my Self, and so it would be possible for me to distinguish between my own memories and any q-memories I might have acquired.

Although Taber (1990) suggests that this interpretation of Butler and Reid has been forgotten, it is worth noting that it is one of the arguments offered for the substantial Self in Ewing (1951), and is used by Lewis in "The Elusive Self" chapter of *The Elusive Mind* (Lewis 1969).

I will begin from the version of the argument that Taber attributes to the Mimamsa school, and particularly to Sabarasvamin and Kumarilbhatta. The Mimamsa version, Taber says, was used as an argument for the existence of the Self, as it was claimed "that a substantial self is made evident to us by the very notion 'I' " as it occurs in memory." (Taber 1990)

According to Taber, some Buddhists argued that a person is not a continuously existing substance, but a series of "person stages", each of which is a collection of states and/or events. Each stage lasts only for an instant, but causes a new stage to follow it. Each state was causally determined by the preceding state, and therefore there is an affinity between causally related thoughts. This affinity accounts for the feeling of personal identity. However, the unity of "I" is a unity of the stream of states only. There is no permanent entity, no substantial or persistent mind.

In order to account for memory it was suggested that each stage causes "memory traces" in the next stage. The momentary Self *b* inherits the memories of Self *a* that caused it because it inherits the entire nature of *a*. Eventually a stage can have a "memory experience" similar to the original experience. No continuous Self is needed to account for memory.

(I have great difficulty accepting this theory. A "memory trace" cannot be the whole, full memory. If there is only a series of conscious Selves, and each memory is transferred to the following Self, all my memories would be part of my consciousness and so I would be conscious of all my memories at once. My present experience would include the experience of remembering everything. But this is not the case. Indeed, sometimes not only are memories not present, they are not available. I forget things and cannot recall them when I try, and then later remember them.

According to the memory trace theory, all my memory traces must present in my mind now, although I only become aware of them when they unfold into full memory experiences. This means that there must be something *unconscious* that is passed on. Now the idea of a transient Self comes from examining conscious states alone. If we accept that memory traces must be unconscious, then we are accepting that there is an unconscious part of the mind. There is no reason for supposing that this unconscious part is transient, and the fact of memory suggests that the unconscious part is in fact permanent. But this renders the explanation of memory in terms of memory traces redundant.)

The argument from Self recognition was used to reply to the above mentioned Buddhist claim. Our present experience is that of experience being had and unified by a subject, and of acts performed by an agent. Likewise, our memories are those of experience had and unified by a subject, and acts performed by and agent. To quote Taber:

> But Vatsyayana goes on to say that the Buddhist is also wrong in thinking that the object of memory is merely the thing that was previously experienced. Memories of an absent object in fact apprehend the object *as having been experienced in an act of knowledge by a knowing subject*. Thus, typically, we say something like, "I knew that thing," or "that thing was known to me". (Taber 1990, p. 9)

There is an impression, an impression that seems like tacit knowledge, that the remembered subject/agent is the same as the subject/agent I am now.

It is recognized as "me again". A thing is seen on one day. The notion "*I* saw this" arises on a later day. "I" cannot refer to a person stage, because the current person stage "I" would be different from the person stage in the memory, whereas in fact I recognize it as being the same. It seems, then, that "I" refers to some continuous entity, an inner Self. This is the conclusion Taber attributes the Mimamsa school.

While "I" must refer to a continuous entity, could that entity be something other than a continuous Self, such as a body, or a series of Selves? I have already shown that the Self cannot be a series of Selves. Here I will show that the subject I remember cannot be the body or a collection of mental states.

The "I" I remember cannot be a body. A body could not be quite identical. The body I remember having when I was twelve is rather different from the one I have now. I remember what it felt like, and it did not feel like the one I have now. What I recognize in my memories is not 'that was the body from which this one originated" but 'that was me embodied in that body". It is not the body I recognize as me.

The same is true of mental states. The mental states I had when I skied in the forest in Sweden are all gone. I have a very different set now, and yet the subject I find in the memory of skiing in Sweden is the same subject as the one that remembers it.

However, the capacity for consciousness and the capacity for agency I remember are the same as the capacities I have now. Therefore there is something that I recognize as being at least the *same sort of thing* in spite of it having the different mental states. The *same sort of thing* cannot be the mental states. It can only be the subject that has the mental states. This seems to indicate that there is something other than a collection of mental states involved in being a Self. Thus far, the argument from self-recognition suggests at least that the subject is not identical with either the body or a collection of mental states.

I recognize the subject of experience in memories as being the same sort of thing as the subject of experience I am now, but I recognize more than that. When I remember something I am certain that I remember *me* and not just *some subject of experience or another* undergoing that experience. Thus, as Taber points out, the argument is an appeal to an intuition.

I shall try to explain the source of the intuition, by showing how it arises. I will also to argue that the intuition is correct, in that the Self remembered can only be the current Self.

False memories, that is, apparent memories of things that never happened, need not detain us here. If I have the delusion that I starred in several James Bond films, I will automatically imagine myself into the centre of the false memories as I create them. The issue is not whether I can be mistaken about whether the events happened, but whether I can be mistaken about which subject experienced them.

There seem to be two ways in which I recognize that p1 at t1 and p2 at t2 are in fact the same individual. The first, which I will call recognition by complete similarity, is that is that p1 and p2 have all the same characteristics. The second, which I will call recognition by continuous awareness, is that I have observed p continuously from t1 to t2 without noticing any discontinuity. Applying these two types of recognition to Self recognition, I find there are at least four possibilities that can explain the intuition.

(1) I see an immediate congruence between the Self remembered and the Self I am now, and so assume they are the same because they are the same sort of thing. This is recognition by complete similarity.

However, in exactly the same way, I might assume the person before me now is the same person as the person I remember seeing yesterday, and yet this person may be the twin brother of the person I saw yesterday. The Self I remember may be a twin of the Self I am now.

Thus, recognition by complete similarity may be mistaken, and yet the recognition is immediate and unquestioned. There is no sense of a deduction being made, and no sense of checking or noting any similarities. Even when we seriously consider the possibility of the Self being different, we cannot shake off the certainty that in our own case the Self in memory is identical with the Self I am now. We do not investigate the memory to see if it could be from a different Self.

Furthermore, I do not ever change my mind after identifying myself as the subject. I never deny that a memory has me in it. I never say 'that was not me in that memory." (Taber attributes this point to Kumarila.) I am much more likely to consider that I have misremembered an event, or made up a false memory, than decide that I am not the person at the centre of the memory.

Now this may be simply because I have, in fact, never been wrong, not because I cannot be mistaken, but the force of the certainty is such that, as Reid noted "no philosophy can weaken it, without first producing some degree of insanity." (Reid 1975, p. 107) The idea that the recognition is based only on the similarity of the Self remembered with the current Self does not seem adequate to explain this certainty, and so should not be accepted unless no better explanation can be found.

(2) The general characteristics of the Self (e.g. the capacity for consciousness and the capacity for agency) are common to all Selves. However, there may be some other characteristic of my Self which is distinctive to my Self alone, and which *cannot* be shared by any other Self. It is this distinctive characteristic I somehow recognize, even though I cannot discern any phenomenal content to this characteristic. There may be some tacit knowledge of such a characteristic which has no phenomenal content, somewhat similar to the knowledge of body position. (Chisholm seems to suggest this in *Person and Object* (1976) where he writes of a person being aware of that person's individual essence.) Nonetheless, it seems possible to deny the existence of such an essence or such a characteristic unless some evidence can be presented for its existence. The only evidence is the fact that we believe we recognize ourselves, but that is the very belief we need evidence to justify.

Furthermore, again, there is no sense of deduction, no sense of thinking 'that is like me, so it must be me". The recognition is immediate. Of course, when I see my wife walk into the living room, my recognition of her is also immediate, without any sense of checking. I expect her to be in the living room from time to time. I do not expect her to be in the University library, so if I saw her there, I would be inclined to check that I had not misidentified someone similar in appearance. Naturally, I expect to find myself at the centre of the memories that are immediately accessible to me (I always have done) so it is plausible that I recognize myself instantly.

(3) There are two acts of recognition. I recognize the remembered Self as being the same sort of thing as the current Self, and I recognize the mind it is associated with as being continuous with the mind I have now. I therefore assume that it is the same Self.

The mind I have now is the result of a continuous period of development, during which a network of associations, background knowledge, emotional content, was built up, and memories are part of that network.

Memory is detailed, rich in emotional content, and connected with other memories. As the memory arises I recognize that it has a place in the same network as that in which my current state is placed.

I have shown that the Self is aware of its own continuity, and that it cannot divorce itself from a continuous stream of consciousness. I have shown that a single stream of consciousness will have a single subject for as long as it continues, so the change can only occur when the Self has at some state stopped acting on or illuminating its original mind. Now even in pure consciousness the Self is still controlling, and so associated with the mind. I suspect that during sleep the Self continues to illuminate the contents of the mind, although does not greatly attend to them. Under these circumstances too, the Self would notice a discontinuity if it lost contact with the mind. The Self has been constantly monitoring the mind, and so knows that it has not acquired a new mind. The Self also knows that it has existed continuously. Thus I have good reason for believing that the Self in the memories of this mind is the same Self as the Self I am now.

There are two problems with this suggestion. The first is, yet again, that the recognition is immediate. There is no sense of deduction or checking being made, even though the process is more complex than in the previous cases.

The second is the question of whether, if I had an apparent memory that had no associations, no connections with anything else, I would recognize it as being me from anything other than the fact that it is "remembered" from the first person point of view.

This seems to be the case for some people who claim to have memories from a previous incarnation. They recognize the memories as memories of their own previous life, that is, they do not doubt that they were the subjects of the experiences the remember, even though the personality and mind in the memory is different from the mind they have now. Those who do not take these alleged memories seriously will say that this is only to be expected when the memories are false memories created by the imagination. Since I do take at least some seriously, it presents a difficulty for the claim that what is being recognized is the mind that the Self is attached to.

A possible escape from this difficulty might be that the presence of the memories from the previous life shows that some of the mind of the previous life has survived as well. I am ignoring the possibility that memory is an act of the Self in which it illuminates past mental states, because discussion of this idea would take me too far afield.

(4) I have shown that the Self is aware of its own existence as well as its own continuity. From one moment to the next the Self is aware that it exists from the "just past" to the "just future" of the specious present, and that this overlapping awareness is unbroken. The Self has, in fact, been constantly observing itself from the time remembered until now. The self recognition is not recognition by matching characteristics of the item in memory with the item now present, but recognition by continuous awareness.

An analogous case of this sort of recognition is that of a continuously experienced object. If I take a coin, and carry it around in my hand all day, I will, for most of the day, not concentrate on the coin. But the sensation of the coin in my hand will be continuous, even if unattended, throughout the day. When, at the end of the day, I remember the coin I picked up in the morning, I will immediately recognize it. I will know it as the coin I am carrying. I will recognize it not because it looks like the coin I picked up in the morning, but because it has been sensed continuously. Even though I may have no memory of the events around lunch time, I know that the coin was in my hand because I know there was no break in sensing it. If I do have a memory of the time just after lunch time, and remember the feel of the coin, I know it was the same coin as the coin I hold now.

Similarly, the Self is sensed continuously, and so the Self in memory is known to be the same one as is now remembering. The experience of the Self is a continuous experience.

There is an important difference between the recognition of the coin and self recognition. Perhaps a cunning pickpocket could sneak the coin from my hand and replace it with a copy in such a way that I did not notice any change in sensation. But my Self could not be replaced by a copy, and so I could not be mistaken about whether the Self in a memory was the same Self as the current Self. I recognize a memory as being one of mine because my current Self is connected with the Self in the memory. It is the Self that authenticates the memory, and places it within the stream of my life. If an attempt were made to give me a q-memory from someone else, that memory would include memory of a different Self, one which had not been constantly sensed, and so the memory would be recognized as one which came from another person.

An End to Q-memory?

The third and fourth possibilities show how it could be impossible to misidentify the Self in memory with the current Self. If we accept the claim that what we remember is the same Self, and that we cannot be mistaken, then all the arguments about q-memory are irrelevant, for it would be immediately obvious to me that a memory was a q-memory if I could not recognize the Self in that memory as being myself. When Parfit attempts to give Jane one of Paul's memories of Venice, Jane would know that the Self in the Paul-memory was not her own. Thus the argument from Self recognition shows that accounts of personal identity built on q-memory are likely to fail.

Advocates of q-memory have, of course, attempted to defuse the argument, either by denying that the subject in memory is recognized or by denying that there is a subject in memories.

Noonan (1989) describes a version q-memory, which he refers to as q-memory (G), as memory "from the inside", although he does not specify what aspects of "insideness" are relevant. Q-memory (G) is a capacity for direct, non-inferential knowledge of the past not restricted to what person has experienced himself. E.g., of past of parents, or of all people alive when he was born.

Noonan imagines a world in which people spontaneously report events of the past lives of their parents by means of q-memory (G), and claims that in such a world the q-memories (G) would not be reported in first person terms as "I remember skiing down the Matterhorn and seeing an elephant on the ski lift." If I were one of those people I could have an apparent memory "from the inside" of seeing an elephant on a ski-lift without thinking that apparent memory was of "*me* seeing an elephant on a ski-lift", and a memory of skiing down the Matterhorn that I did not believe was of "*me* skiing down the Matterhorn".

To make this seem more possible, Noonan claims (without any justification I can find)

> The reason why our memories of experiences and actions are spontaneously first-personal is that this is how we were brought up, trained, to report them by our elders, who themselves spontaneously reported their memories of their own experiences and actions in the same way. (Noonan 1989, p. 183)

But this leaves unanswered the question of why our elders reported memories in the first personal way. The answer that they learned this from their ancestors leads to an obvious regress to the prelinguistic protoplasmal primordial atomic globule that Pooh-Bah and the rest of us are descended from. The most reasonable alternative reply is that they reported in this way because the memories are accompanied by self recognition, that is, accompanied by the knowledge of the fact that it was me that saw and skied.

If Noonan's G-rememberers can accurately report the content of their q-memories (G) without making them first personal it must be because q-memories (G) are not accompanied by the knowledge that the subject in the memory is the same as the subject G-remembering. But in such a case q-memories (G) would be clearly distinguishable from real memories. The "from the inside" of real memories includes self-recognition.

Parfit denies that in memory a person is aware of being "a persisting subject of experiences, a separately existing entity that is not his brain and body?" and particularly that he is not aware of being a Cartesian Ego. (Parfit 1991, p. 223)

Now the mention of a Cartesian Ego is a red herring. The argument from self-recognition does not require me to be aware of the subject being a Cartesian Ego, or of it being a separately existing entity that is not my brain or body. I may deduce that is an entity logically distinct from brain, body, or mind, but the argument does not require me to be immediately aware of this.

Is Parfit denying that he is aware of being a subject? If he denies he is aware of being a subject, this is inconsistent with his claim that "I am not a series of experiences, but the person who has these experiences." (Parfit 1991, p. 223) Is he denying that he finds a subject/agent at the centre of his memories? If so, either his memories are very different from mine in quality, or he has not paid sufficient attention to the content.

Memory must have a subject/agent at the centre of the memory to seem like memory. If I remember thinking about Q-memory, I remember not only the thoughts but also the process of thinking, and this includes memory of the sustained mental causation. Similarly, if I remember skiing, I remember not only the sensation of the skis on my feet, but also the agency of the activity. As Filice has argued, causation is inalienable from the sense of self. Thus, all memories of doing something, of being an agent, must contain the memory of an agent Self. Selfless-memories have no subject/agent at the centre and so such memories cannot be memories of actions. They can only be memories of perceptions.

However, for perceptions to seem like a memory they must be unified. Unification requires a subject, and the memory of the subject must be included in the content of the memory.

Suppose a skier has recorders attached to his optic nerves and to the sensory nerves of his body. He skis down the Matterhorn, and the sensations coming through the nerves are recorded. The recordings are then played back into my nerves, so that I have all the sensations that the skier had, without any of the feelings of agency. Self-less memories would be like this.

If the first time I have a Self-less memory is like this, then it would seem to be a strange sort of experience, but it would not seem like real memory. Although the various experiences have been recorded, they will not been unified into a single stream of consciousness until I receive them. When the experiences are played into my nerves, they would give me the feeling that the experience was happening to me *now* as I unified them into a single stream of consciousness.

This is not like memory. Memory requires that the experiences are unified before I remember them, and unification requires a subject. If the experiences had been unified before being played into my nerves, the subject of experience would be part of the memory.

The main point of Parfit's denial seems to be his denial that he is aware of being a *persisting* subject. In Parfit 1971 he states "it cannot be a part of what I seem to remember about this experience that I ... am the person who had this experience. That I am is something I automatically assume." Here he refers to arguments to that effect by Palma. The essence of Palma's (1964) argument is that the content of memory is about the past. The identification of the present person with the past person is an identification made in the present, so the identity cannot be part of the *content* of the memory. I quite agree with Palma on this. I further agree with him when he says that my inclination to call one of the persons in a remembered scene "myself" cannot be accounted for on the basis of what is given in a memory image. The argument from self recognition does not require that knowledge "I now am the person in the memory" to be part of the content of the memory. The argument only requires that the knowledge *accompany* the memory.

On p. 224 of *Reasons and Persons* Parfit claims that the content of experience gives us no more than the continuity of our stream of consciousness, and buttresses this with reference to the suggestion that there may be a series of subjects. However, I have already shown that there cannot be a series of subjects. I cannot say what Parfit is or is not aware of, but I believe that I am aware of the continuity of my own existence. If we regard the phenomenal content of the stream of consciousness as thoughts and sense perceptions, there is indeed no item that can be separated out as "awareness of persistence". Nonetheless, we do normally regard ourselves as continuant beings. We do not merely believe in our own persistence as an intellectual fact, but also take it for granted in the conduct of our lives. The vast majority of people never doubt their own persistence. These facts suggest that the "awareness of persistence" forms part of the unchanging background awareness of the Self.

My theory provides an explanation for the immediate self-recognition. Parfit has no explanation for the "automatic assumption" that the Self I remember is the same as the Self I am now.

Shoemaker admits that one's Self is in the content of the memory, but claims that it "enters, not as the subject of the past action or experience (although in fact it will be that) but as the subject of the present remembering." (Shoemaker 1984, p. 105)

Now Shoemaker may claim that, just as a false memory can be fabricated around the subject of experience, so a real memory can have the current subject inserted into it. But a false memory is fabricated by unifying various items around the subject. A real memory comes as items already unified around a subject. In order for the memory to be "as experienced by a subject" it has to be "as unified by a subject at the time of experiencing" and so it must include a subject. When I remember taking my test for third Dan, I remember visual images of the *dojo*, the sound and feel of my feet on the mats, the image of Takahashi making a *yokomen-uchi* attack, the sense of causation, of agency, appropriate to the *shiho-nage* defence, the feel of his wrist, the kinesthetic sensations of the activity. I am not having those sensations or exercising that agency at the time of remembering, nor am I remembering them as independent items and then unifying them at the time of remembering. I remember them as a unified whole. They have already been unified by a subject/agent. This is clearly memory of a Self as subject/agent at the centre of the memories.

What Shoemaker suggests, then, is that memory of the subject who experienced the event has been removed from the content of the memory, and replaced by the present subject. This seems both an unnecessary and an implausible revision.

It seems plausible, then, that the automatic, immediate Self recognition that occurs when we remember something is not mistaken.

Conclusion

It is time to draw together the threads of my argument. In my defence of the Butler-Reid position, I have argued that there is a Self, distinct from mind, and that the Self is consciousness and agency. It is the Self that makes mental states conscious, and the Self that performs conscious acts. The Self is a simple item, and criteria for its identity cannot be given. For the Self, survival, that is, continuous existence, is identity through time. This concept of the Self proves to be a very powerful explanatory concept, accounting for the unity of consciousness. The Self illuminates and, by illuminating, unifies the stream of consciousness. The Self continues to exist and be conscious throughout life. I have suggested that we have an awareness of the Self underlying our normal experience, and that we have knowledge of the continuity of the Self.

In examining the question of what is necessary for me to survive, I have shown that my desires for survival are desires, first and foremost, for the continued existence of my Self. If the person I am is to survive, continuity of my Self is a necessary condition. The survival of the Self is necessary for survival of the person.

I have also shown that, from the first person point of view, the arguments drawn from the fission and fusion arguments can be ignored, since the logical possibility of fission has not been established, and we have good reason to deny the possibility. (Also, even if we accept the possibility of fission, we are not required to accept that this affects the identity of the Self.)

Now to apply these results to the question of personal identity. There are three popular types of theory about personal identity. They are the Physical Continuity theories, the Psychological Continuity theories, and the Simple view.

The Physical Continuity theories hold that personal identity consists in the continued existence of a particular body. Of course, allowance is made for the fact that the body changes slowly over time. A person survives for as long as that person's body continues to exist. However, I have shown that from the first person point of view continuity of the body is not a necessary condition for continuity of the Self, and so not a necessary condition for the survival of the Self. It is logically possible for the Self (accompanied by the mind) to move from one body to another, and even to survive without a body at all. (Of course, it may be *nomologically* impossible for the Self and mind to exist or survive without permanent connection with a specific body.) Thus, survival of the body is not sufficient for survival of the person. That which is not sufficient for survival of the person cannot be sufficient for identity of the person.

The Psychological Continuity theories hold that personal identity consists in the continued existence of a particular mind. Again, allowance is made for the fact that minds change. According to the Psychological Continuity theories, connections of intention, memory, personality, etc. constitute survival of the mind. However, the survival of the mind is not sufficient for survival of the person. I have shown that those psychological connections can all be lost without the Self ceasing to exist. I have further shown, in the rejection of Parfit's relation R, Brennan's S - relation, and the discussion of replicas, that theories of survival of the mind are inadequate for continuity of the Self. My views on memory and Self recognition have also added to the doubts about whether the psychological criterion can be non-circular by suggesting that the attempts to use the notion of q - memory are bound to fail.

Thus, neither the Physical Continuity theories nor the Psychological Continuity theories provide a satisfactory account of personal identity. However, the Simple view, that a person is an entity (Self, or soul) distinct from mind or body which is a simple continuant, and that the diachronic identity of that entity is sufficient for personal identity, also seems unsatisfactory, for it restricts the notion of a person to being that Self or soul. Now when we think about the persons we meet, and the persons (human and non-human) we fantasize about, we usually regard them as having more to them than a bare locus of consciousness and agency. We expect persons to have personality, ideas, beliefs, desires, and intentions. We usually recognize that these can change, and so we are likely to say things like "He seems like a completely different person."

Thus I claim that although the survival of the Self is a necessary condition, it is not a sufficient condition for *personal* identity. For a person P1 at time t1 to be identical with a person P2 at time t2 entails that the Self of P1 has survived from t1 to t2 and is the Self of P2, but there must be a certain degree of continuity of mind and/or body as well. However, I shall not try to formalize how much or what sort of continuity is required.

What Butler Saw

According to Butler, the idea of personal identity arises from comparing the "consciousness of one's self, or one's own existence" (Butler 1964, p. 167) at one time with the consciousness of oneself at another time. He compares the case with that of gaining the concept of equality from encountering equal numbers, or gaining the concept of similarity from encountering similar objects. Butler does not say that he *infers* identity from the similarity of the remembered Self with the present Self. He does not deduce from their similarity that they are the same Self. In order to infer identity from similarity one must have the concept of identity to begin with. He sees directly that they are the same Self, and so the concept of personal identity arises in him.

Thus, each of us knows his own identity. Each person recognizes the continuity of his Self, and knows that personal identity consists in the survival of the Self associated with the changing body and mind.

References

Anderson, Susan Leigh, (1978) "The Substantive Centre Theory Versus the Bundle Theory" *Monist*, Vol. 61, No. 1, January

Ayer, A. J., (1991) *The Central Questions of Philosophy* London, Penguin Books

Baillie, J. (1990) "Identity, Survival, and Sortal Concepts" *The Philosophical Quarterly*, Vol. 40, No. 159, April

Beck, Simon, (1991) "Finding ourselves: Personal identity and the limits of possible - world arguments." *South African Journal of Philosophy,* Vol. 10, No. 1

Block, R. A. (1979) "Time and Consciousness" in *Aspects of Consciousness* (Vol. 1) (Ed. Geoffrey Underwood and Robin Stevens) London and New York, Academic Press

Bolton, R. A. N. (1992) *Personal Identity: A Neoplatonic Theory of the Principle of Personality.* Ph. D. Thesis, University of Exeter

Borowski, E.J., (1978) "Puzzle Cases: The Wrong Approach to Personal Identity" *Metaphilosophy*, Vol. 9, Nos. 3 and 4, July/October

Bradley, F.H. (1928) *The Principals of Logic* London, Oxford University Press. (Second Edition, 1922 Edition, corrected impression)

Brennan, A. (1988) *Conditions of Identity.* Oxford, Clarendon Press

Broad, C. D. (1925) *The Mind and Its Place in Nature.* London, Routledge and Kegan Paul

Brooks, D. (1985) "Hume's Bundle Theory of the Mind" *South African Journal of Philosophy*, Vol. 4, No. 3, August

Brooks, D.H.M. (1994) *The Unity of the Mind.* Basingstoke, Macmillan

Brueckner, Anthony, (1993) "Parfit on What Matters in Survival" *Philosophical Studies*, Vol. 70, No. 1, April

Butler, Joseph, (1964) "On Personal Identity" in *Body, Mind, and Death.* (Ed. Antony Flew) New York, The Macmillan Company

Campbell, C. A. (1951) "Is 'Freewill' a Pseudo-Problem?" *Mind,* Vol. 60, No. 240, October

Carruthers, Peter, (1986) *Introducing Persons.* London and Sydney, Croom Helm

Cherry, Christopher, (1984) "Can My Survival be Subrogated?" *Philosophy* Vol. 59, No. 230, October

Chisholm, Roderick, (1976) *Person and Object.* London, George, Allen, and Unwin

Clark, Stephen, R.L. (1991) "How Many Selves Make Me?" in *Human Beings* (Ed. David Cockburn) Cambridge, Cambridge University Press

Comans, Michael, (1990) "The Self in Deep Sleep According to Advaita and Visistadvaita" *Journal of Indian Philosophy*, Vol. 18, No. 1, March

Dainton, Barry F. (1989) *The Nature and Identity of the Self.* D. Phil. thesis, Oxford University

Dainton, Barry F. (1992) "Time and Division", *Ratio,* (New Series) Vol. 5, No. 2, December

Dement, William C. (1974) *Some Must Watch While Some Must Sleep.* San Francisco, W.H. Freeman and Co.

Dennett, Daniel, (1976) "Are Dreams Experiences?" *The Philosophical Review,* Vol. 5, No. 2, April

Dennett, Daniel, (1992) *Consciousness Explained.* London, Allen Lane

Descartes, Rene (1991) *The Philosophical Writings of Descartes,* Vol. III - The Correspondence. (Tr. J. Cottingham, R. Stoothoff, D. Murdoch, A. Kenny) Cambridge, Cambridge University Press

Eco, Umberto, (1984) *The Name of the Rose.* (Tr. William Weaver) London, Picador

Ehman, Robert R. (1974) "Temporal Self-Identity" *Southern Journal of Philosophy,* Vol. 12, No. 3, Fall

Ehring, Douglas, (1985) "Personal identity and the Causal Theory of Memory" *The Modern Schoolman,* Vol. 63, No. 1 November

Ehring, Douglas, (1987 a) "Survival and Trivial Facts" *Analysis,* Vol. 47, No. 1, November

Ehring, Douglas. (1987 b) "Personal Identity and Time Travel" *Philosophical Studies,* Vol. 52, No. 3, January

Elliot, Robert. (1991) "Personal Identity and the Causal Continuity Requirement" *The Philosophical Quarterly,* Vol. 41 No. 162, January

Empson, Jacob, (1989) *Sleep and Dreaming.* London, Faber and Faber

Evans, C. O. (1970) *The Subject of Consciousness.* London, George, Allen and Unwin

Ewing, A.C. (1951) *The Fundamental Questions of Philosophy.* Routledge and Kegan Paul, London and Henley

Filice, Carlo, (1986) "Sustained Causation and the Substantial Theory of the Self." *International Philosophical Quarterly,* Vol. 26, No. 2, June

Flew., Antony, (1985) "Personal identity and the Imagination" *Philosophy,* Vol. 60, No. 231, January

Flew., Antony, (1992) "James Giles on Personal Identity", *Philosophy,* Vol. 67, No. 261, July

Flew, Antony, (1976) *The Presumption of Atheism.* London, Elek/Pemberton

Flew, Antony, (1987) *The Logic of Mortality, London,* Basil Blackwell

Forman, R. K. C. (1986) "Pure Consciousness Events and Mysticism", *Sophia*, Vol. 25, No. 1 April

Forman, P.K.C., (Ed.) (1990) *The Problem of Pure Consciousness.* New York, Oxford University Press

Forman, R. K. C. (1991) "Mystical Consciousness" *Sophia*, Vol. 30, Nos. 2 &3, 1991

Foster, John, (1991) *The Immaterial Self: a defence of the Cartesian dualist conception of the mind,* London and New York, Routledge

Foulkes, D. (1962) "Dream Reports from Different Stages of Sleep." *Journal of Abnormal and Social Psychology,* Vol. 65, pp 14 - 25

Garrett, Brian, (1988) "Identity and Extrinsicness" *Mind*, Vol. 97, No. 385, January

Garrett, Brian, (1990) "Personal Identity and Extrinsicness" *Philosophical Studies,* Vol. 59, No. 2, January

Garrett, Brian, (1992) "Harold Noonan, *Personal Identity*" (Review article) *Nous,* Vol. 26 No. 1, March

Geach, P. T. (1969) "Immortality" in *God and the Soul.* London, Routledge Kegan Paul

Giles, James, (1991) "Bodily Theory and Theory of the Body" *Philosophy* Vol. 66, No. 257, July

Giles, James, (1994) "A Reply to Antony Flew." *Philosophy*, Vol. 69, No. 257, January

Gillett, Grant, (1986) "Brain Bisection and Personal Identity." *Mind* Vol. 95, No. 378, April

Gillett, Grant, (1986b) "Disembodied Persons" *Philosophy,* Vol. 61, No. 237, July

Green, Michael B, and Wikler, Daniel, (1980) "Brain Death and Personal Identity" *Philosophy and Public Affairs,* Vol. 9 No. 2, Winter 1980

Hannay, Alastair (1987) "The Claims of Consciousness: A Critical Survey." *Inquiry,* Vol. 30 No. 4, December

Hazlitt, William, (1969) *An Essay on the Principles of Human Action* (Facsimile edition, Ed. John R. Nabholz) Gainesville, Scholars' Facsimiles and Reprints

Hearne, Keith, (1990) *The Dream Machine.* Wellingborough, The Aquarian Press

Hirsch, Eli,(1982) *The Concept of Identity* Oxford, Clarendon Press

James, W. (1891) *The Principles of Psychology,* Vol. 1. London, Macmillan and Co. Ltd.

Jersild, P. C. (1982) *En Levande Själ* Stockholm, Bonniers Förlag

Johnston, Mark, (1992) "Reasons and Reductionism" *The Philosophical Review,* Vol. 101, No. 3, July

Kant, Immanuel, (1929) *Critique of Pure Reason,* (Tr. Norman Kemp Smith) London, Macmillan and Co. Ltd.

Kinsbourne, M. (1980) "Brain-Based Limitations on Mind" in *Body and Mind* (Ed. Reiber) London and New York, Academic Press

Knox, John (1969) "Can the Self Survive the Death of its Mind?" *Religious Studies,* Vol. 5, No. 1, October

Knox, John (1970) "Reply to Professor Woodhouse" *Religious Studies,* Vol. 6 No. 3, September

Kolak, Daniel and Martin, Raymond, (1987) "Personal Identity and Causality: Becoming Unglued" *American Philosophical Quarterly,* Vol. 24, No. 4, October

Korsgaard, Christine M. (1989) "Personal Identity and the Unity of Agency: A Kantian Response to Parfit" *Philosophy and Public Affairs,* Vol. 18, No. 2, Spring

Kupperman, J. (1984) "Investigations of the Self." *Philosophy East and West,* Vol. 34, No. 1, January

Lewis, D. (1983) *Philosophical Papers* Vol. 1 Oxford, Oxford University Press

Lewis, H.D.(1969) *The Elusive Mind* London, George Allen and Unwin.

Lowe, E.J., (1991) "Substance and Selfhood", *Philosophy,* Vol. 66, No. 255, January

McCloskey, M. (1986) "Review of *Reasons and Persons*" *Australasian Journal of Philosophy,* Vol. 64, No. 3, September

McGinn, Colin, (1982) *The Character of Mind* Oxford, Oxford University Press

McGinn, Colin, (1993) "Consciousness and Cosmology: Hyperdualism Ventilated." in Davies, M., and Humphreys, G. W., *Consciousness: Psychological and Philosophical Essays.* Oxford, Basil Blackwell

McKay, D.M. and McKay, V. (1982) "Explicit dialogue between left and right half-systems of split brains" *Nature,* Vol. 295,pp 690 - 691, February

MacKay, Donald, (1987) "Divided Brains – Divided Minds?" *Mindwaves,* Eds. C. Blakemore and S. Greenfield, Oxford, Basil Blackwell

Mackenzie, Nollaig, (1982?) "Can I Cease to be a Person" *Dialogue (Canadian Philosophical review)* Vol. 21, No. 2

MacKenzie, P.T. (1983) "Personal Identity and the Imagination", *Philosophy,* Vol. 58, No. 224, April

Madell, Geoffrey, (1981) *The Identity of the Self,* Edinburgh, Edinburgh University Press.

Madell,Geoffrey, (1985) "Derek Parfit and Greta Garbo" *Analysis,* Vol. 45, No. 2, March

Madell, Geoffrey, (1991) "Personal identity and the Idea of a Human Being." in *Human Beings* (Ed. David Cockburn) Royal Institute of Philosophy Supplement Vol. 29., Cambridge, Cambridge University Press

Martin, Raymond, (1987) "Memory, Connecting, and What Matters in Survival" *Australasian Journal of Philosophy,* Vol. 65, No. 1, March

Martin, Raymond, (1988) "Identity's Crisis" *Philosophical Studies* Vol. 53, No. 2, March

Martin, Raymond, (1992) "Self - Interest and Survival" *American Philosophical Quarterly* Vol. 29, No. 4, October

Martin, Raymond, (1993) "Having the Experience: the Next Best Thing to Being There" *Philosophical Studies* Vol. 70, No. 3, June

Matheson, Carl, (1990) "Consciousness and Synchronic Identity", *Dialogue* Vol. 29, (pp. 523 - 530)

Matthews, E. (1990) "Review of Noonan's *Personal Identity*" *Philosophical Books,* Vol. 31, No. 4, October

Mills, Eugene, (1993) "Dividing without Reducing: Bodily Fission and Personal Identity." *Mind.* Vol. 102, No. 405, January

Moody, Ernest A. (1967) "William of Ockham" in *The Encyclopaedia of Philosophy.* Vol. 8 (Ed. Paul Edwards) New York, Macmillan and The Free Press.

Morick, Harold, (1970) "Introductory Essay - The Privacy of Psychological Phenomena" in *Introduction to the Philosophy of Mind,* (Ed. Harold Morick) Glenview, Scott, Foresman and Co.

Nielsen, Kai, (1987) "God, Disembodied Existence, And Incoherence" *Sophia,* Vol. 2, No. 3, October

Noble, W.G. and Lundie, R.E. (1974) "Temporal discrimination of short intervals of dreamless sleep." *Perceptual and Motor Skills,* Vol. 38, April, (pp. 445 - 446)

Noonan, H. (1989) *Personal Identity,* London, Routledge

Oaklander, L. Nathan, (1984) "Perry, Personal Identity, and the 'characteristic" way." *Metaphilosophy,* Vol. 15 No., 1, January

Oaklander, L. Nathan, (1987) "Parfit, Circularity, and the Unity of Consciousness" *Mind,* Vol. 96 No. 384 October

Oderberg, David S. (1993) *The Metaphysics of Identity Over Time,* Basingstoke, Macmillan

O'Shaughnessy, Brian (1986) "Consciousness" *Midwest Studies in Philosophy,* Vol. 10 Minneapolis, University of Minnesota Press

Paine, Thomas. "The Age of Reason" in *The Theological Works of Thomas Paine*, London, J. Watson, 1842

Palma, A. B. (1964) "Memory and Personal Identity." *Australasian Journal of Philosophy,* Vol. 42, No. 57

Parfit, D. (1971) "Personal Identity" *Philosophical Review,* Vol. 80, No. 1 Jan

Parfit, Derek, (1991) *Reasons and Persons,* Oxford, Clarendon Press,

Parfit, Derek, (1993) "The Indeterminacy of Identity: a Reply to Brueckner," *Philosophical Studies,* Vol. 70, No. 1, April

Pendleton, Gene, (1988) "Forman and Mystical Consciousness" *Sophia,* Vol. 27, No. 2 July

Penelhum, Terence, (1970) *Survival and Disembodied Existence,* Routledge and Kegan Paul, London

Perry, J. (1972) "Can the self divide?", *Journal of Philosophy* , Vol. 69. No. 16, September

Perry, J. (1975) "The Problem of Personal Identity" in *Personal Identity* (Ed. Perry, J.) Berkeley and Los Angeles: University of California Press

Perry, J. (1976) "The Importance of being Identical" in *The Identities of Persons,* (Ed. Rorty, A. O.) Berkeley: University of California Press

Plato, (1985) *The Symposium,* (Tr. Walter Hamilton) Harmondsworth, Penguin Classics

Popper, K, and Eccles, J. C. (1983) *The Self and its Brain.* London, Routledge and Kegan Paul.

Price, H. H. (1972) "Two Conceptions of the Next World" in *Essays in the Philosophy of Religion,* Oxford, Clarendon Press

Prigge, Norman, and Kessler, Gary E., (1990) "Is Mystical Experience Everywhere the Same?" in *The Problem of Pure Consciousness.* (Ed. Forman, P.K.C.) New York, Oxford University Press

Reid, Thomas (1975) "Of Identity" in *Personal Identity* (Ed Perry, J.) Berkeley and Los Angeles, University of California Press

Rey, Georges, (1976) "Survival." in *The Identities of Persons,* (Ed. Rorty, A. O.) Berkeley, University of California Press

Robinson, Daniel N. (1982) "Cerebral Plurality and the Unity of Self" *American Psychologist,* Vol. 37, No. 4, pp 904 - 910, August

Robinson, J. (1988) "Personal Identity and Survival', *Journal of Philosophy,* Vol. 85, No. 6, June

Rorty, A. O. (Ed.) (1976) *The Identities of Persons,* Berkeley, University of California Press

Schechtman, Marya, (1990) "Personhood and Personal Identity" *Journal of Philosophy,* Vol. 87, No. 2, February

Shear, Jonathan, (1983) "The Experience of Pure Consciousness: A New Perspective for Theories of the Self" *Metaphilosophy,* Vol. 14, No. 1, January

Shoemaker, S. (1984) "Personal Identity: A Materialist Account" in Shoemaker and Swinburne, *Personal Identity.* Oxford, Basil Blackwell

Silkstone, Thomas, (1973) "My Self and My World" *International Philosophical Quarterly*

Sperry, R.W. (1985) "Consciousness, Personal Identity, and the Divided Brain", *The Dual Brain* (Ed. Benson and Zaidel) New York and London, The Guildford Press

Sprigge, T. L. S. (1988) "Personal and Impersonal Identity" *Mind,* Vol. 97, No. 385, January

Squires, Roger (1973) "The Problem of Dreams" *Philosophy.* Vol. 48 No. 185 July

Stone, Jim, (1988) "Parfit and the Buddha: Why There Are No. People" *Philosophy and Phenomenological Research,* Vol. 48, No. 3, March

Strawson, P. F. (1966) *The Bounds of Sense.* London,, Methuen and Co.

Stroud, Barry, (1977) *Hume.* London, Routledge, Kegan Paul

Swinburne, Richard, (1984) "Personal Identity: The Dualist Theory" in Shoemaker and Swinburne, *Personal Identity.* Oxford, Basil Blackwell

Swinburne, Richard. (1986) *The Evolution of the Soul* Oxford, Clarendon Press

Taber, John A. (1990) "The Mimamsa theory of self-recognition" *Philosophy East and West,* Vol. 40, No. 1, January

Thurber, James, (1953) "The Secret Life of Walter Mitty" *The Thurber Carnival.* Harmondsworth, Penguin Books Ltd.

Unger, Peter, (1986) "Consciousness and Self-identity" *Midwest Studies in Philosophy,* Vol. 10 Minneapolis, University of Minnesota Press

Unger, Peter, (1990) *Identity, Consciousness, and Value* New York, Oxford University Press.

Vendler, Zeno, (1984) *The Matter of Minds* Oxford, Clarendon Press

Watterson, Bill, (1993) *Scientific Progress Goes "Boink"* London, Warner Books

Wei, Tan Tai, (1990) "Bodily Continuity, Personal Identity and Life after Death." *Sophia,* Vol. 29, No. 2, July

White, Stephen L. (1989) "Metapsychological Relativism and the Self." *Journal of Philosophy*, Vol. 86, No.6 June

Wiggins, D. (1967) *Identity and Spatio-Temporal Continuity.* Oxford, Basil Blackwell

Williams, B. A. O. (1973) *Problems of the Self.* Cambridge, Cambridge University Press.

Woodhouse, Mark B. (1970) "Selves and Minds: a Reply to Professor Knox" *Religious Studies,* Vol. 6 No. 3 September

Woodhouse, Mark B. "On the Possibility of Pure Consciousness." in *The Problem of Pure Consciousness.* (Ed. Forman, P.K.C.) New York, Oxford University Press

Zuboff, Arnold, (1990) "One Self: The Logic of Experience" *Inquiry,* Vol. 33, No. 1, March

Index